The Team Handbook For Educators
How to Use Teams to Improve Quality

Peter R. Scholtes

with assistance from
David L. Bayless
Gabriel A. Massaro
Nancy K. Roche

with other contributions by
Brian L. Joiner, Bill Braswell, Lynda Finn,
Heero Hacquebord, Kevin Little, Sue Reynard
Barbara Streibel, Lonnie Weiss, and John Woods

Joiner®

The Team Handbook For Educators

How to Use Teams to Improve Quality

Production and Adminstrative Staff:

John Woods Project Manager, Editor, Production Coordinator, and all-around problem solver

Sue Reynard Inside consultant, quality disciple, and proofreader

Dale Mann Who does great cartoons

Reed Jones Production and Manufacturing Chief

Customer Service Staff An extraordinary and delightful group of professional people who answer phones and process orders

Production Notes:

Layout was done electronically at Impressions, A Division of Edwards Brothers, Inc. (Madison, WI) using QuarkXPress. The production manager at Impressions was Claire Huismann, a conscientious book publishing professional. The book was printed at Straus Printing Co. (Madison, WI).

About Joiner Associates Incorporated

Joiner Associates Incorporated is an internationally recognized consulting firm specializing in helping companies learn how to use quality management principles and techniques to build market strength. Our consulting practice is led by Dr. Brian L. Joiner, one of the leading quality proponents in the world. Our other consultants, with backgrounds in manufacturing, service, and education, represent disciplines as diverse as statistics and organizational development. All have extensive experience in using quality management tools to better understand customer needs, solve problems, and achieve long-lasting improvements in processes and products. We focus on helping top executives, middle managers, professional employees, and internal resources lead improvement in their organizations.

Dedication

To Dr. William G. Hunter . . .

When he died in December of 1986, Bill Hunter left behind a considerable body of new statistical insights and methods, and an army of students who learned from him not only how to appreciate statistics and how to appreciate Dr. Deming's teachings, but, most of all, how to appreciate life. He left, as a legacy, scores of organizations knowledgeably engaged in the new industrial revolution. He left many, many friends.

The authors of this book, and the many who contributed to its development, were among Bill's students and friends. For Bill Hunter there was no clear distinction between the two—he befriended his students and taught his friends. Perhaps his greatest gift was his enthusiasm. Bill so obviously relished exploring any ideas we would share with him that we came to understand and appreciate more deeply the things we already knew. He influenced our work—and this book—in countless ways. With fond memories and deep gratitude, therefore, we dedicate this book to Bill Hunter.

Biographical Notes

- Born March 27, 1937
- Died December 29, 1986
- One of the foremost proponents and teachers of Dr. Deming's teachings; worked with organizations around the globe
- Co-Founder of the Center for Quality and Productivity Improvement at the University of Wisconsin-Madison
- Professor of Statistics and of Industrial Engineering, University of Wisconsin-Madison, 1963-1986; held several Visiting Professorships abroad
- Founding chairman of the Statistics Division of the American Society for Quality Control
- Co-Author of *Statistics for Experimenters: An Introduction to Design, Data Anlysis, and Model Building*

Foreword

Changes in the style of Western management are essential if we are not to be smothered by other parts of the world. American products were in heavy demand after the War. The gold of the world flowed into Fort Knox. Everyone expected the good times to continue. Somehow, the balance has changed. Imports of manufactured product from Japan and from other parts of the world demonstrated need for new thought and better understanding about quality. Service industries such as banking, real estate, hotels and department stores are yielding to invasion of foreign capital. Restrictions to foreign trade, in which the U.S. tops other countries, have hindered our exports, not helped them.

Change is required. There is a process of change, just as there is a process of manufacturing, or for growing wheat. How to change is the problem. Mr. Scholtes provides the route in this book for change. He has my respect and best wishes.

W. Edwards Deming
Washington
May 1988

Foreword

This is a book for which I have been waiting for some time.

I have greatly admired Dr. Deming's contributions to quality improvement, but I have felt his methods and principles should be blended in more systematically with the qualitative principles of adult learning and group dynamics. Then the whole package needed to be put together in the context of business operations. Here we have that package, beautifully wrapped.

I first became aware of this need several years ago when people started describing problems they were encountering in their experimentation with quality circles, and project teams. They were discovering that these tools weren't working as well as they should because the leaders and members of the groups lacked sufficient skills in managing group processes—particularly in regard to responsible involvement in planning and decision-making.

I find in this book Peter Scholtes (one of the brightest students I have had) and his associates have taken sound theoretical principles of adult learning and group dynamics and translated them into clear, practical, easy-to-apply strategies and techniques for enabling project teams to do their work effectively and smoothly.

I think we in this field owe them a resounding vote of thanks.

Malcolm Knowles
Professor Emeritus
North Carolina State University
December 1987

Table of Contents

Chapter 6: Learning to Work Together 6-1

It is folly to assume that a group assigned to a task will simply find a way of working cooperatively. Learning to work together is as hard as learning to make improvements. This chapter describes the stages teams usually go through and gives suggestions for building a team and maintaining support within a group. We also discuss common problems and ways to deal with them.

Chapter 7: Team-Building Activities 7-1

These activities will help your team make the transition from a loose collection of individuals to a cohesive team.

Appendix 1: Further Readings A1-1

Appendix 2: Picture Book Format Example A2-1

Appendix 3: The Planning Grid A3-1

Index

Introduction

This is a "how-to" book. Its purpose is to help project teams working in educational systems succeed in improving quality and learning outcomes, and in all their efforts to improve processes.

Those who are responsible for establishing such projects will find suggestions on how to set up the project and assign the team. Administrators who establish a project will learn what to look for as the project unfolds. Those who take part in the project as team leaders, team members, or in some technical advisory role will learn the larger context within which to see their effort. Those directly involved in projects will find detailed recommendations on how to proceed through the project's many phases.

There have been projects and project teams of one kind or another since the first prehistoric tribe grouped together to accomplish something that each member individually was unable to do. Business organizations commonly set up project teams to solve problems or pursue some new development.

Our approach to projects differs from more conventional approaches in three ways:

First: Our approach is focused on the pursuit of quality as taught to us by Dr. W. Edwards Deming, the founder of the new economic and industrial era.

Second: Our approach relies heavily on the understanding and application of data. These data-based methods—which we call the scientific approach—draw from the discipline of statistics and classical logic, which characterize Dr. Deming's teachings.

Third: We include methods for the formation and maintenance of groups, the planning and managing of projects, and the design and conduct of meetings. These approaches we have learned from Malcolm Knowles and other contributors to the field of group and organizational dynamics.

About the Authors

Peter R. Scholtes is one of the few leading proponents of continuous improvement whose professional background is in Organization Development. A widely acclaimed writer and lecturer who has worked closely with Joiner Associates for the past decade, he has more than 30 years of experience in planning and implementing change in a wide range of organizations. Peter believes we can only create a competitive, humane economy through a transformation of the relationships, environment, and the dynamics within and between individuals and groups in our organizations, including educational systems. The cornerstones of his work are training and consultation devoted to educating managers and administrators on the theory, skills, methods, and tools needed to guide the efforts of their employees and staffs. Other publications include "Beginning the Quality Transformation" (see *Quality Progress,* July and August, 1988), "An Elaboration on Deming's Teachings on Performance Appraisal" (available from Joiner Associates), and "Total Quality or Performance Appraisal: Choose One" (see *National Productivity Review,* Summer, 1993). Mr. Scholtes holds a master's degree in educational administration from Boston University, where he studied with Malcolm Knowles, and has completed additional studies in the fields of management science, philosophy, and psychology.

It is our strong conviction that for a project team to succeed in its task, it needs much more than technical knowledge of the work area under investigation. Expertise in the subject at hand is indispensable. But participants in a successful project must also know how to work as a team, plan, conduct good meetings, manage logistics and details, gather useful data, analyze the data, communicate the results, and implement changes.

The methods in this book result from the experience of many project teams and many trainers and consultants who work with project teams. Someone looking at the title page of this book and seeing so many names listed as authors might wonder about how so many can genuinely co-author a single publication. As its principal author, I know that *The Team Handbook for Educators* wouldn't exist without the contributions of those listed.

David Bayless, Gabriel Massaro, and Nancy Roche, educational consultants, worked as a team to help us transform the original version of *The Team Handbook* into this version for educators. They have tirelessly sought to revise language and examples to place all the ideas in this book into a context that is readily applicable by teachers, administrators, and everyone involved in improving educational processes.

Brian Joiner is the principal author of Chapter 5 in the original book, and contributed to all other sections. But he contributed far more than words to this publication. Brian's wisdom, insight, values, and support have enriched all of us who participated in *The Team Handbook.*

John Woods managed the project from its inception, working with me and the other members of the team to keep the project moving ahead and carried the workload over the final steps to completion.

We also want to acknowledge the contributions of the following educators and give special thanks for all their suggestions, insights, and examples: Carol Litman and Denise Jones and the staff of the Educational Studies Area at Westat, Inc., for all their valuable resources; the staff of the Evaluation Center and the Center for Research on Educational Accountability and Teacher Evaluation (CREATE) at Western Michigan University; Dr. Roy Forbes, Executive Director, Southeastern Regional Vision for Education (SERVE), University of North Carolina, Greensboro; Deer Lake Middle School staff, Leon County School District, Tallahassee, Florida; Gulf Shores Middle School staff, Baldwin County School System, Gulf Shores, Alabama; Magnolia Junior High School staff, Moss Point School District, Moss Point, Mississippi; Scott Elementary School staff, Thomasville City School District, Thomasville, Georgia; State of Louisiana Department of Education; Deridder High School staff, Beauregard Parish, Deridder, Louisiana; Johnson Elementary School staff, Desoto Parish, Mansfield, Louisiana; Beau Chene High School staff, St. Landry Parish, Arnaudville, Louisiana.

All of us who worked on this publication are honored to have contributions from both W. Edwards Deming and Malcolm Knowles. Dr. Deming has been called the Father of the New Industrial Age and the Founder of the New Economic Era. The lives of people in all industrialized countries have been changed as a result of his visits to Japan in 1950 and his work around the world ever since.

At about the same time that Dr. Deming was introducing Japan to the importance of quality and the application of Statistical Thinking, Dr. Knowles was making major contributions to the relatively new discipline of Group and Organizational Development. He is also recognized as one of the most important contributors in the twentieth century to the field of Adult Education.

Dr. David L. Bayless has had 25 years of professional experience as a statistician and corporate executive. He spent 10 years as Vice President and Study Area Director at Westat, Inc., in Rockville, Maryland, and specialized in large-scale surveys of various types for local and national educational systems. He also worked with several state departments of education on the design, analysis, and interpretation of statewide assessments. He established Bayless Associates as a quality consultant to educational systems throughout the United States and other countries. Dr. Bayless received a master's degree from Florida State University and his Ph.D. from Texas A&M University.

Dr. Gabriel A. Massaro is a research associate at Westat with more than 25 years experience in education. He was an associate superintendent of schools for curriculum and instruction, an elementary and high school principal, college professor, elementary and high school teacher, and educational researcher and consultant. He specializes in curriculum development, and planning, implementing, and evaluating training programs. Dr. Massaro consults with school districts seeking to implement quality management throughout their systems. He received his Ed.D. from Columbia University.

Nancy K. Roche is an educational consultant working with Westat, Inc. She has more than 30 years experience in curriculum development, implementation, and evaluation in Montgomery County and Charles County, Maryland, schools. Ms. Roche has designed and presented workshops, conferences, and seminars on quality leadership, tools, and team building. She has been a teacher, a curriculum specialist, and a school principal. She received her master's of education degree in administration and supervision from Western Maryland College.

While many have contributed to this publication, it will be successful only if you—the reader and customer—find it useful. We earnestly seek your feedback and suggestions for improvement. We will practice what we preach and be responsive to your needs. Please let us know what works and what doesn't. You can contact us at the address or phone on the copyright page.

Peter R. Scholtes
Madison, Wisconsin
January, 1994

Chapter 1
Education in a New World

I t is hard to change when you have been doing something the same way all of your life. But in the education world, changes in student and community demands and the increased competition that graduates face will force schools and school districts to examine the entire system of education as we know it today.

Many American schools and school districts are finding they have to do things differently to remain relevant. World competition—powered by a new, smarter leadership style—has never been so intense. The American economy is transforming before our eyes as industry after industry is restructured, reshaped, and reformed to keep up with the worldwide competition. American schools, ideally a reflection of our society, must also change in order to prepare our students for the changing marketplace.

Managers are learning new ways to run their companies. Workers are learning how to contribute their knowledge to improving processes. Chief executive officers are beginning to nurture and grow healthy corporations for long-term strength, not just short-term profit. All are listening to customers more effectively to make certain their products continue to be useful and valuable. If they don't, someone else will quickly jump in and take away those customers. With no customers, there is no company. If schools are to follow the example of their counterparts in industry, administrators must learn new ways to lead and manage. Teachers, students, and community members must learn to work together to continuously improve educational processes. All must see the alignment of a school system's purpose, curriculum, instruction, and assessment. Superintendents must nurture and encourage the development of healthy schools for long-term strength and increased learning, not just short-term achievement measured by often misunderstood and/or poorly designed assessments.

The new approach to management of continuous learning and school improvement allows a school system to keep up with—even ahead of—these rapid changes. American schools, like American companies, are only beginning to understand these management principles, put

Notes...

them into practice, and prepare students to deal with the new world of work and its quickly changing marketplace.

We call this new style of management "Quality Leadership." It is a new world view that shifts emphasis from short-term results to long-term value. By learning how to manage, stabilize, and constantly improve their systems and processes, schools are better able to lead educators and learners at every level to a new standard of excellence in education.

With Quality Leadership, decisions are based on data, not guesswork. Use of a scientific approach, through data-driven problem-solving tools, becomes standard procedure. The focus is on improving the many educational processes and services by improving *how* they get done (the methods) instead of simply measuring *what* is done (the results).

Relationships between staff and administrators are restructured: An administrator's job becomes helping people to do the best job possible, foreseeing and eliminating barriers that prevent educators and learners from doing work they can take pride and joy in. All staff members learn how to use the knowledge and insight they've gained day after day to be active, involved participants in the process of continuous learning and school improvement.

Though Quality Leadership is most often seen in foreign countries, its roots are American. Many of the ideas originated with Dr. W. Edwards Deming, the American statistician who helped Japanese industry recover after World War II (see facing page). His teachings, especially those that have led to the development of Quality Leadership principles, are today drawing attention from more and more American business leaders. Many educators are also becoming interested in Quality Leadership and how it can be applied to education.

Joiner Associates has worked closely with Dr. Deming and extensively studied his teachings. We use a triangle to symbolize what we have

Dr. W. Edwards Deming

The "new" approach to management is not widely practiced in the United States; yet it is not new, nor is it foreign. Its roots go back many decades and its principal prophet is a Sioux City, Iowa, native named W. Edwards Deming. A statistician by profession, Dr. Deming formed many of his theories during World War II when he taught industries how to use statistical methods to improve the quality of military production.

When the war ended, American industry turned its attention to meeting the huge demand for consumer goods. For almost 20 years there was no significant foreign competition. Costly management methods grew up and took hold during a period of unparalleled prosperity. It was hard to fail in such a rising tide.

Across the Pacific—where "Made in Japan" meant junk—people turned to Dr. Deming for help. They invited him to come to Japan so they could learn about his methods. Dr. Deming told them to find out what their customers wanted, then study and improve their product design and production processes until the quality of the product was unsurpassed. He taught them the product was "still in the development process when it was in the customer's hands."

His influence there began in 1950 at a dinner meeting with 45 leading industrialists in Tokyo. Dr. Deming has since recalled that meeting:

"They thought they could not [compete] because they had such a terrible reputation when it came to quality . . . I told them, 'Those days are over. You can produce quality. You have a method for doing it. You've learned what quality is. You must carry out consumer research, look toward the future, and produce goods that will have a market years from now and stay in business. . . .'

"Incoming materials were terrible, off gauge and off color, nothing right. And I urged them to work with their vendors and to work on instrumentation. I told them a vendor is a part of you. A lot of what I urged them to do came very naturally to the Japanese, though they were not doing it. I said, 'You don't need to receive the junk that comes in. You can never produce quality with that stuff. But with process controls that your engineers are learning about, specifications as loose as possible, consumer research, redesign of products, you can. Don't just make it and try to sell it. Redesign it and then again bring the process under control. The cycle goes on and on continuously, with quality ever-increasing.' "

[Footnote: Quotes taken from *The Keys To Excellence* by Nancy R. Mann, Ph.D., Prestwick Books: Los Angeles, 1987.]

Deming told the Japanese that they would have people demanding their products within five years. He was wrong; within four years the Japanese had already captured large shares of some markets.

The rest, as they say, is history.

The Joiner Triangle

We use the triangle to symbolize the relationship that quality, a scientific approach, and a feeling of "all one team" must have if a school district is to be successful. Taken together, these three elements are extremely stable and powerful.

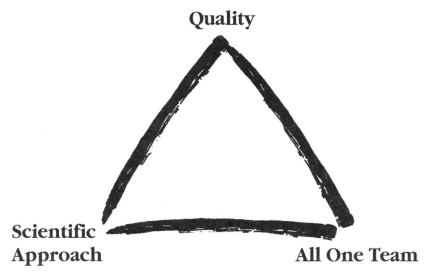

Quality

Scientific Approach

All One Team

learned about translating continuous improvement theories into practice. One corner represents quality as defined by the customer, for that is where the new focus must be. In the context of an education process, the translation of the concept of "customer" is complex and is related at each level of the system—classroom, school, district office, and community—to the particular process with which the person's work is associated. It is crucial to remember that the product is the education that students receive, not the students themselves. The customer for the classroom teacher consists, at various times in the process, of other classroom teachers, certain administrators, the community, the students, and parents. A second corner of the triangle represents the scientific or data-based approach to studying processes, a strategy that leads to long-lasting, fundamental improvements. The third corner represents everyone working together as "all one team" to learn how to apply these principles. These three function like a three-legged stool: When they function together, they are exceedingly stable. When even one element is missing, the result is disaster. Each must be linked to the others for the success of all.

The transformation to Quality Leadership is a tough job and takes the concerted effort of people throughout an educational system, including the commitment of all who make up the system—community, parents, students, classroom teachers, school principals and staff, district superintendent and staff, and the local school board members. This book concerns school improvement and project teams, just one dimension of a quality effort. Other dimensions will be described below. But to explain where project teams fit into an overall quality improvement scheme, we must first take a broader look at how the quality movement got started.

I. Management by Results

American managers are generally a tough lot who have accomplished much. Their efforts have built the strongest economy the world has known, supported by a strong education system.

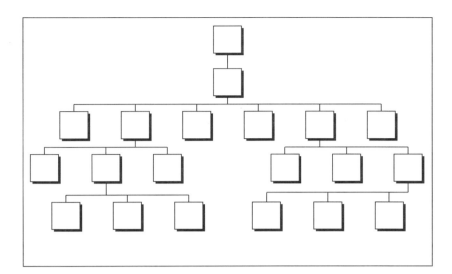

The traditional hierarchy chart of educational organizations reflects many principles of Management by Results. Numerical goals or quotas are set at the top, then passed on down through a chain of accountability.

Yet our nation's competitive edge is blunted. Trapped in an outdated style of running organizations, managers are unable to use the full potential of their workers. Organizations thus fail to keep up with the developing needs of their customers, and lose them. The recent criticism aimed at education indicates it is in a similar position.

Most American managers do business, at least in part, through a management approach that is sometimes called "Management by Results." It is practiced by nearly every major American corporation, taught in almost every American business school. And it is credited by many for the successes we have enjoyed.

Management by Results has its own logic and consistency. As shown (above), it emphasizes a chain of command and a hierarchy of objectives, standards, controls, and accountability. Traditional organizational charts therefore portray a chain of accountability where objectives are translated into work standards, or sales quotas. The performance of all employees is guided and judged according to these numerical goals, the heart and driving force of traditional management practices.

The shortcomings of Management by Results are rooted in the numerical goals. Management by Results pays little, if any, attention to processes and systems: the real capabilities of the organization as a whole. So these standards and quotas are nothing but arbitrary numerical goals. Eventually, workers, supervisors, and managers get caught up in games; looking good overshadows a concern for the organization's long-term success. Too often, they lose sight of the larger purpose of work they do.

Schools too, often are governed by management by results. Curriculum may be a series of objectives measured by standardized assessments that measure part of the total curriculum.

Using numerical goals to judge and direct performance fosters a host of problems:

- **Short-term thinking**
- **Misguided focus**
- **Internal conflict**
- **Fudging the figures**
- **Greater fear**
- **Blindness to customer concerns**

The Consequences of Management by Results

When Management by Results is used, educators are forced to play games to meet their numerical goals.

- Many administrators negotiate safe learning outcomes so they can meet performance standards. Some administrators include on their list educational outcomes that have already been accomplished prior to negotiation.

- A Curriculum Department had developed new strategies for the teaching of science in an effort to raise test scores. Implementing these strategies required an inordinate amount of staff development. To help teachers raise test scores and implement the strategies, a central office curriculum specialist went to several schools to provide in-service workshops. Without knowing for sure that low test scores represented a problem or that lack of training is the cause of the problem, this was an expensive way to respond to a numerical goal.

continued on next page

In short, use of numerical goals to judge and direct performance fosters a host of problems:

- **Short-term thinking**

    In a system of numerical objectives, standards, and quotas, rewarded efforts are measurable and short-term. The near horizon gets attention and countable results get priority even though the education system's survival may depend on unmeasurable activities undertaken to reach long-term goals.

    Top administrators impose goals on their staffs. The staff members struggle to meet their goals, forced to ignore how much they distort efforts at some other time or place in the education system. Everyone struggles to survive distortions inherited from other times or places, and the cycle becomes self-reinforcing. People are too busy meeting quotas to worry about what is happening to learners.

    In this climate, meeting short-term, measurable goals reflects well on an individual and reinforces the legitimacy of the goals themselves. When goals are met, the entire education system can boast of its performance. But this attitude wreaks havoc with quality and staff morale along the way.

- **Misguided focus**

    If administrators and staff truly understand a system's capability, what benefit is added by a numerical goal? A numerical goal cannot expand capability; only improving a system can do that.

    If administrators and staff do not understand the system's capabilities, a numerical goal is nothing more than guesswork. The guess will either overestimate the capabilities or underestimate them. Either way, it does little to help the staff, the education system, or the learner.

- **Internal conflict**

  Systems of numerical controls cause internal conflict. The process conditions that direct one unit's short-term gain more often than not contradict the controls given to another unit.

  For example, when standardized test scores fall, administrators make promises to improve learning. The curriculum office begins to look at making revisions to the curriculum and the instructional program. Planners and policymakers develop programs that educators aren't equipped to provide. The conflicts between departments lead to finger pointing, blame games, and an endless series of excuses ("If it weren't for them . . ."). Each group struggles to conform to its controls independently of other groups. Turf wars flourish.

- **Fudging the figures**

  Frequently, imposed measurable goals are unattainable; they lie beyond a system's real capability. But since people or departments could lose status if they fail to reach the goals, they have to make it look like they are conforming. They are forced by the system to fudge figures, alter records, or just "play the game"—to work around the system instead of improving it. This charade fosters guarded communication and minor, sometimes major, dishonesty. The greater the stress on reaching unattainable goals, the more likely it is that reports and numbers will be given a face-lift. (See Sidebar "The Consequences of Management by Results," facing page and right.)

- **Greater fear**

  The worst shortcoming of Management by Results is fear—fear of what will happen if the standardized test scores do not rise, of being out of favor or losing a job. Fear is the prime motivator in a Management by Results system. The more rigid and unrealistic the control or requirement, the deeper the fear.

- To increase the percentage of students who successfully complete the advanced placement examination, a high school principal permits only the top one percent of students to enroll in the class.

- In September of every year, teachers were asked to write performance objectives for what they expected to achieve throughout the school year. The school principal and supervisor then reviewed, monitored, and evaluated these objectives. The written objectives were always easy to achieve, even for the least experienced teachers. This was because these teachers were so fearful of this process that they wrote only low-level performance objectives.

- An elementary school principal became so cautious in dealing with parents that he always went along with requests for student placement with a specific teacher, even if that was in neither the student's nor the school's best interest.

- A part of the school principal's evaluation included the recording of monthly gas and electric bills. All principals were required to lower the bills by 10 percent.

What to Call the New Quality Movement?

The new approach to quality has many names. In Japan, it is usually called "Total Quality Control," or TQC. But some Japanese firms prefer the expression "Company-Wide Quality Control," or CWQC.

In the United States, these expressions are less appropriate for two reasons. First, "quality control" has been used to describe the traditional inspect-for-quality approach, which TQC seeks to eliminate. Second, the word "control" tends to reinforce an authoritarian approach to the implementation of quality, something also contrary to the spirit of TQC.

Many educators have adapted the term Total Quality Improvement (TQI) or Total Quality Management (TQM) or Continuous Quality Improvement (CQI).

This new way is a holistic, preventative approach, a new way of life for almost every aspect of every school district.

What can we call an approach that involves all employees in pleasing the customer and builds quality into every system and process in the educational organization? Time will tell what label will be popularly accepted in the United States. We at Joiner Associates call this new way of doing business "Total Quality Leadership," or, more simply, "Quality Leadership."

• **Blindness to learners' concerns and the community's needs**

Management by Results encourages a school system to look inward, rather than outward at the world in which the customer operates. Accomplishment comes from meeting a numerical goal, rather than the delight in providing a product or service that works and satisfies.

(You can see where problems like these exist in your school district by working through Exercise 6 in Chapter 7, entitled "Identifying the Consequences of Management by Results," p. 7-22 to 7-23.)

These problems compound each other, each disguising the true shape of the education system. People think they are doing a good job—and they are by the education system's internal standards, which are driven by the logic of Management by Results. The result is a Titanic-like complaisance about the invulnerability of the operations. When people finally realize that the indicators of control may be focused on the wrong measurement, it's too late. The ship is going down and "Nearer My God To Thee" is heard from the afterdeck.

II. Quality Leadership

Administrators often say, "I agree there are serious problems with Management by Results, but what is a better alternative?"

The alternative, we believe, is Quality Leadership. Quality Leadership emphasizes *results* by working on *methods* that solve process problems and lead to lasting educational improvements to the learning environment of the school. Problems are solved, not just layered over. Dr. Deming tells us to give customer concerns top priority. When applied to the school setting, he encourages us to study and constantly improve every work process of the school. Then the resulting learner proficiencies or the internal and external services of the education system exceed everyone's expectations. Simply providing a teaching and learn-

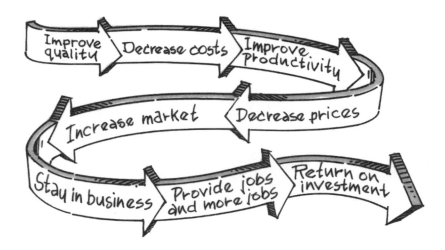

The Deming Chain Reaction

With each improvement, processes and systems run better and better. Productivity increases as waste goes down. Customers get better products, which ultimately increases market share and provides better return on investments.

ing service is replaced by providing a service that surprises others by how well it meets learner needs and even teaches higher order thinking skills they hadn't thought they needed.

This can only be done by building excellence into every system, process, and operation of the school district. Quality Leadership, therefore, focuses on creating a workplace that encourages everyone to contribute. Everyone learns to use a data-driven scientific approach to solving process problems and making improvements.

Indeed, use of a scientific approach becomes pervasive. Each process is carefully described, problems identified, the root causes of problems determined through careful research. Then new error-proof systems are developed. Every process is made stable. The variation in the learning environment is studied, understood, and reduced. Then it is studied and reduced some more. All educators and learners have ownership.

With each improvement, there is better and better execution of the processes of the learning environment. What learners know and can do goes up as waste and inefficiency go down. The learners get educational services of increasingly higher value. As joyous learners receive improved quality, the expectations of their parents and future employers will be satisfied. Dr. Deming summarizes this cycle in what has come to be called the Deming Chain Reaction (above).

Improvements of such scale cannot happen without everyone's involvement, without a fundamentally different view of the relationship between administrators, educators, and learners.

Staff and administrators learn to work together, for Quality Leadership cannot exist where they are adversaries. Administrators are still in charge, but they develop a genuine partnership with staff. Both sides are better armed with the knowledge and methods needed to keep the school system in touch with the people and to provide quality services through continuous improvement. Staff are allowed to make more potent contributions by combining their intimate knowledge of a process with the tools of the scientific approach.

What About the Bottom Line?

Many administrators have trouble understanding why they should focus on improving the processes that serve customers rather than simply pursuing outcomes. The Deming Chain Reaction (above) is how Dr. Deming explained it in 1950.

When quality is increased by improving processes—not by expanded testing—education improves. Better outcomes increase achievement. Customers respond to better quality and increasing achievement. School districts that practice Management by Results, on the other hand, tend to focus only on the end result. This viewpoint is like trying to keep a dog happy by forcibly wagging its tail.

As they work together to improve quality, staff and administrators build mutual respect and trust. The more they help each other employ the scientific approach, the more the quality of teaching and learning improves. This environment of teamwork associated with Quality Leadership cannot be developed under Management by Results; unnecessary bureaucratic mandates and requirements, conflicting goals, game playing, and distrust get in the way.

The Principles of Quality Leadership

Because many of the elements of Quality Leadership have appeared separately in fads that have swept through schools of education and school districts, people fail to recognize how the total package differs from anything they have seen before. Quality Leadership is a new way of operating educational organizations and a better way to work with people.

The combination of characteristics described on the following pages distinguishes Quality Leadership from its predecessors.

- **Customer focus**

   For educators, the customers are the learners and the community. Whereas Management by Results begins with goals, objectives, assessment measures, and cost control, Quality Leadership starts with the customer—the person who is to be satisfied and served. Under Quality Leadership, a school district's goal is to meet and exceed expected needs, to give lasting value to those being served—students and the community. Support will follow as people boast of the quality of their school district's service. Members of a quality school district recognize both external customers, those who use the services of the district, and internal customers, fellow staff members whose work depends on the work of those whom they serve. In such districts, it is acknowledged, for example, that the quality of the second-grade educational process depends upon the quality of the first-grade process.

• **Obsession with quality**

Everyone in the school system becomes obsessed with quality. Quality is relentlessly pursued through services that delight the learners, educators, and the community, and bring joy and pride to the educator. Efficient and effective methods for providing these services are created.

• **Recognizing the structure in work**

Quality Leadership knows that the work to align curriculum development, instruction, and assessment is not haphazard. All work has structure. The structure may be hidden behind inefficiency or rework, but it can and must be studied, measured, analyzed, and improved. Quality Leadership calls upon educators and learners to operationally define and measure processes and characteristics inside and outside the school district.

These numerical measures (not to be confused with the numerical goals of Management by Results) guide the search for better performance, and are recognized as a means rather than an end. They lead the way to a deeper understanding of the collection of many activities of the school district and are not used as criteria for judging individuals.

• **Freedom through control of the processes**

In Quality Leadership there is control, yet there is freedom. There is control over the best-known method for any given process. Staff standardizes processes to make them stable and capable of fulfilling their purpose and then finds ways to ensure everyone learns and understands the standard procedures to meet the learner's needs. They reduce variation in outcomes by reducing variation in

Principles of Quality Leadership

- **Customer focus**
- **Obsession with quality**
- **Recognizing the structure in work**
- **Freedom through control**
- **Unity of purpose**
- **Looking for faults in systems**
- **Teamwork**
- **Continued education and training**

Which Path?

American educators wait while administrators decide whether to take the easy path to higher test scores (and ultimate disaster) . . .

the way the work is done. As these changes take hold, educators are free to spend time working on the system in order to prevent problems, to discover new teaching strategies, to develop new administrative processes to better align curriculum instruction and assessment, and to gain greater mastery over the processes that comprise their roles. There is freedom to find a better method. When it is proven better, it is then standardized.

- **Unity of purpose**

  There is a unity of purpose throughout the school district in accord with a clear and widely understood vision of continuously improving the learning environment and its outcomes. This environment nurtures total commitment from all staff. Rewards go beyond benefits and salaries to the belief "we are family" and "we do excellent work."

- **Looking for faults in the system**

  Quality Leadership recognizes—as Dr. Joseph N. Juran and Dr. W. Edwards Deming have maintained since the early 1950's—that at least 85 percent of an organization's failures are the fault of management-controlled systems. Educators and learners thus can control fewer than 15 percent of the process problems. In Quality Leadership, the focus is on continuous learning and rigorous school improvement of every system and process, not on blaming individual educators and learners for problems. (See "The 85/15 Rule," p. 2-12.)

- **Teamwork**

  Where once there may have been barriers, rivalries, and distrust, the quality school district fosters teamwork and partnerships with everyone in the educational system. This partnership is not a pretense, a new look to an old battle. It is the common struggle of all the educators on behalf of the learners and the community. It is no longer separate struggles for power. The notion of a common

. . . or use Quality Leadership to travel the road to long-term success.

struggle for quality also applies to relationships with suppliers of curriculum and other materials. Departments within the school, schools within the district, regulating agencies, and local community groups must all recognize that they are interdependent parts of a system.

- **Continued education and training**

  In a quality school everyone is constantly learning. Administrators and staff constantly elevate their level of technical skill and professional expertise. People gain an ever greater mastery of their jobs and learn to broaden their capabilities.

The Dimensions of a Quality Effort

The principles of Quality Leadership are easy to understand, but putting them into practice can be difficult. It requires effort on many fronts.

Some people think the route to Quality Leadership can be traveled solely by project teams. While project teams are a crucial tool for quality improvement—and the subject of this book—they are only one dimension of the total package. School districts must adopt other practices if they are to succeed in the long run.

We have identified six dimensions to pursue in the early phases of implementing Quality Leadership. Each requires careful planning before plowing ahead. They are displayed in a cause-and-effect diagram (see page 1-14) to illustrate the steps toward Quality Leadership.

1. **The education, reeducation, and active leadership of top administration**

   The most frequent cause of failure in any quality improvement effort is uninvolved or indifferent top and middle administration.

The Elements of Quality Leadership

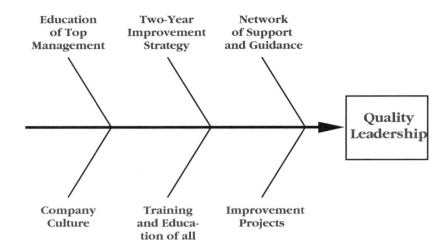

Therefore, the active leadership and participation of administration, beginning at the top, is essential.

Quality can't be delegated to others. Administrators must lead the transformation effort to ensure long-lasting success. They must become leaders instead of bosses, coaches instead of enforcers. They must change their focus from blaming and controlling individuals to preventing and eliminating system problems. Only this will lead to constant improvement.

Administrators must deeply understand Dr. Deming's teachings. (See "Deming's 14 Points," pp. 2-4 to 2-7.) They must learn new skills and approaches for stabilizing and improving the capability of processes. They must understand variation and know how to use data effectively. When top administrators feel these concepts deep in their bones, quality will become second nature.

2. **A multiyear strategy for starting and implementing a quality improvement philosophy**

   School districts commonly make the mistake of involving too many people too soon. It is easy to plant a big garden; hard to tend it. Don't begin a bigger effort than you can realistically support and maintain. Plan to start with a multiyear strategy. A long-range strategy addresses these questions:

   • In which parts of the school district should the transformation or school improvement effort start? Which potential school improvement projects have the best chance of success?

   • What resources, financial and personnel, will be needed to sustain initial education and training linked to important school improvement efforts? Who will provide guidance and technical assistance to administrators, supervisors, teachers, and project teams?

- Who will coordinate logistics and district-wide communication? What systems must be developed for deploying resources, maintaining an information clearinghouse for publications, conferences, and seminars on quality, and a thousand other details?

3. A network of coordination, guidance, and technical support

Identifying and developing resource people within the education system is an initial priority. It is almost always necessary to recruit technical resources from the outside as well. Typically, these include a senior statistician, an experienced organization development specialist, and technical advisors who can assist people engaged in improvement efforts. (In this book we refer to these technical specialists as "Quality Advisors." More details are given in Chapter 3.)

These specialists and quality advisors coach administrators and supervisors about how to lead and guide the effort. Until a school district has an adequate number of these experts, it will have to rely on external consultants and trainers.

4. A school district culture supportive of Quality Leadership

The notion of culture in a school district is complex and elusive. In general, culture refers to the everyday work experiences of the total staff. We urge administrators to address these questions: How do staff experience their roles? What gets in the way of pride in their work and their work groups? Do they feel valued and trusted by the school district?

Sometimes a simple change of policy or administrative practice can have a positive influence on these attitudes (even something as elementary as getting rid of reserved parking spaces for administrators). Administrators must review the school's policies and change those that are contrary to Quality Leadership and a supportive learning environment.

CONVENTIONAL
ADMINISTRATIVE
STRUCTURE

5. Training and education of all

All staff members must understand their jobs and their roles in the school—and how these roles change as quality improves. Such understanding goes beyond the instructions given in manuals or job descriptions. Staff members need to know where their work fits into the larger context: how their work is influenced by those who precede them and how their work influences those who follow. They must learn new skills for improving work.

6. Carefully selected school improvement projects

Having teams work on carefully selected school improvement projects is a useful vehicle for moving Quality Leadership forward. Project teams can tackle larger issues than individuals can. Their access to technical support and guidance from people versed in data-based approaches, project planning and management techniques, and group leadership skills enhances their ability to find permanent solutions to problems.

Early projects must be focused, carefully selected, and of manageable scope to insure the greatest chance of success. Often teams tackle projects that are too large or diffuse for them to handle. The resulting frustration only dampens enthusiasm for the transformation or school improvement effort. (This topic is covered in depth in Chapter 3.)

III. How to Use Project Teams

Though project teams are only one dimension of Quality Leadership, they are, nevertheless, an important one. The success or failure of school improvement projects will have great impact on the school district because they are highly visible efforts. Therefore, you have to clearly understand where project teams fit into the overall quality

TEAMS

improvement plan of the district and know how to use them properly. The figure (above) shows where project teams fit into a school district or school improvement strategy.

Whether you are involved in a pilot project, or one that is part of a later expansion, your project is part of something very big, very long lasting, and very important to your school district. As mentioned above, the main agenda of quality projects is to improve a work process that administrators have identified as important to study for possible change. The team studies this process methodically to find permanent solutions to problems. To do this, members can use the tools and skills described throughout this book. But project teams, especially initial teams, also have a "hidden agenda." They are an instrument of widespread education, a purpose equally if not more important in the long run than their focus on improvement. The first project teams plant the seeds of Quality Leadership in the school district.

They are a classroom through which the entire school district learns lessons such as

• **How to blend teamwork and scientific methods**

Project team members learn how to work as a team and how to improve processes using scientific tools and techniques. The team leader also learns how to plan and manage a project, design and monitor work plans by keeping the improvement project on schedule and within budget, conduct effective meetings, and facilitate group processes. They can all carry these skills beyond the project.

• **Where continuous improvement leadership teams fit in**

Through regular meetings with the project team, the administrators guiding the project also learn about the scientific approach to problem solving. In addition, they learn how to coach and inquire about

The Role of Teams

As school systems become more involved in the quality movement, they discover the benefits of having people at all levels work together in teams. Administrators, often in teams, will learn about and plan for quality. They will identify multiple processes or problems needing improvement, and form leadership teams that oversee project teams assigned to find solutions.

project team progress. They begin to understand both the exciting, successful side of projects and the tedious, confused, and unsuccessful side.

- **Moving the decisions outward**

  In school districts and most other organizations, decisions are made two or three hierarchical levels above where they should be made. Projects provide an opportunity to empower groups at the lower levels, groups that normally include teachers, with authority to decide on important changes to the environment.

- **Making improvements is not easy**

  Everyone in the school learns that the achievement of ever-improving quality is not easy. Administrators learn they need to be patient.

- **How to develop internal experts**

  Most schools develop a network of individuals trained to provide technical assistance to project teams and other quality improvement efforts. In this book we refer to these specialists as "Quality Advisors." Early projects provide an opportunity for Quality Advisors to improve their coaching and consulting skills.

- **How to expand the effort**

  Other people inside and outside the school learn from the project team's work through presentations and by participating in the changes resulting from the team's effort. To aid this process, project teams are typically asked to make presentations to people outside the school.

The project team's importance in this reeducation of all school system personnel cannot be underestimated. The teams should constantly record the projects' progress with clear, attractive visual displays. They should plan carefully any meetings with other groups in the school district, paying attention to what is said and how, and addressing the above-mentioned lessons as well as the outward results of the project.

IV. Hints for Getting Started

The transformation to Quality Leadership is often dramatic, and almost always traumatic. Change is seldom easy. It is unlikely anyone will figure out how to change a school district without requiring its people to change. Therefore, we must all be sensitive to the problems that people will have with the transformation or school improvement.

Keep in mind some of the "laws" of organizational change:

- **Things are the way they are because they got that way.**
  Somebody, sometime had to write the obnoxious policy, create the problem-plagued methods, or establish the backward school organization that you are studying. And often it is the same person asking you to find solutions. Remember that there were probably good reasons for doing things that way at the time the awful system was established. Therefore, it helps to understand the history behind any problem before you attempt to change it.

- **Unless things change, they are likely to remain the same.**
  An exception to this law is that things left unattended or unimproved will change for the worse. However, do not mistake attention and improvement for tampering. Tampering involves introducing change when you don't know what the cause of the

problem is. Tampering is worse than inattention. The methods described in this book will help you decide when you are improving a process and when you are just tampering with it. Pay attention to processes; improve, but don't tamper, with them.

- **Change would be easy if it weren't for all the people.**

  There are other versions of this law: "Administration would be easy if it weren't for all the educators, and teaching would be easy if it weren't for all of the students." The message in the irony of these statements is that people are the organization and the organization is there for the students. Therefore, pay attention to the people as well as the systems. Listen to them, especially if you would be likely to blame them for something down the road. Listening to staff and learners before problems arise will make any change go easier.

- **People don't resist change; they resist being changed.**

  A close corollary of this is that people who lose will find a way to win. Therefore, involve people in every step of an improvement effort: identifying the need for a change, planning and implementing the change, monitoring and acting on the results. Ask for their opinions: What do they fear? What do they hope will happen? What suggestions can they make to insure the success of the project?

Break Down Barriers

The biggest problems you will run into when coping with the transformation to Quality Leadership are the barriers inherent in school districts run by Management by Results. People will be afraid of giving up their control, of getting involved in something they think could risk their security or position. The following guidelines will help you prevent or overcome traditional barriers.

- **Identify informal networks**

  Imagine your district as a small town. Along with its official work system, it has a social system—a loose network of small groups of people. These groups offer their members support and friendship. Loyalty within groups may be stronger than loyalty to the school district. Informal groups have their own leaders and "rules" that can determine, for example, the pace of work or the relationship with the administration. If the informal group and its leaders accept a proposed change, events will proceed more smoothly; if they are opposed, change may be nearly impossible. Identify the informal leaders. Get to know them. Spend time listening to them. When you understand their needs and concerns, you will understand how the changes you seek might be fashioned.

- **Build a critical mass**

  To get any idea rolling, you need to build enthusiasm. When the idea is supported by a sufficient number of diverse people, it reaches a "critical mass." It takes off under its own steam, giving the impression of a growing, formidable movement and a sense of momentum. The size of the critical mass can vary from just a few key people to the entire district. In the early stages of change, the critical mass builds as key opinion leaders shift from a neutral to supportive position, or at least from resistance to indecision.

  When planning a change, identify these key opinion leaders—both in the formal and informal networks. Find out how you can sway their opinions: Do they need to see an idea in action? Do they need to see data you have already collected? Do they need to talk to the people involved in the change?

Onion Patch Strategy

What do you do if no one will listen, if you are having trouble getting the attention of the people on high, feeling like a "lonely little petunia in an onion patch"?

Our advice: Think big but stay close to your roots.

Select improvement efforts within your scope of control. Make certain they will capture the attention of people in administration. Look for projects that focus on desired learning outcomes. Focus on desired learning outcomes or administrative improvements that others, even skeptics, will respect. Involve colleagues in your efforts, sharing credit for a successful job. Slowly build a network of supporters.

Be patient. Be persistent. When someone expresses interest, be prepared to provide more information and detail about implications. Identify the most common questions or objections, and have the answers at hand. Compile success stories. Figure out ways to persuade administration to hear quality leaders in person.

The "onion patch" transformer must keep in mind that efforts should always be geared at involving key leaders of the education system, educating them, and making them believers and champions. Without their eventual buy-in, all transformation efforts will wither on the vine.

(For hints on what to do if there are only a few people in your school district who recognize the need for change, see "The Onion Patch Strategy," left.)

- **Create emotional acceptance**

  Since people resist being changed, transformation or school improvement is a campaign for their hearts as well as their minds. Even when there is a lot of detailed planning and fancy words, very little actually happens as a result of a rational, logical process. Change happens because people as a group accept it.

  Under Management by Results, change is attempted through commands and fear of the administrator. Everyone is told, "All who enter here, put away your brains and follow orders." It might work in the short run. But in the long run, people will spend most of their creative energies designing ways to get around the orders.

  You will need creative, thinking people in a quality learning environment. Talk to the people who will be involved in or affected by a change. Include them in decisions about the change whenever possible. Help them to understand the need to change. Listen and respond to their needs, fears, desires, and concerns about change: make accommodations as necessary.

- **Treat change like a courtship**

  Approach any change as you would a courtship, slowly and with a sense of surprise.

  "Woo" the people. Listen to them. Be responsive to their concerns. When change represents a new lifestyle for people, they need time to warm up to and experiment with it. Permit them to be inelegant and to make mistakes. Help the school stretch itself, but not too much at a time. An idea approached as an experiment or pilot may be accepted more readily than one imposed as a permanent change.

• **Anchor the change**

The individuals or groups on the cutting edge of change will often feel isolated, floundering, or inadequate. Combat such feelings by surrounding them with a network of similar activities, support, and guidance. Make them feel anchored to the direction and main-stream activities of the school district.

With a well-connected network of activity, the people implement-ing change will become part of a common effort to learn and change. If a group falters, let it know help is at hand. Meanwhile, overall progress can be maintained.

SUMMARY

Some people instinctively understand the principles of Dr. Deming and Quality Leadership. "Of course," they say, "how else would you lead a school district? How else would you make decisions? You find out what the learner needs and help the educators do the best job they possibly can. You get good solid data and learn how to interpret what the data tell you. It's common sense. There is no other way."

Such common sense is not so common. In school districts where Management by Results is strongly ingrained, it can be difficult to switch to Quality Leadership. There is no easy way to make a change. We suggest gradually letting go of the old style while growing into the new. Once you make the commitment, it can take several months before you see measurable results, and years to transform the entire dis-trict's school improvement effort.

The rest of this book pulls back from the vision and larger issues of quality improvement to focus on one specific transformation activity: the quality improvement project. We describe the tools, techniques, and attitudes that will make teamwork successful in your district. Most schools have a long road ahead of them. The journey to where teams are an ingrained part of the district is long, but rewarding. We are convinced that school improvement projects conducted as described here will not only lead to substantial improvements in your district, but educate the scores of people who, in one way or another, are touched by these efforts.

Chapter 2
The Basics of Quality Improvement

A statement that expresses the very essence of Quality Leadership is, "Total Quality begins with education and ends with education." Any educational system hoping for long-term improvement must adhere to this philosophy, educating and re-educating everyone from the board of education members, college professors, and superintendent's staff, to the teachers, support staff, faculty members, and all other employees as well as members of the community. These efforts will lead to LASTING improvements when everyone is busy studying and improving some part of the school district.

What do you teach people? There is a lot to learn because the Quality Leadership approach differs so greatly from the way school districts have traditionally been run. This chapter is an overview of the most important principles and concepts, including both the basic philosophy of quality improvement and the problem-solving tools needed to practice this philosophy.

I. Practical Quality Improvement Concepts

As you learn about Quality Leadership and apply the scientific approach to making improvements, there are some basic concepts that everyone who has a role in the education system will find useful. Understanding these concepts allows teams to figure out what their goals should be, what kinds of problems they should be looking for, where to look for them, and what solutions are appropriate. The underlying philosophy is drawn from Dr. Deming's 14 Points (pp. 2-4 to 2-7). It will take many discussions to fully appreciate the significance of these ideas, but here is a quick overview to get you started. There is a worksheet at the end of this section (p. 2-21) to help you begin thinking about these concepts.

Notes. . .

Key Quality Improvement Concepts

- **Processes and Systems**
- **Customers and Suppliers**
- **Quality**
  - § of target values and features
  - § of execution
- **Scientific Approach**
- **Complexity**
  1. Mistakes/defects
  2. Breakdowns/delays
  3. Inefficiencies
  4. Excessive variation
- **Variation**
  - § common causes
  - § special causes
- **Statistically Designed Experiments**

Processes and Systems

We tend to think of educational systems as places where countless tasks or activities get done: teaching classes of children, developing lesson plans, putting grades on report cards, assessing what learners know and can do, clearing the copy machine, calling parents, and on and on. Dr. Deming's view of an organization (above, right) challenges us to look at these tasks in a new light, to think of them as steps or activities in a process. How is a curriculum developed, and what are the best processes for teaching it? How do we determine if the content has been learned or not? What is real learning, and how do we know when it has taken place? What do grades mean, and how, precisely, will they be derived? What are the steps in the assessment process?

We can define a process by grouping in sequence all the tasks and activities directed at accomplishing one particular outcome. Examples are: the steps in producing a lesson, checking pupil attendance, developing a curriculum, hiring or training or evaluating a new teacher, responding to the district office about a change in policy, admitting students to college, or interacting with a parent regarding a discipline problem. In this light, we begin to see that every activity is part of a process, and there are thousands upon thousands of processes in every educational system.

This idea may not seem as glamorous as other quality improvement concepts, but thinking in terms of processes is perhaps the most profound change that occurs during the transformation to Quality Leadership. Whole new insights open up when you begin to see activities as related series of events. You start to see how jobs throughout your school district are related. You can focus your thinking: Since your school district works through processes, you can only improve your work by improving processes. Better processes mean better quality and improved learning environments, which mean longer-lasting improvements that result in better-educated students.

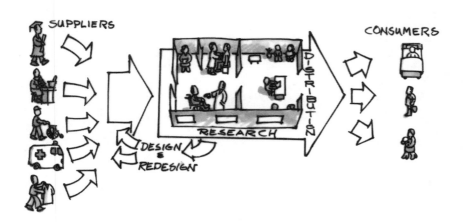

Dr. Deming's View of an Organization

Dr. Deming sees organizations as systems designed to serve customers. Processes and tasks are linked together and affect one another. To excel at meeting customer needs, an organization must constantly improve these systems.

When people begin to look at processes, they will, often for the first time, develop a unified language and understanding of what their roles are. Someone can talk about specific steps in a process, and everyone will understand where those steps fit into the larger picture.

United in a common understanding, people can define starting and ending points to a process, and explain what has to happen in between to continuously improve and create the learning outcomes or other outputs they want. They will be able to focus on errors, waste, and other problems, and determine what data will help them improve the effectiveness of this collection of tasks and activities. And they will have a better idea of where to look for solutions. "What is the process now? What outcomes do we want from this process? What do we have coming in? What must we do to get from one step in the process to the next one? What do we do that is necessary to reach our goals? Which activities of the process are unnecessary? Where do we run into problems?"

People who view work as processes understand how the quality of what comes out is largely determined by the quality of what goes in. How well people can do their jobs depends on the quality of services they receive: A teacher depends on the students' prior preparation, on the quality of the curriculum materials provided. The parents depend on information provided by the school. Everyone depends on the policies, methods, and equipment provided by administration and the board of education.

If a series of related activities can be called a process, a group of related processes can then be seen as a *system*. Teaching a class, for example, is a system that involves thousands of interrelated processes. If a school improvement team feels overwhelmed by its assignment at first, perhaps it is being asked to study a system instead of a process. Unless such a team narrows the project's focus or scope, it stands a good chance of getting mired down and never making any progress. Any improvement team should study one process at a time; the only excep-

Chapter 2

Deming's 14 Points Applied to Education

Over the years, Dr. Deming has developed 14 Points that describe what is necessary for a business to survive and be competitive today. At first encounter, their meaning may not be clear. But they are the very heart of Dr. Deming's philosophy. They contain the essence of all his teachings. Read them, think about them, talk about them with your colleagues or with experts who deeply understand the concepts. And then come back to think about them again. Soon you will start to understand how they work together and their significance in the true quality organization. Understanding the 14 Points can shape a new attitude toward work and the work environment that will foster continuous improvement.

Transformation Through Application of the 14 Points

1. Create constancy of purpose toward improvement of product and service, with the aim to become competitive and to stay in business, and to provide jobs.

For Educators:

- Educators must be clear and constant about the purpose of education.
- The educational system must be focused and persistent in pursuit of that purpose.
- Schools, teaching staff, curricula, programs, and teaching methods have value only as they contribute to that purpose.
- Graduates of our schools will apply their education to their personal life, their family life, their community life, and their work life. The measure of quality in education is how well our graduates can function in and contribute to these parts of their lives.
- Graduates of our schools will help sustain and develop America's place in an interdependent world. The quality of our educational system is crucial to the shaping of America's—and the world's—future.

2. Adopt the new philosophy. We are in a new economic age. Western management must awaken to the challenge, must learn their responsibilities, and take on leadership for change.

For Educators:

- The premises and methods of management have changed. The change began in Japan in 1950, first affecting the consumer electronics and automobile industries. Since then it has spread to all industries—manufacturing and service—and all parts of the world. And it is now extending into the public sector.
- We cannot use old methods to lead in a new era. Those administrators who do not adapt to the new leadership philosophy will put their schools, staff, and students—and their community—at a long-term disadvantage.
- The impact on education is four-fold:
    § It will affect what is taught to students
    § It will affect how students are taught.
    § It will affect how educational systems are lead and administered.
    § It will affect learning outcomes.

3. Cease dependence on inspection to achieve quality. Eliminate the need for inspection on a mass basis by building quality into the product in the first place.

For Educators:

- When a test shows us that a student has not learned, it is too late to improve the educational process for that student. We are left with remedial activities and rework.
- The educational system that relies on testing to measure success is thereby acknowledging the unreliability of its educational processes and methods. If these are not reliable, then why should we trust the same educational system's ability to obtain reliable information from test results.
- We must develop educational systems, processes, and methods that consistently and

reliably educate students with diverse backgrounds and aptitudes for learning. Our knowledge and practice of these processes and methods must be such that there are no failures, no need for rework and remedial activities and therefore no need for testing.

4. End the practice of awarding business on the basis of price tag. Instead, minimize total cost.

For Educators:

- The price tag of a school building is the amount that we must pay to have it built. The cost consists of the price tag plus the useability, adaptability, and durability of the building. You don't know the cost of a school building until you have finished using it. School boards, administrators, and staff too often develop budgets and make decisions based on price tag, not cost.
- To make budgetary decisions based on cost, leaders of educational systems must be clear and constant about the purpose of their organization. Budgets and purchases must accommodate the purpose of the system, not vice versa. Without clarity of purpose and without a long-term, system-wide perspective, these decisions will almost always be based on price tag.

5. Improve constantly and forever the system of production and service, to improve quality and productivity, and thus constantly decrease costs.

For Educators:

- Much of the activity in school systems represents rework, remedial activities, and wasted effort, and tasks which contribute nothing to the educational purpose. We will improve quality and productivity by finding ways to eliminate this work that adds no value.
- In American schools, we are better at change than we are at improvement. And we are better at replacing what we have than we are at improving it. We would realize enormous savings if our changes were all improvements.
- Improvement requires careful study and an intimate awareness of the educational process. Change is easy. Improvement is hard work.

- The methods and strategies of improvement must be mastered throughout the school system and applied continuously. Improvement involves everyone, and it never ends.

6. Institute training on the job.

For Educators:

- The leaders of the system have the responsibility to elevate the level of skill and capability throughout the organization. Next year we should all be able to do things we couldn't do this year.
- Each individual in the system must learn what his or her job is, what constitutes excellence in his or her work, and how to improve his or her work.
- There are no quick fixes in the "Quality School" process. Training and support are prerequisites for success. Research points out that school staff members can and do improve their performance as a result of on-the-job training. As administrators and teachers learn new skills on the job, they become more effective in their roles.

7. Institute leadership. The aim of leadership should be to help people and machines and gadgets to do a better job. Leadership of management is in need of overhaul, as well as leadership of production workers.

For Educators:

- Because the premise of work has changed, the premise of leadership and management has changed. The leader's job is to remove ambiguity, to help everyone understand and respect the interdependence of the entire system, to foster an environment of trust and teamwork, to have an obsession for developing well-educated learners and provide an educational system in which participants experience joy and for which the whole community can take pride.
- Boards of education and administrators who define success simply as the containing of costs and the accomplishment of some numeric goals have abdicated leadership and neglected their responsibility to be leaders of people.

Chapter 2

8. **Drive out fear, so that everyone may work effectively for the company.**

   For Educators:

   - The elimination of fear is an important responsibility of the administrator. Fear can take many forms: fear of making a mistake; fear of change; fear of losing one's job; fear of lack of knowledge; and fear of doing things a new way. Leaders must create an atmosphere of trust and mutual respect, a place of security where risks can be taken and where learning never ceases.
   - Where there is fear, important information and opinions will be withheld or distorted, communication will be inhibited, rumors and negative attributions will abound, relationships will be adversarial, and distrust will be pervasive. Leaders must eliminate fear in order to lead.

9. **Break down barriers between departments. People in research, design, sales, and production must work as a team, to foresee problems of production and in use that may be encountered with the product or service.**

   For Educators:

   - Schools, departments, grades, staff, teachers, administrators, and members of the board of education must work as a team. They are all on the same side, working together in a common system for a common and noble purpose.
   - When parts of the system are at war with each other, what suffers is the output of the system and the quality of educational services provided to the community and its students.
   - Teamwork should extend to the community, its other educational resources, the business sector, social services, government agencies, churches, etc. "It takes a whole village to raise a child."

10. **Eliminate slogans, exhortations, and targets for the work force asking for zero defects and new levels of productivity. Such exhortations only create adversarial relationships, as the bulk of the causes of low quality and low productivity belong to the system and thus lie beyond the power of the work force.**

    For Educators:

    - The key concept that Dr. Deming teaches is that most causes for poor quality and low productivity are attributable to the system. A negligible amount of problems is attributable to individuals.
    - If every individual teacher, student, administrator, and school board member did his or her best, without improvements in the systems, processes, and methods, the increase in quality and productivity would be minuscule. Asking students to improve their knowledge and skill is a waste of time unless the system is changed to allow that to happen. Asking teachers to prepare better and work harder—without improving the system—is equally useless.

11. **(a) Eliminate work standards (quotas) on the factory floor. Substitute leadership. (b) Eliminate management by objective. Eliminate management by numbers, numerical goals. Substitute leadership.**

    For Educators:

    - If a school system accomplishes its purpose, it will have graduates successfully applying what they have learned to their personal, family, social, and professional lives. Graduates will also have learned how to continue learning.
    - Any other measures of success—test scores, GPAs, merit scholars, sports victories—are surrogates that we hope will indicate whether or not education is taking or has taken place. When we focus on these indicators, we risk displacing the purpose of schools from education to grade making, test taking, scholarship winning and game winning. These surrogates become an end in themselves. Looking good replaces doing well.

12. **(a) Remove barriers that rob the hourly worker of his right to pride of workmanship. The responsibility of supervisors must be changed from sheer numbers to quality. (b) Remove barriers that rob people in management and in engineering of their right to pride of workmanship. This means, *inter alia,* abolishment of the annual or merit rating and of management by objective.**

    For Educators:

    - Administrators and educators who believe they can motivate the unmotivated are deluding themselves. Motivation starts within each of us, but we learn demotivation from others. Administrators and educators must ask what they may be doing to demotivate their staff.
    - To be proud of one's work is a source of self-motivation. But when people are placed in a situation where they compete with their peers for recognition and merit pay, great harm to individuals and the organization results. Colleagues and teammates become rivals. The appearance of accomplishment supersedes true accomplishments. Instead of how people feel about themselves and their work, they are told that the judgment of others is what counts. Instead of all of us working together for the good of the whole, each of us works individually for the good of him- or herself. Pride of work is destroyed.
    - School boards and administrators of educational systems should ask staff and teachers in their organizations, "In order to do a good job, what do you need from us that you're not getting?" and "What are you getting from us that you don't need?"

13. **Institute a vigorous program of education and self-improvement.**

    For Educators:

    - Point 6 talks about helping individuals understand their jobs, learn the necessary skills and techniques, and learn how to constantly improve their work. Point 13 stresses the need to encourage people to grow and develop in a variety of ways.
    - We must challenge everyone in our system to pursue a deeper and broader view of the work we do. We must challenge everyone to pursue what Dr. Deming calls "profound knowledge."
    - We must make available the means for people to develop themselves. We must value education for ourselves and our people, not just our students. We cannot predict what new learnings will contribute directly or indirectly to the improvement of any individual's work. We must value learning for its own sake and foster in our people a desire for lifelong learning.

14. **Put everybody in the company to work to accomplish the transformation. The transformation is everybody's job.**

    For Educators:

    - Improvement is not a prerogative reserved for school boards, administration, schools of education, or teachers. Improvement is not the property of some technically elite group. *Everyone* has a stake in improvement. *Everyone* has an indispensable perspective. The need for improvement is so vast and pervasive and continuous, we cannot afford to leave anyone out.

Dr. Deming occasionally modified the wording of these lessons as he gained new insight. This version is from December 1988. The comments for educators were added by the author.

tion is where there are two or three processes that are so closely related it would be difficult to study them separately. One school improvement team recently selected the problem of revising the junior high school curriculum as its assignment. As they proceeded as a team to collect and analyze data, they began to realize the enormous scope of their proposed project. They were, in fact, attempting to study a system rather than a process.

Customers and Suppliers

The concepts of customers and suppliers follow readily once you understand the idea of a process. Suppliers are organizations, groups, or individuals who are associated with the series of tasks preceding the activities you identify as a process. Those who use the outcome of those activities are "customers." These definitions differ from what we are used to because they include customers and suppliers both inside ("internal") and outside ("external") the educational system.

The external customers of a school system are those who depend on the successfully educated student: The student him- or herself, and those with whom the student will work or interact in the future (family, school, the community, etc.). Obviously, it is important to satisfy these external customers. Meanwhile, inside the educational system, people pass on their work to others, who are their internal customers. The educator who writes the lesson plan for the concept that will be studied today is the "customer" of the teacher who wrote the lesson used yesterday.

Similarly, external suppliers are the people outside the educational system who sell materials, information, or services, such as textbook publishers and school bus manufacturers. Inside the school district, people receive work (activities or information) passed on from others in the school district, also internal suppliers. School boards are internal suppliers of policies and financial resources also.

Each person, therefore, *is a customer* of preceding persons and their associated activities. And each *has customers,* the people to whom the person passes on his or her work.

In the day-to-day operations and practices in schools, it is sometimes difficult to decide who is a customer or supplier, and who is not. When educators have difficulty defining the customer for a particular activity, it usually means they failed to define precisely the process they are studying. For example, a school improvement team working on "improved communication" could never define a customer except in the most general terms ("everyone"). If, instead, the team were working on "Improved methods for communicating expectations regarding homework assignments to parents," then the team would have less difficulty identifying the customers (parents) and suppliers (teachers) of this particular communications process.

Each person or collection of activities of the learning environment, therefore, is a customer of preceding persons and their associated activities. The school librarian is the supplier to the pupils and teachers when he/she distributes or "checks out" equipment, materials, and books. However, when a pupil or teacher returns materials and books to the library, the librarian becomes the "customer." In turn, this network of processes—library services—must work as a whole to serve the needs of the outside customers, those who depend on the successfully educated student.

Quality

Once you understand what processes are a part of the learning environment and who the customers are, you will be able to appreciate what quality means in the new education world. Only those who benefit from your work—the customers—can determine what quality is. The community, parents, and students are all partners in defining the quality of education and the learning process. Only they can tell you what they want and how they want it. That's why a popular slogan of the quality movement is "Quality begins with the customer."

You cannot focus solely on a learning outcome from a lesson or a classroom activity in isolation. Quality is determined by both process and outcome. You must build quality into every activity of the process in the educational system. You must work with all internal and external customers to determine their needs, and collaborate with them and with internal and external suppliers to develop a continuously improving education system. With this systems perspective, any person in a school delivering a service will be able to deliver quality to his or her customers, while respecting the needs of the whole educational system.

Providing quality outcomes and services in today's society requires you to think of quality's two dimensions: quality of educational outcomes, and quality of instructional and administrative processes.

• **Quality of educational outcomes**

Are schools doing the right things? Are students learning the right content? Are they proud and delighted? Are the learners achieving the needed learning outcomes when and how they need them? A school can provide learning outcomes or offer a superior service, but all those resources are wasted if it isn't what the learner needs or society wants. A goal of high quality education means choosing learning outcomes that are based on the needs and wants of the community and the students, and the abilities of each individual learner.

• **Quality of instructional and administrative processes**

Are you doing things right? How efficient are the processes used to design, deliver, and provide instructional and supplemental services in the educational system? How well are services for learners planned and delivered?

The final thing to remember about quality is that, as Dr. Deming says of the business world, the responsibility for quality ultimately rests with top management. Only the leaders of the educational system can establish the commitment to quality and prescribe the definition of quality. Only they have the power and influence to provide employees with the support needed to deliver quality products and services to customers.

Teams and Teamwork

A single person using quality improvement practices can make a big difference in an educational system. But rarely does a single person have enough knowledge or experience to understand everything that goes on in a process or system. Therefore, major gains in quality and desired learning outcomes most often result from teams, groups of people working together by pooling their skills, talents, and knowledge. With proper training and coaching, teams can often tackle complex and chronic problems and come up with effective, permanent solutions.

Besides this pooling of skills and understanding, teams have another distinct advantage over solo efforts: the mutual support and synergy that arises between team members. Quality improvement is hard work and takes a long time. It is all too easy for one person's commitment and enthusiasm to flag during a long project. It will be difficult for any classroom teacher to find the time and energy to consistently devote to a continuous improvement effort. The synergy that comes from people working together productively on an important project is usually enough to sustain their enthusiasm and support them through difficult times and hectic school schedules.

As a spirit of teamwork invades the educational system, people everywhere will begin working together towards quality—no barriers, no factions, "all one team" moving together in the same direction.

The 85/15 Rule

There is a widely held belief that an organization would have few, if any, problems if only workers would do their jobs correctly. As Dr. Joseph M. Juran pointed out years ago, this belief is incorrect.

In fact, the potential to eliminate mistakes and errors lies mostly in improving the *systems* through which work is accomplished, not in changing the *people*.

This observation has evolved into the rule of thumb that at least 85 percent of problems can only be corrected by changing systems (which are largely determined by administration) and less than 15 percent are under a worker's control—and the split may lean even more towards the educational system.

For example, a teacher cannot do a top quality job when working with an outdated curriculum; a speech therapist cannot do a good job with equipment that does not work.

Even when it does appear that an individual is doing something wrong, often the trouble lies in how that person was trained, which is a system problem.

Once people recognize that systems create the majority of problems, they will stop blaming parents, students, and individual teachers. They will instead ask which system needs improvement, and will be more likely to seek out and find the true source of a problem.

Scientific Approach

Understanding Quality Leadership is not just rethinking where you are going; it's looking at **how** you will get there. Paying attention to method as well as outcomes is one of the distinguishing features of this new way of leading and managing the educational system.

The core of quality improvement methods is summed up in two words: scientific approach. Though this may sound complicated, a scientific approach is really just a systematic way for individuals and teams to learn about processes, those sets of activities or rules that interact to achieve a desired outcome. It means agreeing to make decisions based on data rather than hunches, to look for root causes of problems rather than react to superficial symptoms, to seek permanent solutions or improvements rather than rely on quick fixes.

A scientific approach, which includes using a variety of basic management tools, can, but does not always, also involve using sophisticated statistical methods. Later in this chapter, we describe the tools of the scientific approach. These tools enable us to go beyond quick fix methods that merely cover up problems to find permanent improvements.

To understand where to apply scientific tools and methods, you must understand what causes problems in processes and how they surface.

Complexity

Many times, the root causes of a problem are buried deep in the procedures and processes used to create and deliver instruction and other services in the learning environment. But even when the original source of the problem is hidden, you can usually detect the complexity—the added work—that was generated to compensate for the problem. Complexity is a general term for unnecessary work, anything that

makes a process more complicated without adding value to the desired outcome.

Typically, complexity arises when people repeatedly try to improve a process without any systematic plan. They try to change one activity by adding or rearranging steps, not realizing that they are distorting other parts of the process. For example, adding lecture time on some subjects, forcing others to be skipped or eliminated entirely. As the problems resulting from distortion start to surface, more and more steps are added to compensate. Almost all processes include work that would not be necessary if systems and processes worked flawlessly.

There are at least four types of complexity: (1) mistakes, (2) delays and breakdowns, (3) inefficiencies, and (4) excessive variation. The odds are high that a process or system will have at least one of these process problems; many will have several. Project teams should examine their processes to identify tasks, jobs, and activities that fall into one of these categories, then work to track down the root causes. As they perform the problem-solving process, they should keep in mind the 85/15 Rule (left) and the Pareto Principle (right).

1. Mistakes

When a mistake occurs, work has to be repeated and extra steps added to correct the error. Dr. Deming calls this "scraping burnt toast," that is, fixing the problem rather than preventing it. Example: Permission slips for a field trip are sent out with the incorrect date, creating a chaotic situation. This includes contacting each parent by phone or retyping or reprinting the permission slip with the correct date and sending it to each parent again. These steps, needed because of the mistake, add no value to the outcome. The solution lies in finding ways to error-proof the process, making sure such problems never arise.

Pareto Principle

This principle is sometimes called the 80-20 rule: 80% of the trouble comes from 20% of the problems. Though named for the turn-of-the-century economist Vilfredo Pareto, it was Dr. Juran who applied the idea to management. Dr. Juran advises us to concentrate on the "vital few" sources of problems and not be distracted by those of lesser importance.

Many educational systems concentrate their efforts on fixing mistakes instead of preventing them.

Examples of Inefficiencies

A large school district was caught with a limited supply of curriculum guides, which had been written by teachers to implement a new approach to the study of mathematics in grades K–5. Several schools in the district were without the mathematics curriculum guides necessary to implement the new program. The supervisor of mathematics tried to correct the mistake by ordering a special printing of the needed guides from the school district's printing office. Unfortunately, the school district's printing office could not print the number of curriculum guides needed in a timely fashion, and the school district had to pay an outside printing company to complete the order. This added considerable cost to the budget.

# # #

Secretaries who enter attendance data were concerned and wondered why they made so many errors when entering records into the computer. They discovered that the information to be entered on a form designed years ago. The format no longer applied to the computer system. After the forms were redesigned to match the sequence in which the computer requested the information, the errors were greatly reduced.

continued on next page

2. Breakdowns/Delays

Sometimes the output of a process has been without mistakes, but the process has broken down and work has ground to a halt. Real work is put on hold and displaced with waiting.

Examples:

a. A poorly maintained copying machine keeps breaking down. This causes delays all along the process, and much confusion as people try to keep track of exactly where materials were before the machine stopped.

b. Several parts are missing from a science kit, so it is labeled and stored on a shelf and the activities related to the science curriculum are no longer taught until the missing pieces are replaced.

c. A PTA president wants to notify people of an upcoming meeting, but has an incomplete list of telephone numbers and addresses. More calls are needed to get the information.

d. The school bus is constantly late because the district is trying to save money by creating long bus runs. As a result students are chronically late for class.

3. Inefficiencies

Even when there are no mistakes and the work flow isn't interrupted, sometimes more instructional material, time, and movement is used than absolutely essential. Often the inefficiency arose because something happened that upset the process, and the effects remained long after the problem was gone. In some cases, there is a clear reason why the process was established the way it was. At other times, there is no way of knowing how the inefficient process began. Example: By tracing their movements on a floor plan of their work area, teachers discovered they crisscross their paths many times to get all the instructional material they need. No one is sure exactly how the floor plan got the way it was. Still, they redesigned the layout to reduce these movements, eliminating the complexity of unnecessary movement.

4. Excessive Variation

When outcomes of some activity are highly diverse, educators or policymakers are forced to add steps to a process in order to remedy inadequate outcomes. Example: "All students with scores below a certain point receive extra tutoring." Usually, remedial steps seem so natural that everyone thinks it is normal to have this remediation. It doesn't even occur to those involved that it's possible to have educational methods that produce outcomes so uniform that a remedy is not needed. The key is to understand that variation needs to be studied and reduced.

Variation

If you had your choice of working in a learning environment that was predictable, consistent, and had minimal waste of time or effort, or one where the environment was erratic, whose learning outcomes were high one day and low the next, which would you choose? It doesn't take a genius to recognize the benefits of having a process whose capability and results are consistent and well understood.

Variation is one of the main culprits working to make processes unreliable or erratic. Every learning environment or system has variation in its input, process, and outcomes. In fact, there are a vast number of potential causes of variation in every system. And that means that no two outcomes will ever be exactly the same. If, for example, your aim is to teach simple addition, there will always be some differences in the way the lesson is planned and the instruction is delivered. Among learners there will be variation regarding how fast and thoroughly they comprehend and master the skill. There will be variation no matter how well you perform your role.

At budget time, the principal of a rural school (without a gym) consistently requested that the blacktop portion of the school playground be repaved. Rainy weather created flooding and caused the entire student body to remain indoors for long periods of time throughout the school year. The cost of the repaving was approximately $8,000. The school district only approved $1,500 for cinders to be dumped into the holes, which quickly washed away. After four years, the school district finally approved the $8,000 budget for repaving, after wasting time and money with cinders, which did not solve the problem.

\# \# \#

Each February, students who are identified as being two grade levels below their grade level placement in language arts are assigned to a special remedial class. Since the special class meets at the same time as their regular language arts class, they do not receive the regular language arts instruction. They thus fall farther and farther behind as the remedial curriculum emphasizes seat work over activity, breadth over depth, and rote memorization over critical thinking.

Though we can't eliminate all the variation in a process, we do have tools and methods that allow us to reduce variation. The goal is to improve the outcome by reducing variation as much as possible. That way you will be able to predict more accurately how much you can achieve and what level of quality is possible, given your current process.

One approach to reducing variation is standardization: getting staff to pursue common outcomes using agreed-upon curriculum, materials, procedures, methods, use of technology, and so forth. This alone has enormous potential to create more-uniform outcomes and approaches, providing a basis for a common interdependent educational system. A second approach is to study the process as it now operates, looking for potential sources of variation to study further. What can we learn about these students' learning patterns? Does the time of day affect their learning? What about changing the learning environment? You can then structure data collection to see if these process conditions do affect the outcomes. (See "Stratification," p. 2-34.)

There is some overlap in these two approaches (standardization, identification and reduction of certain sources of process variation) because they share a common goal: to improve the outcomes to a desired range. However, each has a contribution to make in our quest to control variation. (See the Improvement Strategies "Develop a Standard Process," p. 5-54, and "Reduce Sources of Variation," p. 5-59.)

Use of these strategies often highlights obvious sources of variation that can be eliminated or reduced relatively easily. But they can take you only part of the way to creating processes and learning environments that are truly consistent and predictable. To reach this state, you must understand the concept of having a process that is "stable," and understand the difference between "common causes" and "special causes" of variation. From a quality perspective, the ultimate goal is to determine the limits of the inherent (common cause) variation, which specifies what the capability of the process is.

• **Common causes of variation**

Common-cause variation is typically due to a large number of small sources of variation. The *sum* of these small causes may result in a considerable amount of variation with widely diverse learning outcomes or other outputs. This variation results from a large number of conditions and factors. The instruction time it takes to teach simple addition will vary from class to class. There are many things that can contribute to these differences; we will never know them all. It is the sum of the common causes that determines the inherent variation of a process and thus statistically determines its limits and its capability as it is currently practiced.

• **Special causes of variation**

Special causes of variation are not part of a process all the time. They arise because of specific circumstances. A learner who is visually impaired may have difficulty learning because he may not be able to see the chalkboard adding greatly to the variation in the class's test scores. A teacher being sick or a tragedy among a group of students are not ordinary occurrences. These would be special causes of variation.

Dealing with each type of variation requires distinctly different approaches. If you respond to common-cause variation as if it were due to special causes, you will make matters worse and increase variation in a teaching/learning process. If you fail to notice the appearance of a special cause, you will miss an opportunity to search out and eliminate a source of process problems.

Though these concepts are difficult to explain in the abstract, they are implemented in the school or classroom through use of "control charts." Control charts show the measurements of a process characteristic (daily attendance, number of children who complete their homework daily, number of students who buy lunch) or the outcomes of the process. All process and outcome data are plotted in time order.

In addition to showing the data, these charts have two lines ("control limits") that indicate limits to the common-cause variation inherent in the process or its outcomes as it operates over a specified period of time. These control limits are calculated from the measurements actually taken on the process. They are *not* simply theories of what should be happening, nor are they indicators of what you would like to have happen. They simply tell you how much variation you must expect to see in today's process. They provide a basis for action when unusual patterns or amounts of variation appear.

Use control charts to monitor a process. Points that fall outside the limits or that fall into any of several specified patterns are *signals* to search for a special cause. React to these signals by tracking down and eliminating the special cause. As you do so, you slowly bring your processes into a stable, more consistent condition called "statistical control." The result is a stable process. (See Dr. Deming's notes, p. 2-19.)

Elimination of special causes is a critical first step. But once the process is stable, or in statistical control, the harder job begins because eliminating common causes requires in-depth knowledge of the subject matter. As Dr. Deming points out, sometimes simple changes can improve a stable process. Other times, you will only be able to improve a process through laborious hard work and clever thought. Statistically designed experiments are sometimes helpful.

Some notes on a stable process and on tampering by Dr. W. Edwards Deming

Understanding and controlling variation is a subject at the very heart of Dr. Deming's theories. Here's what he has to say on the subject.*

A stable process, one with no indication of a special cause of variation, is said to be, following Shewhart, in statistical control or stable with respect to the quality-characteristic measured. It is a random process. Its behavior in the near future is predictable. Of course, some unforeseen jolt may come along and knock the process out of statistical control. A system that is in statistical control has a definable identity and a definable capability (see *Out of the Crisis,* p. 339).

Suppose that you have brought a process into statistical control. This you have accomplished with effort. You have searched for each special cause one by one when a point went beyond control limits. Certain patterns of points on a control chart may also indicate a special cause. You have tried, with apparent success, to identify each cause, and to remove it.

Once you reach statistical control, the difficult problem commences—improve the system. Improvement nearly always means reduction of variation (narrower control limits), though it may also require movement of the average (the central line) to a higher or lower level. Improvement of a stable system requires fundamental change in the system. This fundamental change required may be extremely simple. Example: provide better illumination in a room.

On the other hand, the fundamental change required may be complex or even costly. It may require authorization and effort higher up. Example: develop better understanding between the upper management of the customer and the upper management of a supplier.

Specification limits are not control limits. (*Out of the Crisis,* p. 335). [They represent wishes, hopes and needs, not process capability.]

If the system is not worth the cost of improvement, it might be wise to abandon the control chart and direct effort to other systems more in need of attention. We should study with the aid of the Taguchi loss function (William J. Scherkenbach, *The Deming Route,* pp. 42ff.) the economics of shrinkage of variation.

A system may be stable, yet turn out faulty items and mistakes. To take action on the system in response to production of a faulty item or a mistake is to tamper with the system. The result of tampering is only to increase in the future the production of faulty items and mistakes, and to increase costs—exactly the opposite of what we wish to accomplish.

Of course we wish to stay within specifications. No one wishes to turn out faulty product and mistakes. We know also that it is not sufficient just to meet specifications; we should try to reduce variation of a stable system (*Out of the Crisis,* pp. 139–142; Scherkenbach, *The Deming Route,* pp. 40–46).

A special cause may turn out to be one that cannot possibly recur. An example might be a mishap from foreign material received in a batch. The vendor has already taken steps to ensure nonrecurrence.

On the other hand, a special cause may be one that will recur. If the recurrence is periodic (every Monday at 1000 h), clues to the source may be unmistakable. Sporadic recurrence will require detective work.

---

*These are excerpts from a note Dr. Deming sent to us on 16 May 1988.

A Sample Designed Experiment

The school administrators learned that the board of education was going to mandate a change in the curriculum. The administrators recommended a pilot program to study the implementation of the proposed curriculum change.

The first results were unsatisfactory even though the staff carefully followed the board of education recommendations. Since many factors could influence quality, they decided to collect and analyze the data from a second pilot project.

The second pilot revealed that most of the changes had little or no effect on performance. But in subsequent pilots, the staff team controlled various factors: class size, the pace of teaching, and the type of interaction between students. They learned what combination of factors optimized the results.

As a result of these studies, the process in question was better than the original process. Thus the school system was able to extend the curriculum change to other schools in the district.

Statistically Designed Experiments

Statistically designed experiments are a wide range of efficient, systematic, and flexible protocols for running experiments. Though not terribly difficult to use after you've had experience, it takes a while to learn how to use them properly, which is why you should always start off under the guidance of someone who has used designed experiments. Here we provide only a brief overview.

The distinguishing characteristic of designed experiments is testing many factors in each experiment, rather than testing one factor at a time as in traditional experiments. It is this multifactor approach that makes designed experiments efficient: Testing many factors at one time means you can get more out of your research and project dollars. To avoid confusion, the factors are tested systematically in predetermined patterns and combinations. The designs are flexible and can be adapted to everything from school labs to the classroom. In the most common designs, 3 to 15 factors are tested at 2 levels apiece, but the number of factors or levels can exceed this range. After choosing the factors and levels, the experimenter selects a set of experimental trials, or runs. Each run is one specific combination of the factors and levels being tested. (See the example described, left, and the one in Chapter 5, p. 5-64.)

Uses for statistically designed experiments

- Pilot test alternative methods for implementing changes to determine the right combination of conditions and approaches.

- Increase your process capability by finding optimal operating procedures.

- Design a method for teaching a particular lesson which will turn out well even when conditions are less than perfect.

Practical Concepts Worksheet

Instructions: Read through the descriptions of the practical quality improvement concepts given on the preceding pages. The questions below should help you apply these concepts to your organization. Work alone and jot down your answers on a separate page, or use the questions to stimulate discussion in your team.

1. What is your job? Into what process or processes does it fit? What product or service results from that process?

2. Who are your external customers? Internal customers?

3. Who are your external suppliers? Internal suppliers?

4. What are the quality characteristics of the product or service? What criteria are important to your customers (both internal and external)?

5. Give examples of quality characteristics related to:

    - Quality of the educational outcomes. (what you do)
    - Quality of the instructional process. (how it gets done)

6. Review the descriptions of the sources of complexity. Give examples of each that you have seen on the job.

    - Mistakes
    - Delays/Breakdowns
    - Inefficiencies
    - Excessive Variation

7. What would it take to reduce or eliminate this complexity. Keep in mind the lesson of the 85/15 Rule.

8. How would you go about measuring variation? How could you determine its impact on the quality of your process?

9. What kinds of common causes of variation do you think you will find in your process? What kinds of special causes? (Record these answers and later on compare them with what you actually find out.)

10. Though not every team will need to use designed experiments, more of them should be using experiments than actually do. How would you know whether your team should investigate this possibility? (Hint: One answer to this question is related to special versus common causes of variation.)

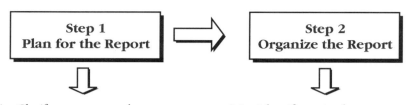

II. Tools of the Scientific Approach

The main purpose of this book is to get a school improvement team started and working effectively and efficiently. Reviewing a variety of tools used most frequently in a scientific approach to quality improvement is a part of this process. These tools help your team visualize a process, pinpoint problems, find their causes, and determine solutions. They also provide a way to evaluate proposed changes.

These tools look deceptively simple. "Is that all there is?" is a common reaction. However, most teams will need an expert's help in the early stages to choose appropriate tools, and to know when and how to use them. Successful improvement teams work with experts to internalize the application of these tools so that the team becomes more self-sufficient in doing its own work. Study these tools and practice applying them under an expert's guidance.

Most tools can be used in several stages of a project. The sequence given here generally reflects one order in which they might be used.

Flowcharts

Flowcharts are step-by-step, schematic pictures used to plan stages of a project or describe a process being studied. As outlines of a sequence of actions, they provide team members with common reference points and a standard language to use when talking about an existing process or project. They can also be used to describe a desired sequence and order of activities of a new, improved process.

Four types of flowcharts have proven particularly useful: top-down flowchart, detailed flowchart, work-flow diagram, and deployment chart. Each highlights different aspects of a process or task. The detailed flowchart is most time-consuming and least useful; the other three are simpler and usually more effective visual tools for describing what really happens in a process.

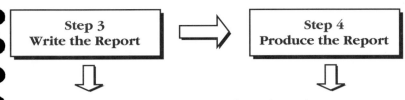

| Step 3
Write the Report | ⟹ | Step 4
Produce the Report |

⇩ | ⇩

3.1 Write report.

3.2 Edit for flow, completeness.

3.3 Refine text.

3.4 Incorporate charts and graphs

3.5 Copyedit (typos, errors).

4.1 Design layout.

4.2 Type or typeset the text; get final draft of charts.

4.3 Do paste-up.

4.4 Proofread and correct.

4.5 Photocopy or print.

Top-Down Flowcharts . . .

Are simple, easy-to-construct charts that emphasize the major steps of a process. The one shown here can be used to develop a team report.

• Top-down flowchart

A top-down flowchart is a picture of the major activities in a process or project. By limiting the amount of information that goes on any single chart, top-down flowcharts force people to narrow their thinking to only those steps absolutely essential to the process. The resulting picture therefore represents only useful work, omitting other activities that have evolved to detect or respond to quality problems.

Why is this so useful? Every process changes slowly over time, usually by accumulating complexity (steps put in to fix process problems that shouldn't occur in the first place). The productivity drops accordingly. Top-down flowcharts free people to consider only what should happen in a process rather than what actually does. Once they chart the major steps and sub-steps, they can then ask, "Where do we go off track?" and "What causes us to go off track?" This helps them determine which steps are complexity and which are necessary. These answers point them towards potential sources of problems, not just the problems themselves. Typically, this approach is faster and more efficient than spending weeks or months constructing a detailed flowchart of every step that occurs.

The same concept applies when the top-down flowchart is used for planning. Teams can avoid haggling over details, and instead spend their energies on looking at the whole project. Once developed, a top-down flowchart of a project is a quick overview of how a project is likely to unfold. Particular steps can be developed in more detail by the team members involved in carrying out that part of the plan.

Constructing a top-down flowchart

To construct a top-down flowchart, first list the most basic steps in the process being studied or project being planned. You should end up with no more than six or seven steps. List these steps across the top of the page or flipchart. Then below each one, list the major substeps (again no more than six or seven).

Detailed Flowcharts . . .

Describe most or all of the steps in a process, with varying levels of detail. Often this level of detail is unnecessary, but when needed, the team as a whole will usually develop a top-down version, then smaller work groups can add levels of detail as needed throughout the project.

• Detailed flowchart

A detailed flowchart, as the name implies, is a flowchart that includes a lot of information about what happens at every stage in a process. The chart shows all or most of the steps in a process, including loops caused by the need for rework or remedial activities. Sometimes teams need more detail in order to understand where problems arise. Use detailed flowcharts sparingly, however, because the detail they provide is often unnecessary, and it can take weeks to get one that all team members agree on. By that time, everyone is discouraged about the lack of progress.

In creating the detailed flowchart, its purpose or use helps determine what level of detail is needed. It is important to get the right amount of detail in your flowchart. If an outline of the major steps is all you need, then spending time with additional details is wasted time. However, the more detail you capture, the more information you have about how the process actually works.

If you decide you need a detailed flowchart, make sure everyone on the team agrees about how much detail to include. Will "fill out the form" be sufficient or do you want "enter your name and the data on the form; describe the item; check the appropriate boxes"? If such decisions aren't clear, team members' preparations will probably be incompatible.

Chapter 7

Detailed Flowchart of
Pupil Attendance Checking Process

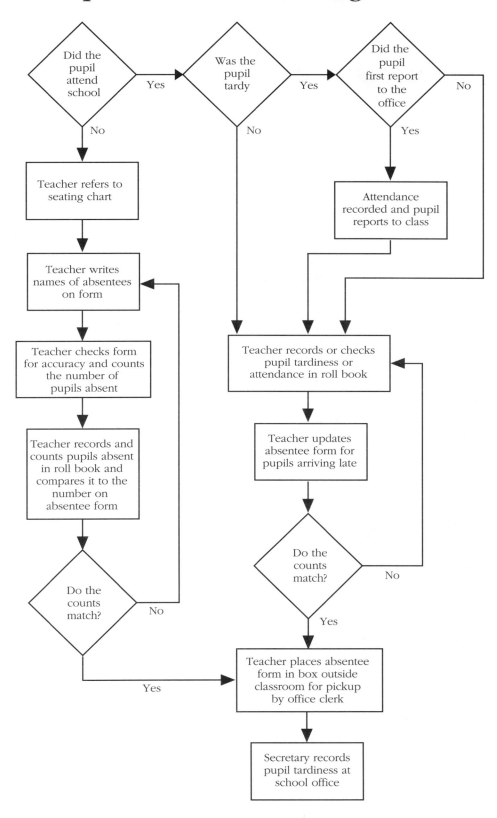

Work-flow diagrams . . .

Show the flow or movement of materials, people, or information within any space.

• **Work-flow diagram**

A work-flow diagram is a picture of the movements of people, materials, documents, or information in a process. It is created by tracing these movements on a sketch of the floor plan or some similar map of the work space. The power of these sketches lies in illustrating a system's inefficiency in a clear picture. Places where work can be simplified will jump off the page. The example on the facing page, for example, shows how people in a school health room were able to redesign the work space to minimize movements.

For example, teachers and students can draw lines on a school floor plan to show how they move around during a normal work day; attendance specialists can similarly mark copies of forms they use to see whether information is arranged in a logical sequence; secretaries can track the flow of forms and invoices through the school district. In each case, the interest lies in whether there is excessive or unnecessary movement. If so, have the people involved think about what an ideal layout would be, then see if the work space or forms can be rearranged to eliminate the problem.

Before...

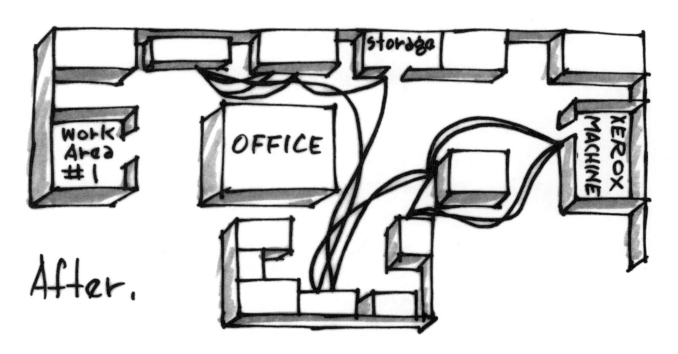

After.

Deployment Charts . . .

Show both the flow of a process and which people or groups are involved at each step. The one shown here depicts how the "report preparation flowchart" described previously (p. 2–22 and 2–23) might look as a deployment chart. The shaded boxes indicate who has primary responsibility for that step; the ovals indicate a helper or advisor.

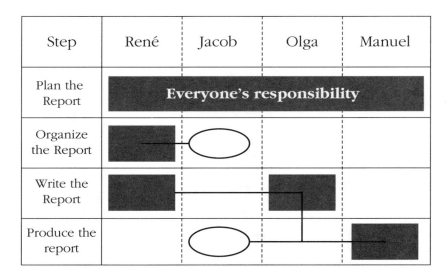

Step	René	Jacob	Olga	Manuel
Plan the Report	**Everyone's responsibility**			
Organize the Report	■	◯		
Write the Report	■		■	
Produce the report		◯		■

• **Deployment chart**

A deployment chart combines two ideas: what happens in a process or project (the tasks or activities accomplished) and who is responsible for each step. These charts show the major steps of a process, just as in the top level of a top-down flowchart, along with which person or group is the center of activity for that step. These charts are useful for school project teams and district-level teams to keep track of what each person or group is supposed to do, where the people involved fit in the sequence, and how they will relate to the other people at that stage.

To construct a deployment chart, use the following steps:

1. Clarify the purpose.

2. Agree on the level of detail and the start and end steps.

3. List the key people and groups across the top of the page.

4. Draw lines from the top to bottom to create columns.

5. Arrange steps.
   • Place the first step in the column of the person or group responsible for it. Use other symbols to indicate groups or people who play a role but do not have primary responsibility.
   • Place each succeeding step lower than the preceding step, and in the column of the person responsible for it.

6. Check to be sure the time sequence flows down the page.

7. Check for completeness and add any missing steps.

8. Add flow lines.

When you use different symbols, anyone can read the chart to discover how the process operates at each step, which people are involved, and what kind of responsibility each has.

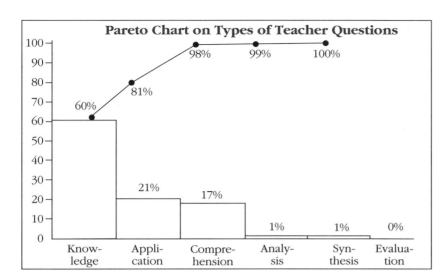

Pareto Charts . . .

Focus improvement efforts by ranking problems or their causes.

Pareto Charts

A Pareto chart is a series of bars whose heights reflect the frequency or severity of problems. The bars are arranged in descending order of height from left to right. This means the categories represented by the tall bars on the left are relatively more important than those on the right. The name of the chart derives from the Pareto Principle ("80% of the trouble comes from 20% of the problems"). Though the percentages will never be that exact, teams usually find that most trouble comes from only a few problems.

Pareto charts are useful throughout a project: early on to identify which problem should be studied, later to narrow down which causes of the problem to address first. Since they draw everyone's attention to the "vital few" important factors where the benefit is likely to be greatest, Pareto charts can be used to build consensus in a group. In general, teams should focus their attention first on the biggest problems, those with the highest bars.

Cause-and-Effect Diagrams . . .

Identify and organize possible causes of problems, or factors needed to insure success of some effort. The problem, situation, or event is listed on the right. Branches off the central arrow indicate main categories of items. Use of this format allows people to easily see the relationship between factors.

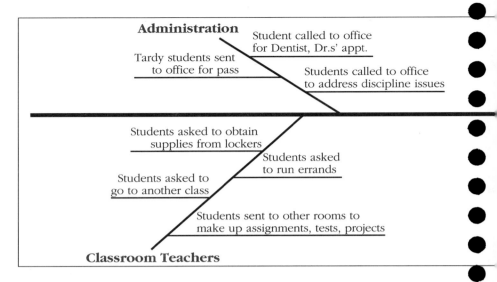

Cause-and-Effect Diagram

The cause-and-effect diagram, also called a "fishbone diagram" because of its appearance, allows you to map out a list of factors or process characteristics thought to affect a problem or desired outcome. This type of diagram was invented by Kaoru Ishikawa, and hence is also called an "Ishikawa diagram." It is an effective tool for identifying and organizing possible causes of a problem in a structured format.

This diagram is a kind of map showing possible cause-and-effect relationships. The lines fan out to show ever deeper possible causes and the relationships among them. Once you have identified the possible causes, you must verify them with data to confirm that they actually are real causes. In developing a cause-and-effect diagram, remember that

- The "head" of the diagram is a brief description of the problem.

- Each of the "bones" represents a potential cause of the problem.

- The smaller "bones" represent deeper causes of the larger "bones" they are attached to.

A cause-and-effect diagram helps solve problems by

- Identifying potential causes.

- Making relationships among factors visible.

- Helping structure ways to think about possible causes.

- Providing a framework for documenting verified causal relationships.

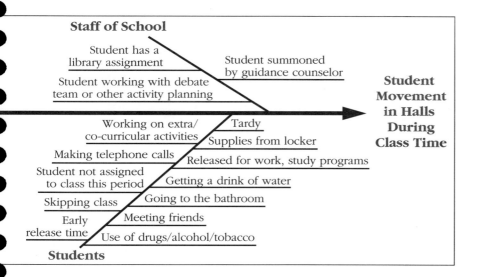

This tool often leads to greater understanding of factors that contribute to a problem. For example, if one potential cause of a problem is "equipment failure," then the smaller bones are causes of equipment failure such as lack of maintenance or part failures. You can generate deeper causes for each level of problem by simply asking questions such as, "What could cause Part A to fail?" The answers help you extend your diagram in a way that can help you effectively solve the problem.

Cause-and-effect diagrams are most effective after the process has been described and the problem well-defined. By then, team members will have a good idea of which potential causes to include on the diagram. When creating a cause-and-effect diagram, consult with colleagues not on the team who are familiar with various aspects of the process. This way your team will be less likely to miss important potential causes.

Remember that cause-and-effect diagrams identify only *possible* causes. Even when everyone agrees on these possible causes, only data will point to *actual* causes.

Operational Definitions

An operational definition describes *what* something is and *how* it is measured. For example, an operational definition of "a student with a handicap" could be: the learning disabled student, a student who has an individualized educational plan (IEP) and receives appropriate services and instructional intervention. An operational definition of a "report handed in on time" could be one that is given to the teacher by the end of class on the day it is due.

Each team must discuss what quality characteristics or other quantities it will be measuring, and decide how these will be measured. The goal is to get a definition that all team members agree to, and that gives consistent results no matter who does the measuring. Having these common definitions is critical for gathering meaningful data. To be useful, they must represent a consensus on precisely what criteria everyone will use in studying or measuring a problem, what procedures and instruments will be used, and so forth.

The need for operational definitions arises because we tolerate a lot of imprecision in our everyday conversation—"When I'm out too late, I feel miserable the whole next day!" What does this person mean by "out," "too late," or "feel miserable"? Would these words mean the same thing to everyone?

To collect meaningful data, we must know precisely what to observe and how to measure it. In an educational context, what do we mean by "mastery," "on-time," "gifted," "alignment," "user-friendly," "at-risk students," or "above average"?

Suppose you are responsible for taking attendance at the beginning of the class. Sounds clear enough doesn't it? But then a bus arrives 15 minutes late, and you are told via the intercom that these students are to be admitted to class and should be marked "excused absent." Another student arrives late and says she doesn't think she should be marked absent or tardy because she was meeting with the guidance counselor. Unless you have operational definitions of "absent" or "tardy," you cannot record attendance data in a consistent way.

To avoid this imprecision when your team collects data, have people envision or walk through the procedures they will use. Discuss similarities and differences between different data collectors. Decide exactly what everyone will measure, how they will measure it, how far off something can be and still be counted, what equipment or criteria will be used, and so forth. Even if one procedure does not stand out as clearly superior, choose one that every person will agree to use.

Run trials where everyone taking data will measure or categorize the same items. Compare outcomes, discuss differences, and continue to run trials until there is agreement. If customers or suppliers will be involved in data collection, include them in these trials. For example, if a change to a checklist describing types of student behavior is to occur, parents, students, and school staff should work together to accomplish the change.

All these considerations are part of an operational definition.

Stratification and Is/Is-Not Analysis . . .

Help pinpoint a problem by exposing where it does and does not occur. Such analysis lets teams avoid wasteful effort, directing their energies to the most potentially fruitful areas.

Stratification and Is/Is-Not Analysis

Stratification and Is/Is-Not analysis are both ways to split, or "stratify," data in ways that expose underlying patterns. Discovering such patterns helps localize a problem, making it easier to identify the cause of the problem. This analysis both precedes data collection (so the team will know what kind of differences to look for) and follows it (so the team can discover which factors actually affected the results).

To stratify data, first examine the process to see what characteristics could lead to biases in data; these are not necessarily factors that actually *do* cause differences, only ones that *could*. For example, might the way critical thinking skills are taught across classrooms differ appreciably between regular and honor classes? Is classroom behavior different when special art, music, and physical education teachers are being used instead of the regular classroom teachers? Are the routine mistakes made by new teachers much different from those made by more experienced teachers? Do outcomes in mathematics on Mondays differ substantially from those for the rest of the week?

As a team, make a list of the characteristics you think could cause systematic differences in your results. Incorporate the information into data collection forms (for example, record the day of the week so you can later see if results depend on which day you measured). Once your data collection is complete, look first for patterns related to time or sequence. Then check for systematic differences between days of the week, classroom, people, and so on.

One structured form of stratification is the Is/Is-Not matrix (facing page) based on ideas developed by Charles H. Kepner and Benjamin B. Tregoe. It helps you sort out observed characteristics so you can speculate on possible causes of patterns you identify.

The Is/Is-Not Matrix

Instructions: Identify the problem or situation you want to analyze. Use this matrix to organize your knowledge and information. Your answers should help you pinpoint the occurrence of the problem, and guide data collection so you can verify your conclusions/suspicions.

	Is Where, when, to what extent, or regarding whom does this situation occur?	**Is Not** Where, etc., does this situation NOT occur, though it reasonably might have?	**Therefore** What might explain the pattern of occurrence and non-occurrence?
Where The physical or geographical location of the event or situation. Where it occurs or where it is noticed.			
When The hour, time of day, day of week, month, time of year of the event or situation. Its relationship (before, during, after) to other events.			
What kind or how much The type or category of event or situation. The extent, degree, dimensions, or duration of the occurrence.			
Who (Do not use these questions to blame.) What relationship do various individuals or groups have to the situation or event? To whom, by whom, near whom, etc., does this occur?			

Chapter 2

Time Plots . . .

Are used to examine data for trends or other patterns that occur over time. A time plot is just the data points plotted in time order.

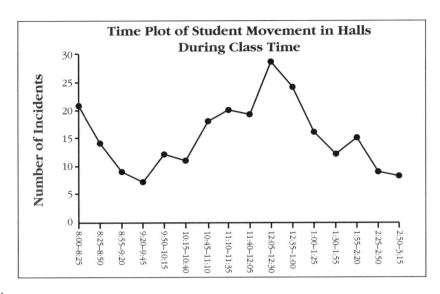

Time Plot

Many factors that affect a process change over time: new teachers are hired; attention span falters as the day continues; classroom behavior seems to have a cycle reflecting the day of the week and or proximity to grading periods; response to curriculum changes or world events cause materials to become outdated. Any of these changes can affect data you collect from a process over time. Detecting these time-related shifts, trends, or patterns is an essential step in making long-lasting improvements. And the best way to detect the effect of these types of changes is to plot relevant measurements in time order.

When you collect data over time, the first step is to make a time plot because the presence of a time-related trend can invalidate other forms of data analysis (such as the dot plot, described on p. 2-38).

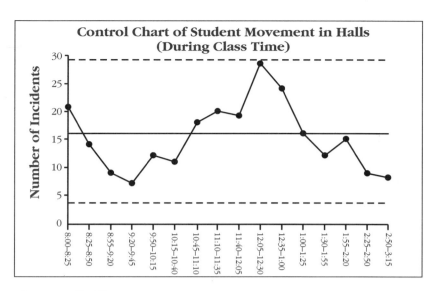

Control Chart of Student Movement in Halls
(During Class Time)

Control Charts . . .

Are used to monitor a process to see whether it is in statistical control. The UCL and LCL—or upper and lower control limits, respectively—indicate how much variation is typical for the process. Points that fall outside the limits or into particular patterns indicate the presence of a special cause of variation, a cause that deserves investigation.

Control Chart

A control chart is a time plot with one extra feature: It also indicates the range of common cause variation built into the process. The boundaries of this range are marked by upper and lower statistical control limits, which are calculated according to statistical formulas from data collected on the process.

Control charts help you distinguish between variation inherent in a process (variation from a "common cause") and variation arising from sources that come and go unpredictably ("special causes"). Points that occur outside the control limits or that fall into specific patterns are signals of special causes of variation, meaning it should be relatively easy to track down that source and prevent its recurrence. Data points that fall randomly within the control limits indicate that most variation is coming from common causes. The only way to make improvements in a system that only has common cause variation is to fundamentally change some aspect of the process (materials, procedures, equipment, training, etc.).

Note: Control limits are not the same as specification limits (a cut-off score for an admissions test or a graduation examination), nor are they related to budgets, targets, or objectives. (See the discussion earlier in this chapter under "Variation," starting on p. 2-15). Control limits say nothing about how a process is supposed to perform or what administrators or policymakers hope it can achieve. They only indicate what the process is capable of doing.

Chapter 2

Dot Plots and Stem-and-Leaf Displays . . .

Show which values occur and how often. Can be used to quickly check the distribution, or spread, of the data.

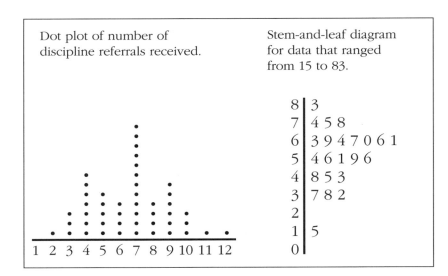

Dot plot of number of discipline referrals received.

Stem-and-leaf diagram for data that ranged from 15 to 83.

```
8 | 3
7 | 4 5 8
6 | 3 9 4 7 0 6 1
5 | 4 6 1 9 6
4 | 8 5 3
3 | 7 8 2
2 |
1 | 5
0 |
```

Dot Plot and Stem-and-Leaf Displays

A dot plot starts as a line marked off in units corresponding to data measurement. A dot is then placed above a value for each time that value appeared in the data. Dot plots are easily constructed, display all the data points, and readily convey information. A quick look at one tells you right away the range of measurements you found, what the central value or average is, and how data points are distributed around the average (whether they are symmetric or not). Sometimes they are used to get a quick look at data before further analysis. Any data plotted on a time plot is usually converted to a dot plot to watch the distribution (spread of points) as well as the pattern over time. Note: Do not make a dot plot of data that shows time-related patterns. In many cases, the plotted points will fall into the outline of a bell, a shape familiar to statisticians. The bell is formed by a natural tendency in data points to cluster about a central value (called the "average" or "mean") and taper off symmetrically on both sides. Other times they may show abnormal data patterns such as those caused by error or inspector bias.

A stem-and-leaf diagram is a minor variation on the dot plot. Here, a line (or "stem") is drawn vertically, and the units that would be marked below the line on a dot plot are put on the left of this line. The rest of the digits from the actual measurements are entered on the corresponding rows. For example, in the diagram shown above, the units of ten are shown on the left side of the stem, and the units of one are on the right.

The advantage of stem-and-leaf diagrams over the dot plot is that you can easily reproduce the actual measurements; in a dot plot you may have trouble deciding at a later time exactly where the measurement fell. However, as shown in the examples above, dot plots work well where there are many repeated values.

A simple checksheet for monitoring classroom interruptions

Date: _____

Teacher Name: _____

Types of Interruptions (Causes)	Period of the Day							Total
	1	2	3	4	5	6	7	
01 Intercom	I					I	I	3
02 Classroom								0
03 Assignments					II	II		4
04 Borrowing								0
05 Clarification								0
06 Asst. Principal								0
07 Parent Helper								0
08 Intercom Students								0
09 Check Out								0
10 Errands	I	I		I		I		4
11 Visit Teacher								0
12 Prin/Supervisor								0
13 Guid. Counselor	I	I				I	I	4
14 Admin Duties								0
15 No Cause Given								0
Total for each period (Daily Total)	3	2	0	1	2	5	2	15

Checksheets . . .

Are structured forms that make it easy to record and analyze data.

Checksheet

Checksheets are used to record data. They are therefore used in every project stage that includes data collection, so we could have put them anywhere in our sequence and been correct. The best checksheets are simple to use, make use of your operational definitions, and visually display the data in a format that can reveal underlying patterns.

Here are some hints that will make your checksheets more effective:

- Incorporating a visual element is an extremely useful trick because it lets you get information from the data without having to do any calculations. For instance, if you are collecting information on the number of errors made on a form, consider making check marks right on copies of the form. That way you can instantly know both how many times an error occurred and whether its position on the form affects how easy it is to pick out. A sketch of a playground can be used as a check sheet to record the locations where accidents occur.

- Make sure educators collecting the data will interpret the check-off categories in the same way, using agreed-upon operational definitions; if they don't, the data will probably be useless.

- Keep checksheets separately for different days, different people, and so on. That way you will be able to look for patterns related to time or sequence as well as patterns related to differences in people and other factors.

- Test the checksheets before a project begins, and make improvements as you see necessary.

Scatter Diagrams . . .

Display the relationship between two process characteristics.

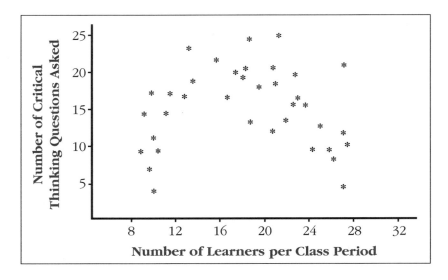

Scatter Diagram

Whereas a dot plot allows you to look at only one process characteristic at a time, a scatter diagram lets you look at the relationship between two characteristics.

Suppose the number of critical thinking questions (for example, the number of questions regarding analysis, synthesis, and evaluation) is an important quality characteristic of a classroom process. To see what other process characteristic (for example, the number of learners for a specified class period) influences or is associated with the number of critical thinking questions asked, you measure both process characteristics in the study. For each class period in the study, there are a pair of measurements: number of critical thinking questions asked, and number of learners in attendance. Instead of making two separate dot plots, you can combine the two, indicating number of learners in the class period along the horizontal axis (sometimes called the *x* axis) and number of critical thinking questions asked along the vertical axis (sometimes called the *y* axis). You place points where the value of each pair intersect.

The shape of the resulting scatter of points tells you if the two process characteristics are related. If they are unrelated, the points will be randomly scattered around the graph. If larger values of one occur with larger values of the other, the points will group towards a line running from lower left to upper right; if larger values of one are associated with smaller values of the other, the points will cluster on a line running from upper left to lower right. However, in this case, the scatter of points are shaped like a horseshoe where the number of critical thinking questions asked increases as class size increases up to 16 pupils and decreases for class sizes above 16.

III. Tools for Making Team Decisions

Though any of the scientific tools may be used only a few times during a project, there are some tools a team will use at practically every meeting: those that help them explore ideas and make decisions. Anyone who has any experience working in groups will appreciate how difficult it is to develop creative ways to approach a task. It is sometimes even more difficult to select only one or two items to work on from all the possibilities generated. The following techniques should help; teams can modify portions of these instructions if they want to be more informal in their meetings.

Brainstorming

Before team members can make a decision, they should make sure they have examined as broad a range of options as possible. One of the easiest and most enjoyable ways to generate a list of ideas is to brainstorm. A successful brainstorm lets people be as creative as possible and does not restrict their ideas in any way. This free-form approach can generate excitement in the group, equalize involvement, and often result in original solutions to problems.

Rules for conducting a brainstorming session are

- Encourage everyone to freewheel; don't hold back on any ideas, even if they seem silly at the time; the more ideas the better.

- No discussion during the brainstorm. That will come later.

- No judgment. No one is allowed to criticize another's ideas, not even with a groan or grimace!

Brainstorming

The objective of a brainstorming session is to collect ideas from all participants without criticism.

- Let people hitchhike—build upon ideas generated by others in the group.

- Write ALL ideas on a flipchart so the entire group can easily scan them.

The general sequence of events in a brainstorm is to

1. Review the topic, defining the subject of the brainstorm. Often this is done best as a "why," "how," or "what" question. ("What are the possible ways to inform and train principals and teachers?" "How can we get all the information we need on a regular basis to complete these forms on time?")

2. Give everyone a minute or two of silence to think about the question.

3. Invite everyone to call out their ideas. The meeting facilitator should enforce the ground rules ("No discussion! Next idea . . .").

4. One team member should write down all ideas on the flipchart, pausing only to check accuracy.

Feel free to modify this procedure to fit the group and the topic. For instance, you could have everyone write down his or her ideas, then go around the group and have each person say one idea, continuing in this way until everyone's list is complete. Or you could do the entire sequence in stages: first, have everyone think of the minimal or partial solutions to a problem; then, the most outrageous, unconventional, or expensive solutions; then try to meld the two together into reasonable alternatives. Be particularly alert for ways to combine suggestions.

Multivoting

Multivoting is a way to conduct a straw poll or vote to select the most important or popular items from a list with limited discussion and difficulty. This is accomplished through a series of votes, each cutting the list in half—even a list of 30 to 50 items can be reduced to a workable number in 4 or 5 votes. Multivoting often follows a brainstorming session to identify the few items worthy of immediate attention.

How to conduct a multivote:

1. First, generate a list of items and number each item.

2. If two or more items seem very similar, combine them, but only if the group agrees that they are the same.

3. If necessary, renumber all items.

4. Have all members choose several items they would like to discuss or address by writing down the numbers of these items on a sheet of paper. Allow each member a number of choices equal to at least one-third of the total number of items on the list (48 item list = 16 choices; 37 item list = 13 choices).

5. After all the members have silently completed their selections, tally votes. You may let members vote by a show of hands as each item number is called out. If there is a need for secrecy, conduct the vote by ballot.

6. To reduce the list, eliminate those items with the fewest votes. Group size affects the results. A rule of thumb is: If it is a small group (5 or fewer members), cross off items with only 1 or 2 votes. If it is a medium group (6 to 15 members), eliminate anything with 3 or fewer votes. If it is a large group (more than 15 members), eliminate items with 4 votes or fewer.

Crawford Slip Method

Another analytical method that is extremely good for organizing information within groups is the "Crawford Slip Method." This method, pioneered by Dr. C.C. Crawford of the University of Southern California, is a structured but flexible way to gather and organize information. Individual thoughts or pieces of information are written on slips of paper, and can be arranged or rearranged in many ways to stimulate further thoughts on a subject or find patterns or similarities.

As of the publication date of this book, materials on this subject were available by writing: Professor Gilbert Siegel, School of Public Administration, U.S.C., Los Angeles, CA 90086-0041.

What Is Consensus?

Any group's goal should be to reach decisions that best reflect the thinking of all group members. We call this "reaching consensus"—a phrase used repeatedly throughout this handbook. It is easy to be confused about what consensus is and isn't, so here are some guidelines:

Consensus is . . .

- Finding a proposal acceptable enough that all members can support it; no member opposes it.

Is not . . .

- A unanimous vote—a consensus may not represent everyone's first priorities.
- A majority vote—in a majority vote, only the majority gets something they are happy with; people in the minority may get something they don't want at all, which is not what consensus is all about.
- Everyone totally satisfied.

Requires . . .

- Time
- Active participation of all group members
- Skills in communication: listening, conflict resolution, discussion facilitation
- Creative thinking and open-mindedness

Aiming for consensus at a meeting requires a much different strategy than if you were just going to keep on arguing until you had a unanimous vote (or even a majority vote). To reach consensus, the team must let each member participate fully in the decision. This probably means going through several rounds of the outlined process. How do you know when you have reached consensus? Probably no one will be completely satisfied with the decision, but everyone can live with it. The decision-making processes described in this chapter can help you reach consensus, particularly when the group is new.

Not every decision need have the support of every member—in fact, it is impossible to have such agreement in any group. Your group should decide ahead of time when you will push for consensus. Decisions that may have a major impact on the direction of the project or conduct of the team—such as which problem to study or what ground rules to establish—should belong to the whole team and be supported by consensus.

The brainstorming, multivoting, and nominal group technique methods described in this chapter are very structured ways to reach consensus. Other less-formal methods exist, and a team can explore them as members become more relaxed in working with each other.

7. Repeat steps 3 through 6 on the remaining list with the choices reduced accordingly. Continue this until only a few items remain. If no clear favorite emerges by this point, have the group discuss which item should receive top priority. Or you may take one last vote.

Nominal Group Technique

The nominal group technique (NGT) is a more structured approach than either brainstorming or multivoting to generating a list of options and narrowing it down. It is called "nominal" because during the session the group doesn't engage in the amount of interaction typical of a real team. Because of its relatively low level of interaction, NGT is an effective tool when all or some group members are new to each other. NGT is also good for highly controversial issues or when a team is stuck in disagreement.

NGT, Part One: A formalized brainstorm

1. Define the task in the form of a question, just as you would for brainstorming. (Often done by the team leader or quality advisor before the meeting.)

2. At the meeting, describe the purpose of this discussion and the rules and procedures for this technique.

3. Introduce and clarify the question. The facilitator reads the question aloud and either writes it on paper taped to the wall or hands out sheets of paper with the question written on them. This way anyone may refer back to the question whenever he or she wants to be reminded of the session's purpose. Anyone who does not understand the question should ask for more explanation. Do not let this develop into a discussion of the issue itself.

Results of an NGT session

Team members first rank the items selected from the brainstorming session by filling out cards as shown (near right). The item number, taken from the brainstorming session, is placed in the upper left. Key words identifying the item are in the middle. The score, or rank, appears in the lower right. This person ranked item 7 as 4th. All votes are tallied (see flipchart, far right), then entered on a Pareto chart (next page).

7	
Write a few words here about the item.	
	4

Flipchart Tally of Votes

1. Improve Quality 8, 8, 8, 6, 7, 5, 3, 2, 6, 8	61
2. Reduce Absenteeism 1, 3, 2	6
3. Improve Planning 8, 8, 7, 6, 4, 3, 1, 1	38

4. Generate ideas. This is the most important step in the entire nominal group technique. It is important to have team members first write down their answers in silence. Experience shows this is the best way to elicit good ideas. Do not allow any distractions at this stage: no joking, no moving around, no whispering. People who finish first must sit quietly until all are finished.

5. List ideas. When everyone is done, go around the table and have each participant read one idea from their list; write down every answer on a flipchart. Continue the round robin until everyone's list is complete or until time runs out (we suggest you stop at 30 minutes). No discussion, not even questions for clarification, is allowed at this point because the exercise rapidly becomes tedious and the facilitator must move the group through it as quickly as possible.

6. Clarify and discuss ideas. Display all the flipchart pages in full view of the entire group. The facilitator asks if anyone has question about any items listed. The person who contributed the idea should be the one to answer a question, but other members may join in the discussion to help define and focus the wording. The facilitator may choose to change the wording, but only when the person who originally proposed the idea agrees.

When there are no more questions, the facilitator condenses the list as much as possible. If the originators of the ideas give their approval, combine ideas. If someone suggests combining several items, but the originators think there is a difference, then leave the ideas listed separately.

NGT, Part Two: Making the selection

The second part of the NGT is much like multivoting, but again more formal. Use this to narrow the list of options and select the choice or choices preferred by the team.

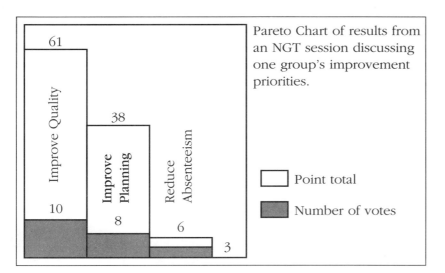

Pareto Chart of results from an NGT session discussing one group's improvement priorities.

1. If there are more than 50 items, use some method to reduce the list to 50 or fewer items, if possible. You could use one or two rounds of multivoting, or simply let members withdraw the less serious items they put on the list. No member is allowed to remove an item that originated with another member, unless the originator agrees.

2. Give each participant from 4 to 8 cards (three-by-five inch, or similar-sized pieces of paper). The number of cards is a rough fraction of the number of items still on the list. Hand out 4 cards apiece for up to 20 items; 6 cards for 20 to 35 items; 8 cards for 35 to 50 items.

3. Members individually make their selections from the list. They write down one item per card, one card per item (4, 6, or 8, depending on how many cards they have).

4. Have members assign a point value to each item, based on their preferences. Each person assigns the highest point value to the most important item. The value again depends on the number of items selected (4, 6, or 8). In an 8-card system, the most preferred item is numbered 8, the second most preferred item is numbered 7, and so on until the least preferred item is numbered 1. This system is the same for groups with 4 or 6 selections, except, of course, the highest point values are 4 and 6, respectively. (See sample card above, left.)

5. After each participant has given point values to the items selected, the cards are collected and the votes tallied. It is easiest to mark the flipchart page with the original list, noting the value of each vote an item received, then adding up these values. The item that ends up with the highest point total is the group's selection.

6. The group reviews the results, and discusses the reaction. If you have the time, display the results on a Pareto-like diagram so you can easily see which items received the most votes and which

have the greatest point total (these are not always the same items). Were there any surprises? Any objections? Does anyone want to lobby for or against certain items and ask for another vote?

If members agree on the importance of the item that got the highest score, the NGT can end the discussion, and the team will have to decide what to do next. If members do not agree, the team could focus its efforts on investigating the two or three items that received high scores.

SUMMARY

Quality improvement techniques represent a whole new way of examining the learning process. Teams must understand that it is critical to view tasks as steps in some process instead of unrelated events. In doing so, they will come to understand why quality can be defined only by the learners and others who receive the outcomes of the educational system. They must begin to learn where to look for problems in a process, and which problems they have the ability to change. By familiarizing themselves with decision-making and scientific tools, team members can better handle process problems they uncover and make changes for lasting improvement. In the next chapter, we will examine some of the activities that must be completed before the project team can meet and begin using these tools.

Chapter 3
Setting the Stage for a Successful Project

When your educational system joins the quality movement, all participants will wrestle with a natural urge to start many projects right away. It's tempting to get your feet wet and find out what quality improvement really is.

While admitting that it's better to do something than nothing at all, we must also caution educational organizations to take their time. Discovering a month or two down the road that a project has bombed is much worse than waiting longer and having it succeed.

An educational system that takes time to set the stage properly will reap the benefits in improved processes, improved performance, and desired learning outcomes. This will also result in higher staff morale, in more satisfied students, staff, and community, and in an improved learning environment. The guidelines in this chapter will help you avoid the most common problems encountered in setting up improvement projects, and increase the chance of success.

I. Selecting a Project

As outlined in Chapter 1, quality improvement projects are only part of a larger effort to transform education as we experience it today. Improvement projects are usually taken on because a principal, department chair, or staff member decides that change must occur. But school improvement projects that lack leadership, concern, and commitment from policymakers and top-level administrators often suffer from neglect and are eventually displaced with other priorities. It is a great advantage to have everyone committed to a project's success.

The leaders involved in the transformation are probably the best qualified to select improvement projects. Ideally, they will select projects only after widespread consultation with others. A lot is at stake, particularly if a project is to be one of the first quality improvement projects in the organization. All eyes will be focused on the project's success or failure.

Notes. . .

Common Errors in Selecting Projects

Educational organizations just starting out in a quality improvement effort commonly make mistakes in selecting projects, including

- **Selecting a process that no one is really interested in**

A common error in selecting initial projects is picking one neither the administrators nor project team care about. As a result, the study is likely to die from inattention. Studying a process is hard work, and sometimes the only motive that sustains the effort is the commitment of the people involved.

- **Selecting a desired solution, instead of a process**

Sometimes administrators, thinking they already know what improvements need to be made in the process, pick a solution to be studied rather than a process. Instead of telling a team to come up with ideas about what change to make, they tell them what the results should be. They will say, "Replace textbooks" or "Tighten up sick leave policy" rather than "Study the textbook selection process" or "Study patterns and problems in sick leave."

It may be that the predetermined change is the best way to improve the process. If so, the study will arrive at that conclusion. But team members should be free to recommend whatever actions they conclude stand the best chance of success. Some of the most creative and best solutions may not have even been dreamed of before the study; the team should be allowed to discover them.

Common Errors in Selecting Projects

- **Selecting a process that no one is really interested in**
- **Selecting a desired solution, instead of a process**
- **Selecting a process in transition**
- **Selecting a system to study, not a process**

- **Selecting a process in transition**

Picking a process that is, or soon will be, undergoing transition will only waste resources. For example, avoid studying the current personnel process if someone else is independently computerizing the system.

- **Selecting a system to study, not a process**

In their eagerness to make improvements, administrators often select too ambitious a project. Instead of selecting a single process, they select a system that consists of many smaller processes—hiring new employees, for example. A project team has a better chance for success if it focuses on one aspect, such as recruiting candidates for entry-level clerical positions. Once the improvements are implemented in one small area, the project team can methodically move on to improving other areas.

The following guidelines are written for selecting initial projects; some of the criteria would be modified for projects undertaken months or years into the transformation. Using these criteria will increase your chances for a visibly successful improvement project.

Select a process that

- Has a direct impact on the educational system's external customers—the parents, businesses, students, families, and general population of the community.
- Has a cycle that is completed in a reasonable period of time. The effects of changes you make will then likely show up within a few weeks.
- Is not already undergoing major transitions or being studied using other methods (unless the improvement project is to study how to make a transition).
- Is relatively simple, with clearly defined starting and ending points. Even if you would rather target a large or complex system, such as how curriculum is developed and implemented, break it down into smaller components.
- Is something a substantial group of leaders agree is important to the school district and its customers. The participants should be concerned about each of the selected processes and have a gut feeling that the chosen targets are the right ones to study.

Select an area

- Where the supervisors, principals, department chairs, and staff can be expected to cooperate in the improvement efforts.
- That is highly visible in the educational system so that the results of the effort could be noticed by people throughout and outside the system.

Balance projects so that

- At least half the improvement projects have the potential to realize significant learning improvements, or time or dollar savings.

Project Selection Checklist

Instructions: If you have selected and defined an appropriate project, you should be able to check most, if not all, items listed below. If you can't check all of these items, you may want to reevaluate your choice.

_____ 1. The process or project is related to key educational issues.

_____ 2. The process targeted for improvement has direct impact on the external customers. (This is especially important when selecting demonstration projects early in a quality improvement effort.)

_____ 3. The process has a lot of visibility in the school system.

_____ 4. All the key administrators concerned with this process—at all of the levels of the school district—agree that it is important to study and improve.

_____ 5. Enough administrators, supervisors, and teachers in this area will cooperate to make this project a success.

_____ 6. This process is not currently being changed in any way, nor is it scheduled to be overhauled in the near future. (This criterion does not apply if the project team is being commissioned to study how the change might occur.)

_____ 7. The project is defined as one clearly defined process that has easily identified starting and ending points.

_____ 8. The process is not being studied by any other group.

_____ 9. One cycle of the process is completed in a reasonable period of time. (That is, there is quick turnaround time. Again, this is most important when selecting initial projects. Once a team has some experience, it can tackle longer, more complex processes.)

_____ 10. The mission statement for this team describes a problem to be studied, or an improvement opportunity, not a solution to be tried.

- At least half, but not necessarily all, of the improvement projects involve people from noninstructional positions in the system, such as food services workers, personnel and transportation departments, clerks, custodians, and students.
- At least one project is a collaboration between different parts of the organization, perhaps involving an interaction between the central office and the classroom, support and instructional staff.

The Project Selection Checklist (left) summarizes the main points of this discussion. Using it can help administrators and staff to select projects with a good chance for success. (See also "Common Errors in Selecting Projects," p. 3–2.)

II. Choosing the Players

Most improvement projects touch the lives of many people in the educational system. Even people not directly involved can learn by watching the team's progress. However, the most important roles to clearly define are those of the active participants:

- *Leadership Team*, which supports the project team's activities, secures resources, and clears a path in the educational system.

- *Team Leader*, who runs the team, arranging logistical details, facilitating meetings, and so forth.

- *Quality Advisor*, who is trained in the scientific approach and in working with groups, who helps keep the team on track and provides training as needed.

- *Project Team Members*, who form the bulk of the team, carry out assignments, and actually make improvements.

Enthusiastic, hardworking improvement project team members contribute most to the success of a project. But they must be given an effective team system within which to work. And that depends on the leadership team, team leader, and quality advisor. A successful improvement project requires careful selection of people to fill these roles, and orchestration of their activities. The following guidelines will help the leaders in an educational system make these choices.

Leadership Team

The leadership team is the group of administrators and other key leaders who oversee and support the activities of one or more project improvement teams. Typically, these include the same leaders who chose the improvement projects and appointed the teams in the first place, but other people may be involved.

The leadership team has members with
- Diverse skills and resources (occasionally a nonadministrator who has necessary qualifications will be included).
- A stake in the chosen process.
- Authority to make changes in the process under study.
- Clout and courage.

One or two members of the leadership team may include the superintendent or his/her designee, or principals or other administrators who have established authority and responsibility regarding the process they want studied. One problem is that in conventional educational systems, decisions are made by the wrong people. Decisions that should be made by the people working with a process daily are typically made by superintendents or central office supervisors. For those administrators, membership on the leadership team carries an additional challenge: letting go of some responsibilities. A project team has to study and define the process, and eventually will want to make changes. Participation on a leadership team is a perfect opportunity for these superintendents, supervisors, and even principals in some situations, to learn to delegate control and pass decision-making to those closer to the process.

Leadership team members do not conduct the actual project; they guide the efforts of the project team. They appoint the project team leader, and together with that leader determine the project's boundaries and select the other team members. (The project team leader is therefore the "internal customer" of the leadership team.) They make certain the project team has whatever resources it needs to be successful.

The duties of the leadership team occur in two phases:

   1. Before the project, the leadership team should

   - Identify the goals.
   - Prepare a mission statement.
   - Determine needed resources.
   - Select the team leader.
   - Assign the quality advisor.
   - Select the project team.

   Each of these activities is described in detail later in this chapter (see "Doing the Groundwork," p. 3–15) and reviewed in Chapter 4.

   2. During the project, the leadership team

   - Meets regularly with the project team (their "internal customers").

- Develops resources and improves processes that allow team members to bring about change. This includes opening communication lines between the team and the rest of the educational system.
- When necessary, "runs interference" for the project team, representing its interests to the rest of the educational system.
- Insures that changes made by the team are followed up; implements changes the project team is not authorized to make.

The responsibilities of the leadership team are not finished until these changes are introduced, the improvements accomplished, or the new methods standardized and the project officially completed. This may take from several weeks to over a year.

Team Leader

The team leader is the person who manages the team: calling and facilitating meetings, handling or assigning administrative details, orchestrating and planning all team activities, and overseeing preparations for reports and presentations. The team leader should be interested in solving the problems that prompted this project, and be reasonably good at working with individuals and groups. Ultimately, it is the leader's responsibility to create and maintain channels that enable team members to do their work.

Ordinarily, team leaders are leaders or managers in the school or the part of the school system where the project is taking place. Their closeness to the process means they will be better able to guide team members. It also means they must take extra precautions to avoid dominating the group during meetings. The leader leaves rank outside the meeting room, facilitating discussions and only occasionally actively participating.

Effective leaders share their responsibilities with other team members and trust their groups to arrive at the best answer, thus giving team members a chance to succeed or make mistakes on their own. They understand that the lessons learned from experience are stronger and last longer than those learned from having the leader tell them what to do.

The team leader

- Is the contact point for communication between the project team and the rest of the educational system, including the leadership team. If any member has difficulty in being released for the project assignment, the team leader may intervene with supervisors or principals to resolve the conflict or seek assistance of the leadership team. When necessary, the leader meets with the leadership team members in between the joint leadership team/project team meetings, which are typically every four to six weeks.

- Is the official keeper of the team records, including copies of correspondence; records of meetings and presentations; meeting minutes and agendas; and charts, graphs, and other data related to the project. The quality advisor, team members, and others involved in the project may also keep their own records, but the team leader is formally responsible for documenting the project. (Examples of all documentation are described in Chapter 4.)

- Is a full-fledged team member. As such, the team leader's duties also include attending meetings, carrying out assignments between meetings, and generally sharing in the team's work. The only exception, as described previously, is that the team leader may want to restrain his or her participation in discussions so that other team members may be more active.

- Retains authority as an administrator. The leader can immediately implement changes recommended by the team that are within the bounds of this authority. Changes beyond these bounds must be referred to the leadership team or other appropriate level of management.

Because the team is implementing the teachings of Dr. Deming, the team leader must become knowledgeable in his teachings. By understanding this approach, the team leader is better able to handle problems in the team.

For example, the 85/15 Rule tells us that most of an educational system's problems are attributable to a faulty system; few can be attributed to the behavior of individual members within the system. This principle also applies to problems related to the team, its members, its meetings, and its work.

Thus, problems that develop within the team process are much more likely to result from an inadequate team process or management environment than from the inadequate participation of any individual member. Problems are not solved by blaming people, but by improving the systems and processes.

Quality Advisor

Educational systems will find that project teams function more effectively if they are assisted by people with extra training in project management, group process, statistics, and the scientific tools. We call these project team consultants "quality advisors."

Like team leaders, quality advisors will ordinarily have more expertise than the team members. Their job is to help team members discover for themselves what the opportunities for improvement are, not dictate answers to the rest of the team.

**Continuum of Power-Sharing between a
Team Leader and Quality Advisor**

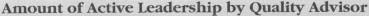

Amount of Active Leadership by Quality Advisor

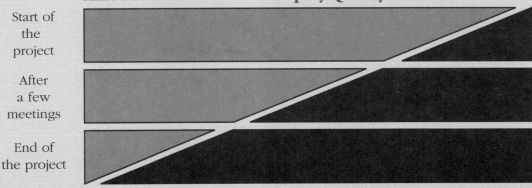

Start of
the
project

After
a few
meetings

End of
the project

**Amount of Active Leadership by Team Leader
(may be shared with others)**

Balancing Team Leader and
Quality Advisor Roles

The descriptions of team leader and quality advisor roles given in the text fit a mature team under ideal circumstances. When a team is inexperienced, or runs into trouble, the roles will not be so clear-cut. In any circumstance, the administrators, team leaders, team members, and the quality advisors themselves must not think of quality advisors as the leaders or as other "workers in the trenches." The quality advisor must remain, as much as possible, the outside consultant to the team.

The diagram (above) illustrates how the proportions of active leadership taken on by the team leader and quality advisor can vary throughout a project. The quality advisor, trained in meeting skills, may run parts of the first team meetings, but the team leader

gradually assumes more of these duties. Throughout a project, the team leader may also choose to share responsibility from time to time with other team members.

While in theory it would be most efficient to have a team leader who was both an administrator and quality advisor—combining two roles in one person—usually the two roles are kept separate unless a school district and its leaders have had long experience in conducting successful projects. The majority of teams and team leaders benefit from the outside, impersonal view that a quality advisor offers—and, in times of crisis or extraordinary needs, the quality advisor is available to step in and temporarily take over more responsibility.

Quality advisors attend team meetings, but are neither leaders nor team members. They are outsiders to the team in many ways, and can maintain a neutral position. One of their most important jobs arising from this neutrality is to observe the team's progress, evaluating how the team functions, and use these observations to help the team improve its process (how members interact both inside and outside of meetings).

A quality advisor's second major focus is instructing team members in the scientific tools, and helping to guide the team's effort when technical expertise is needed.

Quality advisors rarely, if ever, run meetings, handle administrative or logistical details, or carry out between-meeting assignments such as data gathering. Except when teaching the team about the scientific tools or helping the team get unstuck during a meeting, the quality advisor works primarily before and after the team meeting, in conference with the team leader. That is when the two discuss the team's progress and try to find ways to improve the processes by which the team works.

Still, it is important that the quality advisors get their hands dirty, that is, see first-hand the process under study so they can understand the problems facing the team.

The quality advisor

- Focuses on the team's process more than its outcomes; is concerned more with *how* decisions are made than *what* decisions are reached.

- Assists the team leader in structuring or breaking down a task into individual assignments. Most projects consist of several, even hundreds, of individual tasks performed effectively and in a planned sequence to reach the desired goal.

A quality advisor . . .

is versed in the tools and concepts of quality improvement, including approaches that help a team have effective, productive meetings. The quality advisor is there to help facilitate the team's work—coaching team members in needed skills and tools—but not to participate directly in the team's activities.

- Works with the team leader between meetings to plan for upcoming meetings. Together they may have to structure individual activities, discussions, and decisions so the team can work effectively. They revise the plans in response to suggestions from team members, the leadership team, or day-to-day experience on the project.

- Studies and uses the teachings of Dr. Deming; helps explain these teachings to the rest of the team.

- Helps team members become more comfortable with statistics and develop their own facility with the scientific approach; teaches data collection and analysis techniques to the team, showing what conclusions may or may not be drawn from the data.

- Helps team members learn to chart data in ways that make the message clear, particularly to people outside the team; encourages the group to seek the causes of problems before identifying solutions and to distrust any decision unsupported by valid data.

- Helps the group decide what data will be useful and how best to gather that data; works with team members and those outside the team who may be gathering and recording data to develop appropriate forms or checksheets for data collection.

- Prepares teaching strategies on various statistical approaches, with the help of a statistician if necessary, to present to the team at appropriate times.

- Continually develops personal skills in facilitating, group processes, and planning; learns a variety of techniques to control

Selecting and Training Quality Advisors

The ideal quality advisor has a combination of people, technical, and training skills—talents seldom found together. Some of the skills a quality advisor should have or be willing to acquire are

- **People skills**

  Has interpersonal communication, group process, and meeting skills; knows how to form groups, build teams, listen, resolve conflict, and give feedback.

- **Technical skills**

  Understands basic scientific tools, statistics, and the use of data; can organize and plan a project; understands the technical aspects of the project; can ask good questions.

- **Training skills**

  Can teach others all the skills described above; can give effective presentations and teach others how to do the same.

Many school districts are training their own people to become quality advisors. We know of no program open to the general public that offers training in all these subjects, but there are many school districts that offer seminars and workshops in some of these skills. As you select quality advisors in your school district, look for people who are inclined toward all three areas. Start by looking among teachers or others who demonstrate a caring and sensitivity toward people and who also seem capable of learning the technical aspects.

digressive, difficult, or dominating participants, to encourage reluctant participants, and to resolve conflict among participants; learns when and how to employ these interventions and how to teach such skills to team members. (Some helpful hints are explained in Chapter 6, pp. 6-20 to 6-28.)

- Helps project teams design and, sometimes, rehearse presentations to groups such as the superintendent and the executive staff, Board of Education, Parent-Teacher Associations, and Chamber of Commerce.

Finding people with the proper qualifications for becoming quality advisors can be difficult. We provide some hints (left).

Project Team Members

Project team members are the rest of the people on the team other than the leader. The nature of the project dictates who they are: usually people who work closely with some aspects of the process under study; often representing different stages of the process and different groups likely to be affected by the project. They can be administrators, teachers, other school staff, students, community members, and policy makers. They are appointed by the leadership team in consultation with the project team leader. If the project cuts across departments or schools, so should team membership.

Team members

- Should remember that leaders of the educational system have indicated their concern for the project by setting up the project team. Therefore, team members should consider their participation as a priority responsibility, not an intrusion on their real jobs. The project is part of the members' real work.

- Are responsible for contributing as fully to the project as possible, sharing their knowledge and expertise, participating in all meetings and discussions, even on topics outside their areas. They should not be shy about asking what might seem like dumb questions. Each has a right to clearly understand all parts of the process that will be studied during the project.

- Carry out their assignments between meetings: interviewing colleagues or learners, observing processes, gathering data, charting the data, writing reports, and so on. These tasks will be selected and planned at the meetings. If possible, the team should avoid assigning members to study areas outside their own place of work or area of expertise, but if such an assignment is unavoidable, it should be cleared with the appropriate administrators.

III. Doing the Groundwork

The superintendent and executive staff who select the project, or the leadership team, have important issues to consider before a project team gets down to business.

They must

• **Identify the goals**
    What changes are expected to result from this project? These changes are not necessarily stated in numerical terms, but can be described using words like "increase," "decrease," or "sharply

decrease." Avoid using numeric goals. When they are used, make sure everyone knows they only indicate the magnitude of the desired improvement, and must never be used as measures of a team's performance.

- **Prepare a mission statement**

  A proper mission statement enables a project team to set boundaries on the project, know what is and isn't within their domain, understand where the project fits in the educational system's overall improvement efforts, and have a clear idea of where they should begin.

  The mission statement should tell the team
  § What process or problem to study.
  § What boundaries or limitations there are, including limits on time and money.
  § What magnitude of improvements they are expected to make.
  § When they are scheduled to begin the project and, if appropriate, the target date for completion (ordinarily such a date will be included only when some extraordinary circumstance requires it).
  § What authority they have to call in colleagues or outside experts, request equipment or information normally inaccessible to them, and make changes to the process.
  § Who is on the leadership team.
  § How often they are expected to meet with the leadership team (approximately monthly for one or two hours) and the date of the first joint meeting (usually one month after the project team starts its work).

  Sometimes it's best to compose the mission statement by the leaders and project team in a mutual process, perhaps during joint planning meetings. The elements of the statement are the same no matter who prepares it.

Even when the mission statement originates with the leadership team, the project team must be permitted to clarify and negotiate the stated goals.

• **Determine the resources**

What training is needed? Budget? Equipment? Which in-house or external specialists will be needed to advise the team? How much time must be allotted so team members will be able to complete the project? How will their normal work get done? By whom? Substitute teachers and released time for training are a concern and often necessary to complete a project successfully.

• **Select the team leader**

The project team leader is often one of the people responsible for the area where most of the changes are likely to occur. This person should be someone interested in solving the problems that prompted this project, someone reasonably good at working with individuals and groups.

• **Assign the quality advisor**

The leadership team should assign a quality advisor to work with the team leader. The quality advisor is someone experienced in working with groups, someone who knows and can teach others the basic quality improvement concepts and principles, group process approaches, and scientific tools. The quality advisor and team leader will review the mission statement and orchestrate the project's development.

Steps Needed to Prepare for a Project:

- **Identify the goals**
- **Prepare a mission statement**
- **Determine the resources**
- **Select the team leader**
- **Assign a quality advisor**
- **Select the project team**

- **Select the project team**

  The leadership of the educational system will collaborate with the project team leader and the quality advisor to determine what disciplines, academic or administrative departments, and grade levels should be represented on the team. Ideally, team members should represent each area affected by the improvements and each level of educational system affected, e.g., classrooms, schools, school districts, and community.

  Typically, teams should have no more than five members in addition to the team leader and quality advisor. Do not let the team get too large: Not everyone who could contribute something worthwhile need be on the team, and project team members can always consult with experts or other advisors as the project unfolds.

  For similar reasons, project team membership does not have to represent different levels of the chain of command. Even when the nature of the project requires a slice of the hierarchy, be cautious: High-level district supervisors on a team may intimidate teachers and other staff members. However, leaders and supervisors in some educational systems have found that mixing levels is an effective way to improve communication and leadership methods.

  Don't expect team members to take on the project work as additional work. Release time must be provided and built into the project timeline of activities.

SUMMARY

The success of a project depends largely on getting everything set up correctly: choosing an appropriate process to study, selecting appropriate team members, and doing the groundwork so a team will know what the project is all about.

Once the team leader and quality advisor are chosen, they have their work cut out for them. Their responsibilities for starting the project are described in the next chapter.

On the following pages, there appears a long worksheet that will help guide administrators, supervisors, quality advisors, and/or team leaders through the issues they need to address to set up a project team. Use the questions to stimulate discussion of these topics.

Chapter 3

Worksheet for Project Team Groundwork

Instructions: Use these questions to spur discussion of the purpose for having a project. Record the answers and use your notes to generate a mission statement for the team. Attach any relevant documentation to your notes. If the project has not yet been selected, use the "Project Selection Checklist" (p. 3–4) as a guide.

Step 1: Determine the nature of the project (outcomes, expectations).

1.1 What process or system will the team study? What parts of this process or system should the team NOT study?
Note: A flowchart is useful for describing the process or system and showing which parts the teams should target.

1.2 What perceived need led to selection of this project? What data were collected to verify the choice and focus of the project? If you have no data, what kinds should you collect to verify your choice?
Note: Often, data on the project's impact on the business, school district, its customers, and staff, and the needs for resource allocation help frame these issues.

1.3 What are the goals or desired outcomes of this project? What magnitude of improvement is the team expected to make? What changes are expected to result from this project?
Focus on one or two major outcomes, though there may be other results associated with the main changes you want the team to make. These changes are not necessarily stated in numerical terms, but can be described using words like "increase," "decrease," or "sharply decrease." Avoid using numeric goals. When they are used, make sure everyone knows they only indicate the magnitude of the desired improvement, and must never be used as measures of a team's performance.

1.4 How will the process be improved as a result of this project? Will improvement occur in phases? What impact will this have on your customers?

Step 2: Settle team membership and logistics.

2.1 Who is on the leadership team?

2.2 Who will be the team leader?

2.3 Who will be the quality advisor?

2.4 Who else should be on the team? What work areas or specialties must be represented for the team to accomplish its mission?
Collaborate with the team leader and quality advisor to determine what disciplines, departments, or specialties should be represented on the team. Ideally, team members should represent each area and level of staff affected by the improvement project. Typically, teams should have no more than five members in addition to the team leader and quality advisor. Do not let the team get too large: Not everyone who could contribute something worthwhile has to be on the team, and project team members can always consult with experts, staff, or parents as the project unfolds.

2.5 When, where, how often, and for how long will the team meet?

2.6 How often do you expect the team to meet with the leadership team (approximately monthly for one or two hours)? What is the date of the first joint meeting (usually one month after the project team starts its work)?

Step 3: Describe the boundaries and support the team will have.

3.1　When will the project begin? Is there a target date for completion (include only when some extraordinary circumstance requires it)? What limitations are there on the length of the project?

3.2　Will the team need financial resources? What department(s) or school(s) will provide this support? What limitations are there on budgets? Can the team request additional financial support? From whom?

3.3　What decision-making authority will the team have? What authority will the team have to call in other staff or outside experts, request equipment or information normally inaccessible to them, and make changes to the process?

3.4　What training will team members need? In what subjects? Who will provide the training?

3.5　What in-house or external specialists may be needed to provide support on special or specific matters?

3.6　How will team members' normal work get done while they are involved in the project?

3.7　Are there other resources (technical support, equipment, supplies, staff) that this team will need?

Chapter 3

Chapter 4
Getting Underway

"Toto, I've a feeling we're not in Kansas anymore!"

—Dorothy
Wizard of Oz

During your project team's first few meetings, it is not at all un-usual to feel as though you have been transported to the Land of Oz, a place completely different from what you are used to. Most project team members will be participating in an activity unlike any they've done before, perhaps working with people they've never worked with before, and using methods they've probably never used before.

Being less than elegant is understandable and commonplace. If you and your teammates feel self-conscious, awkward, inept, frustrated, or overwhelmed after your first meetings, congratulate yourselves on being normal.

Rest assured that these early feelings of inadequacy have no relation-ship to your team's ultimate success. Some of the most successful pro-ject teams start out looking less like quality improvement leaders and more like The Keystone Kops.

The techniques your team will be using really do work. You are not guinea pigs testing unproven approaches to continuous learning and improving. The problem-solving methods described in this book are superior to any currently available.

This is a new area of learning and improvement. There is a lot for you to learn, and neither you nor your teammates can expect to be experts in all the knowledge and skills you will need immediately. But each of you has something important to contribute: your experience, willing-ness to improve and learn, and expertise. Whatever else you need to know, you can learn together.

Notes. . .

Chapter 4

The initial team meetings are critical for setting a proper tone: There is serious work at hand, but everyone can have fun and contribute to the educational system by working together. This requires a balance between studying the process and learning about each other. The following guidelines will help you develop productive meeting skills, and lead you through the first few meetings.

I. Guidelines for Productive Meetings

Though individual team members carry out assignments between team meetings, much of the team's work gets done when all team members are together during meetings. Many people dislike meetings, but meetings don't have to be disliked. Like other processes, they can be studied and constantly improved. Productive meetings enhance the chance of having a successful project.

It is difficult to have productive meetings because few people know the rules and skills needed. In fact, the goal of having constantly improved meetings may be as hard for the team to reach as the improvement goals set for the project. The best way to have productive meetings is to follow the guidelines given below from the start of the improvement project, a time when team members expect to learn new ways of working together.

General Rules

Through experience, we have learned how to conduct productive, orderly meetings. The basic rules are

- **Use agendas**

  Each meeting must have an agenda, preferably one drafted at the previous meeting and developed in detail by one or two members prior to the actual meeting. It should be sent to participants in advance, if possible. Agendas may be saved as a team record and for future reference. (If an agenda has not been developed before a meeting, spend the first five or ten minutes writing one on a flipchart.)

Agendas should include the following information:
§ The agenda topics (including, perhaps, a sentence or two that defines each item and why it is being discussed).
§ The presenters (usually the person who originated the item or the person most responsible or knowledgeable about it).
§ A time guideline (the estimated time in minutes needed to discuss each item).
§ The item type, and whether the item requires discussion or decision or is just an announcement.

Agendas usually list the following activities:
§ Warm-ups: short (five to ten minute) activities used to free people's minds from the outside world and get them focused on the meeting. (See "Warm-Ups," p. 4-30.)
§ A quick review of the agenda. Simply start each meeting by going over the agenda, adding or deleting items, and modifying time estimates.
§ Breaks for long meetings. If the meeting lasts more than two hours, schedule at least one short break.
§ Meeting evaluation. This is perhaps the most important item on the agenda. Details are given later in the chapter.

Though some of these elements may be unfamiliar, we encourage team leaders to introduce them at the first meeting and include them in all subsequent meetings. Project team members will probably feel awkward at the first meeting anyway, and a new activity will not add much to that awkwardness. As members become more comfortable with the group, they will feel less self-conscious about these activities. (Sample agendas appear on pp. 4-28 and 4-34.)

General Meeting Rules

- **Use agendas**
- **Have a facilitator**
- **Take minutes**
- **Draft next agenda**
- **Evaluate the meeting**
- **Adhere to the "100-mile rule"**

Chapter 4

• **Have a facilitator**

Each meeting should have a facilitator who is responsible for keeping the meeting focused and moving. Ordinarily, this role is appropriate for the project team leader, but your team may rotate the responsibility among its members.

The facilitator's chief responsibilities are to
  § Keep the discussion focused on the topic and moving along.
  § Intervene if the discussion fragments into multiple conversations.
  § Tactfully prevent anyone from dominating or being overlooked.
  § Bring discussions to a close.
  § Be sure the team recorder has had an opportunity to summarize major points of the discussion.

The facilitator should also notify the group when the time allotted for an agenda item has expired or is about to expire. The team then decides whether to continue discussion at the expense of other agenda items or postpone further discussion until another meeting.

• **Take minutes**

Each meeting should also have a scribe who records key subjects and main points raised, decisions made (including who has agreed to do what and by when), and items that the group has agreed to raise again later in this meeting or at a future meeting. Team members may wish to consider either audio or video recording the meeting. This recording should only be attempted when the team members are comfortable with this! Team members can refer to the minutes to reconstruct discussions, remind themselves of decisions made or actions that need to be taken, or to see what happened at a meeting they missed. Rotate this duty among the team members.

- **Draft the next agenda**

   At the end of the meeting, draft an agenda for the next meeting. This step gives each team member an opportunity to shape the next agenda and to participate productively.

- **Evaluate the meeting**

   Always review and evaluate each meeting, even if other agenda items go overtime. The evaluation should include decisions on what will be done to improve the meeting next time and helpful feedback to the facilitator. You may want to experiment with mid-meeting evaluations.

- **Adhere to the "100-mile rule"**

   Once a meeting begins, everyone is expected to give it his/her full attention. No one should be called from the meeting unless it is so important that the disruption would occur even if the meeting was 100 miles away from the workplace. The "100-mile rule" will need to be communicated, perhaps repeatedly, to those who keep taking phone messages or would interrupt the team's work for other reasons.

Effective Discussion Skills

Effective discussions are necessary for effective meetings, which in turn are necessary for effective teams. Every team meeting should include actions that facilitate the process of discussion. Clearly, the team leader should use skills for effective discussion; the team will be even more successful if every team member learns and practices them. The following techniques are presented in the framework of team meetings, but they are useful whenever an effective discussion is important.

Effective Discussion Skills

- **Ask for clarification**
- **Act as gatekeepers**
- **Listen**
- **Summarize**
- **Contain digression**
- **Manage time**
- **End the discussion**
- **Test for consensus**
- **Constantly evaluate the meeting process**

At appropriate times during a meeting, team members should:

- **Ask for clarification**

  If you are unclear about the topic being discussed or the logic in another person's arguments, ask someone to define the purpose, focus, or limits of the discussion. Ask members to repeat ideas in different ways. Ask for examples, pictures, diagrams, data, etc. Use the scientific approach and apply the scientific tools.

- **Act as gatekeepers**

  Encourage more-or-less equal participation among group members by "throttling" dominators. Make openings for less aggressive members by directly asking their opinions or making a general request for input.

- **Listen**

  Actively explore one another's ideas rather than debating or defending each idea that comes up.

- **Summarize**

  Occasionally compile what's been said and restate it to the group in summary form. Follow a summary with a question to check for agreement.

- **Contain digression**

  Do not permit overlong examples or irrelevant discussion.

- **Manage time**

  If portions of the agenda take longer than expected, remind the team of deadlines and time allotments so work can be either accelerated or postponed, or time rebudgeted appropriately.

- **End the discussion**

    Learn to tell when there is nothing to be gained from further discussion. Help the team close a discussion and decide the issue.

- **Test for consensus**

    Summarize the group's position on an issue, state the decision that seems to have been made, and check whether the team agrees with the summary. (See "What is Consensus," p. 2-44.)

- **Constantly evaluate the meeting process**

    Throughout the meeting, assess the quality of the discussion. Ask: Are we getting what we want from this discussion? If not, what can we do differently in the remaining time?

Following these guidelines will help a team have effective discussions and productive meetings. But there is more that goes into the development of teams than learning to have good meetings. These needs are covered in depth in Chapter 6.

II. Setting Up Record-Keeping Systems

The final crucial element in having good meetings and a successful improvement project is to maintain up-to-date files. Good project records are helpful for several compelling reasons:

- Projects often last 6 to 18 months or longer, so the team may lose or gain members. Good records help new members catch up and keep old members informed of developments. This is also an easy way to develop an in-depth case study or historical review of the project.

Action List

- Review previous reports on this subject
  — 2 weeks / Juanita
- Prepare trial data collection sheet
  — Next week / Kim & Joe
- Draft operational definitions
  — Next week / Conrad, Joe & LaVon
- Be prepared to discuss Deming's 14 Points
  — 2 weeks / Everyone!

- Clear, illustrated records help educate and win the support of people in the educational system who may not have time to read or listen to lengthy reports. Include graphs, charts, and other graphics.

- Frequently, presentations about a successful project are widely circulated within the school, the entire educational system, or even to local businesses. Having up-to-date records makes it easier to prepare these presentations and insures a more powerful impact.

- As the project progresses, the team may have to retrace its steps to track down problems or mistakes. Good records make this easier.

For these reasons, document your team's work from the earliest stages. Talk about what kinds of records you are likely to need further down the road and plan how to maintain these records.

We recommend keeping a central file for documents, papers, correspondence, charts, graphs, and other pertinent records. Organize the file around the agendas or a top-down flowchart of the improvement plan developed by the project team. Hint: If you construct a flowchart (or other similar diagram) that depicts likely steps in your project, number or code each step and use that code in all files.

Two specific types of records that have proven particularly useful are meeting records and the picture book format.

Meeting Records

Keeping notes on decisions and problems discussed at each meeting prevents needless rehashing of issues. Agendas, minutes, and the action and the future action list (see next page, and left) are all included here.

• Agendas

The Model Agenda for Regular Meetings discussed in detail later in this chapter (pp. 4-33 to 4-36) incorporates several elements useful in documenting the project. First, the meeting date or number can be used to code all records (reports, handouts, data summaries) associated with that meeting. Secondly, it refers to two lists:

§ *Action List:* Keeps track of the "to do's" decided upon during this meeting, noting who has agreed to do what by when.

§ *Future Action List:* Keeps track of items for action or discussion that the team agrees are worthwhile but should be undertaken later. Putting items on this list means they won't be lost or forgotten, and can be resurrected at a future meeting.

Have the scribe or other designated person keep track of these lists at your meetings.

• Project Team Meeting Minutes

The meeting minutes remind team members about points of discussion, tasks to be performed between meetings, decisions made, and responsibilities assigned. They also help other people within the system who receive copies to understand the issues and challenges facing the project team. Because they are an historical record of the team's progress, minutes may provide useful information for future teams making further improvements to the same process.

In order to fulfill these roles and functions, meeting minutes should contain several types of information: date and time of meeting, names of those attending, topics discussed, procedures used for each topic, main points made in each discussion, action taken or decisions made, tasks to be performed between meetings, and items to be carried over to future agendas. (The last two items can be broken out as the action list and future list described above.)

Chapter 4

Project Team Meeting Record, Part 1

Instructions: Use this page and the next as a blueprint for creating a meeting record tailored to your team. You can then make copies of this form and have the scribe take notes on each topic discussed. He or she would then complete the summary items on this side at the end of the meeting.

Meeting Number _____   **Date** _____   **Location** _____

1. Project Name _____

2. Mission Statement

3. √ To indicate "present"

    Member_____

    Member_____

    Member_____

    Member_____

    Member_____

    Member_____

    Member_____

    Member_____

    Others Attending

4. Agenda: Enter key words indicating the agenda topics. Check off an item when it is completed. Items you do not complete should be carried over to the next meeting.

    ( )   1. Warm-up

    ( )   2. Agenda review

    ( )   3.

    ( )   4.

    ( )   5.

    ( )   6. Set agenda for next meeting

    ( )   7. Meeting review

5. Brief summary of topics, decisions, or conclusions and next steps (on reverse side).

6. Futures file: Items for future consideration but not for the next meeting.

7. Meeting Review

      "+"   "−"

Next meeting:

Date _____   Time _____   Location _____

Recorder: _____

Signature of recorder: _____

Project Team Meeting Record, Part 2

Instructions: Take notes during the meeting on a page like this. Focus on capturing the main ideas associated with topics discussed. Summarize the discussion whenever possible.

Topic 1: (brief description)   **Main points:**

Decisions/Conclusions:

Next Steps:

Topic 2: (brief description)   **Main points:**

Decisions/Conclusions:

Next Steps:

Topic 3: (brief description)   **Main points:**

Decisions/Conclusions:

Next Steps:

Topic 4: (brief description)   **Main points:**

Decisions/Conclusions:

Next Steps:

Chapter 4

• **Alternative Meeting Record Format**

Project teams may use a meeting record format instead of taking minutes at each meeting. The sample format (pp. 4-10, 11) is used like a checksheet. Decide what categories should be permanent parts of the form, and adjust the spacing to fit your team's needs. Filling in a meeting record format is a convenient option to conventional meeting minutes. It is not a substitute, however, for the next form of record-keeping, the picture book format.

Picture Book Format

As its name implies, the picture book format documents a project through descriptive pictures and graphs accompanied by simple text. This format is easy to use, maintain, and read, and helps you keep track of milestones passed by the team. It is constructed in the style of a flowchart with a sequence of boxed information, each box containing a major decision or step in the process and displaying the appropriate data, findings, or plans. The boxes lead the reader through the project's main stages.

A project team leader should begin the picture book report *before* the team's first meeting, filling in the first three boxes labeled "project name," "why selected," and "goals for improvement." At the first team meeting, distribute copies of these boxes to help review the team's mission. As the project progresses, add boxes summarizing each stage the team passes or significant information it discovers.

A partial picture book format is shown on the next page; a completed picture book is in Appendix 2.

Picture Book Format

Description: The picture book format displays the milestones in a project through a series of flowchart-like entries. The project team leader and/or quality advisor should fill in the first two or three entries prior to the team's first meeting. There is a sample picture book format in Appendix 2.

The first three segments of a picture book are standard:

Project

> Enter a brief description of the project.

Reason Selected

> Summarize the issues that led to selection of this project, including its importance to customers.

Situation Analysis

> Summarize any data and include any flow-charts (probably at least a top-down flowchart) or cause-and-effect diagrams that show what the team learned about the status of the process or problem at the beginning of the project. (This box may take up a page or more if you have detailed records.)

Other segments will depend on your project. Some typical items included (not necessarily in this order) are:

Data Collection

> Show charts or graphs of data the team collects.

Data Analysis

> Show conclusions from data analysis. Include charts or graphs as appropriate.

Goal

> State the goal of the next phase of the project.

Actions

> Summarize the actions taken during a certain phase of the project. With a slight twist, a similar box could state actions the team recommends to follow up on its project.

Evaluation

> Present summary data and conclusions from the project. Include evaluation of the project, especially what actions or decisions were most and least effective, and things the team could improve on next time.

Chapter 4

Goals of the First Team Meetings

A. Team-Building Goals for the First Meetings

- Get to know each other
- Learn to work as a team
- Work out decision-making issues
- Determine support services
- Set meeting ground rules
  Attendance, Promptness, Meeting place and time, Regularly scheduled meetings with the leadership team, Participation, Basic conversational courtesies, Assignments, Smoking and breaks, Interruptions, Rotation of routine chores, Agendas, minutes, and records, Other norms or ground rules

B. Educational Goals for the First Meetings

- Explore quality issues
  An overview of the quality movement, Quality, Teams and teamwork, The Pareto Principle, The 85/15 Rule, Processes, Customers and suppliers, Complexity, Variation
- Learn the Scientific Approach
  Operational definitions, Information-gathering tools, Data analysis tools

C. Project Goals for the First Meetings

- Understand your assignment
- Understand the process
- Identify resources
- Develop an improvement plan

III. Goals of the First Meetings

The previous pages explain how project team meetings should work. The challenge is applying these principles to your project.

The goals of your team's first meetings are built around three themes: building relationships among team members, learning about the quality movement, and starting to work towards the desired improvement. Though the temptation is to plunge right into the project, you will be more certain of success in the long run if you spend equal time in the beginning on all three aspects. If anything, concentrate most on building the team—many successful teams spend three or more meetings entirely on team-building activities (see Chapter 7).

The following catalogue of issues a team must address in the first meetings may seem overwhelming. Keep in mind you need not pack them all into one meeting. Some teams take several meetings to get through all of them; some more, some less. The time depends on team members' previous experience and the length of the meetings. You can lessen the time needed by combining several themes into one exercise. For instance, you can discuss quality improvement principles as they relate specifically to your project. You could also practice discussion and feedback skills during these sessions, thus building the team at the same time you are learning about quality and starting on the project.

Helpful hint: If some team members are veterans of previous project teams, invite them to lead discussions on one or more of these concepts.

A. Team-Building Goals for the First Meetings

- **Get to know each other**

  As a team, you're going to be working closely together and will need to rely on each other. Take time to learn each other's background and skills, discover each other's preferences, and find out how each learns and works best. You will be most effective when members can compliment each other without embarrassment and disagree without fear. You may not accomplish this in the first few meetings, but you can take strides in that direction.

- **Learn to work as a team**

  When team membership is drawn from various areas across the educational system or links in the chain of command, allow time for the group to become a team. Find ways to use each member's strengths (see Chapters 6 and 7).

- **Work out decision-making issues**

  Too often decisions just "happen" in a team; members go along with what they think the group wants. Improvement teams should discuss how they will make decisions. This cannot be taken for granted, especially when a diversity of expertise and responsibility is represented. Major decisions belong to the entire team and all members should approve decisions that affect the team's direction.

- **Determine support services and resources**

  How will you get access to personal computers, copying, fax machines, and other current technology? Where can you get supplies for your meetings? Can you get logistical or clerical support?

• **Set meeting ground rules**

Every team establishes ground rules, or "norms," concerning how meetings will be run, how team members will interact, and what kind of behavior is accepted. Some are stated aloud; others are understood without discussion. Each member is expected to respect these rules, which usually prevent misunderstandings and disagreements. A few of the more important ground rules to establish are:

§ *Attendance:* Teams should place a high priority on meetings, regarding them as almost sacred. Talk about what would be legitimate reasons for missing a meeting, and establish a procedure for informing the team leader of a member's absence from a scheduled team meeting. Release time for teachers is a must. There may be a need for others to take on some non-teaching duties such as study hall monitoring. In some cases, substitute teachers may be needed.

§ *Promptness:* Team meetings should start and end on time. This makes it easier on everyone's schedule and avoids wasting time. How strongly does your team want to enforce this rule? What can you do to encourage promptness? What does "on time" mean to your team?

§ *Meeting place and time:* Specify a regular meeting time and place, and establish a procedure for notifying members of meetings.

§ *Regularly scheduled meetings with the leadership team:* Have the project team leader discuss the purpose of these meetings, and when and where they will be held (see "Meetings Between Project Teams and Leadership Teams," p. 4-36). Ordinarily, these meetings will be approximately monthly.

§ *Participation:* Everyone's viewpoint is valuable. Every team member can make a unique contribution to the project.

Therefore, emphasize the importance of both speaking freely and listening attentively. If unequal participation is a problem, structure discussions so that everyone can contribute.

§ *Basic conversational courtesies:* Listen attentively and respectfully to others; don't interrupt; hold only one conversation at a time; and so forth.

§ *Assignments:* Much of a team's work is done between meetings. When members are assigned responsibilities within the project, it is important they complete their tasks on time.

§ *Smoking and breaks:* Decide whether and under what circumstances smoking will be allowed; when to take breaks; how long breaks will be.

§ *Interruptions:* Decide when interruptions (phone calls, for example) will be tolerated; when they won't. (See the "100-mile rule," p. 4-5.) Meetings away from the school and the office can help avoid unnecessary interruptions.

§ *Rotation of routine chores:* Decide who will be responsible for setting up the meeting room, refreshments, and other housekeeping chores, and how to rotate these duties among team members. Everyone should know all the routines.

§ *Agendas, minutes, and records:* The team leader is responsible for keeping the records of team meetings: agendas, minutes, reports, and so forth. However, teams often rotate the responsibility for taking minutes, writing reports, and sometimes setting agendas. Decide how these issues will be handled in your team. Also consider how team members can amend these records and how they can get access to them.

Chapter 4

§ *Other norms or ground rules:* What other guidelines are important for your particular team and situation? Some behaviors that are usually not talked about but nonetheless govern the group's behavior are tacit norms and may include issues such as:

- What kind of language is acceptable in this group (cursing, jargon, etc.)?
- What is OK to talk about? What is not OK?
- What place does humor have? Who or what is an acceptable target for jokes? Who or what isn't?

Sometimes a member, usually in anger, may choose to make one of these "understood" behaviors a subject for open discussion. Then the group can agree on an explicit ground rule governing that behavior.

B. Educational Goals for the First Meetings

There are two primary educational goals: exploring quality issues and learning the scientific approach. Each includes a variety of issues already discussed in Chapter 2.

- **Explore quality issues**

   Begin to explore the key concepts, discussed in Chapters 1 and 2, that should govern and guide your team's efforts. Briefly, the issues to address are:

   § *An overview of the quality movement:* The themes of quality improvement are rooted in the origins of the quality movement. Discuss how these approaches were developed and why they are becoming prominent. Include Deming's 14 Points and the Joiner Triangle.

   § *Quality:* Quality in education takes on a new meaning when measured in terms of learners' needs and society's needs for educated graduates as it relates to stable and improved processes. Discuss what it means in your educational system; compare that with how it is traditionally defined. Ask yourselves who defines quality, where it happens, and whose job it is.

§ *Teams and teamwork:* Talk about the different ways to improve quality and how teams fit into the picture. Discuss why teams are essential to the improvement of processes. Practice team-building concepts and techniques. Be sure to address where your project fits into the educational system's quality improvement effort. Also talk about the importance of spending time building a group into a team.

§ *The Pareto Principle:* Using the Pareto Principle can quickly focus a team's effort on the "vital few" important problems. Review the definition of this principle and discuss how it will govern selection of improvement team activities.

§ *The 85/15 Rule:* As Dr. Juran observed, most problems (at least 85%) are the result of system problems under the control of administration; teachers and other staff have control over relatively few problems (less than 15%). Talk about how this rule should discourage the common instinct to assign blame to individuals—which can cause fear among teachers, other staff members, and students—and replace it with a desire to improve the system.

§ *Processes:* Viewing your work as part of a process can revolutionize the way you approach making improvements. Discuss the concept of processes, what processes are represented in the team, and how these relate to one another.

§ *Customers and suppliers:* Look at the process to be studied by your team and decide which people within and beyond the educational system are its customers or suppliers. How does

the idea of internal vs. external customers and suppliers relate to your project?

§ *Complexity:* Often the only obvious sign of problems in a
process is having complexity: steps that are there only to
correct problems, without adding value to the service.
Review the sources of complexity and think about how you
would determine which sources are present in a process.

§ *Variation:* All processes have variation. Teams must understand what it is, how to measure it, and how it influences
your reactions to the problems.

• **Learn Scientific Approach**

In the quality movement, decisions are no longer made solely on
hunches; they must be supported by information gathered through
a scientific approach. Talk about what the scientific approach is
and how it will influence actions and decisions made by the team.
The tools used in the scientific approach should be taught to the
team by the quality advisor as the project unfolds and one or another tool is needed.

§ *Operational definitions:* When your team is ready to collect
data, members must have operational definitions that say
precisely what is to be measured and how to measure it.
Discuss what kinds of characteristics or data you may need
to define operationally. For example, does everyone agree
what cooperative learning is? Can it be defined operationally?

§ *Information-gathering tools:* Make flowcharts of the process
so you will all have a common understanding of how it
works. Learn the basics of data collection. Anticipate gath-

ering data from teachers, students, other staff members, and people in the community; learn how to design and conduct interviews and surveys; and learn to use focus groups to study a process issue or topic in depth.

§ *Data analysis tools:* Eventually, when your team has data to work with, make basic plots and charts that help disclose patterns and show the frequency and severity of problems. Use cause-and-effect diagrams to help identify the possible causes of problems. Then gather more data and construct more charts and plots, continuing this effort until root causes have been identified and eliminated.

C. Project Goals for the First Meetings

• **Understand your assignment**

Make sure you understand the assignment and the expectations others have of you. (See the team-building exercise "Discussing Your Mission," p. 7-29.)

• **Understand the process**

Concentrate on getting to know the process you are studying. Learn how it functions and all of its activities, steps, tasks, and procedures: review the materials, information, tools, and paperwork associated with the process. (See "Describe a Process," p. 5-52, and the team-building exercise "Information Hunt—A Preliminary Look at a Process," p. 7-24.) Meet its customers and its suppliers. Identify the problems of students, staff, and the community through formal surveys. Build trust with key people.

Chapter 4

At a later stage, you will determine possible causes of process problems. This step will involve such methods and tools as interviewing, surveys, brainstorming, Pareto charts, and cause-and-effect diagrams.

- **Identify resources**

    Discuss what resources you will need: budget, time, people, etc. What expertise or technical abilities will you need that are not represented by team members?

- **Develop an improvement plan**

    An improvement plan is a road map for your team to follow during the project, enabling you to progress steadily and keep on track. The importance of such a plan cannot be overstated. Chapter 5, "Building an Improvement Plan," presents strategies that constitute the core of any improvement plan.

    Before the team meets, the team leader and quality advisor should draft an improvement plan by breaking the larger tasks of the project into smaller tasks and identifying the sequences of activities needed to accomplish the smaller tasks. All team members discuss the plan in detail at one of the first meetings, revising it as necessary.

    The team continues to review and revise the plan as more is learned about what is needed to successfully pursue its mission.

These early sessions are an important learning period for a team. The urge to make improvements can lead teams into neglecting educational needs. Take your time. Include some items from team-building goals, educational goals, and project-related goals in all meetings. Don't try to do them all at once. Take as many meetings as you need to discuss all of these issues.

IV. Preparing for the First Meeting

The team leader and the quality advisor are the driving force behind the first project team meetings. They must draft a preliminary improvement plan. They must also handle all the logistical details, and develop an agenda that blends the three themes of building the team, exploring quality issues, and understanding the project.

More specifically, the quality advisor and team leader must:

• **Review the written mission statement from the leadership team and discuss the project in general**

Will this project work? Are the goals for improvement realistic? Does the proposed improvement fit with your knowledge and observations of the process? What do you like about this project? What are your concerns? Do you anticipate any controversial issues? Is the mission clear? Could you explain the mission to a new team member? List your questions and arrange a meeting with the leadership team to get the answers.

• **Clarify roles**

What responsibilities will each of you have? (Review Chapter 3.) How will you communicate and coordinate with each other? Schedule weekly meetings for the two of you to review the last project team meeting and plan and prepare for upcoming meetings.

• **Draft an improvement plan**

How might this project unfold? Ask what activities are needed to complete the project and in what sequence they should occur. Read through Chapter 5 and decide which strategies may be appropriate for your project; or, if you are experienced, develop a

Team Leader and Quality Advisor Preparations for the First Meetings

- **Review the written mission statement and discuss the project in general**
- **Clarify roles**
- **Draft an improvement plan**
- **Identify pertinent existing data**
- **Set the meeting logistics**
- **Set an agenda**
- **Plan for improving meetings**

Chapter 4

plan on your own. This plan will inevitably change as the team progresses, but preparing one before the team meets makes it less likely that you will stall in the starting gate or get stuck in unimportant details.

• Identify pertinent existing data

Review previous work in this area. To understand the present process, you must understand the history. Find out how the process came to be designed the way it is. Determine if anyone is currently collecting data on the process you intend to study.

• Set the meeting logistics

Setting the meeting time and place well in advance of the first meeting eases the awkwardness and uncertainty of team members.

The first project team meeting should last $2\frac{1}{2}$ to $3\frac{1}{2}$ hours. The time you choose for the first meeting need not be the time members select for regular meetings. Propose several possible meeting times to the team at the first meeting so everyone can decide what is best for regular meetings. Adjust meeting times if team members have conflicting shifts or schedules.

Once the project is well underway, your team will usually meet together weekly for $1\frac{1}{2}$ to 2 hours. You will also meet with the leadership team for at least $1\frac{1}{2}$ hours about once a month.

There should be a regular time and place for all meetings. Holding meetings in the same room at the same time saves members from wondering, "When are we meeting this week? Where do we meet?" Equip the meeting room for effective team meetings. The team leader should make certain there are sufficient:

§ Tables and chairs: Have enough table space and chairs to comfortably accommodate the team and several visitors. A square or round table allows team members to see and hear each other, and encourages equal participation.

§ Flipcharts, markers, masking tape, and other supplies: Each meeting room should have a flipchart mounted on the wall or on an easel. Have adequate flipchart pads, markers, and tape. These are indispensable aids for meetings; chalk boards or grease-pencil boards are not adequate substitutes. Tape the flipchart pages to the wall as the meeting progresses so your team can track its progress. Later, save these pages as records for the minutes. (Team leaders are advised to carry their own markers and masking tape since these items often disappear from meeting rooms.) You may also need regular note paper, graph paper, pencils, and pens.

• Set an agenda

The team leader and quality advisor set the final agenda prior to each of the first several meetings. Questions they can ask themselves are: What are the most important things that people should gain by the end of this meeting? What information? Insights? Attitudes? How can you incorporate the three themes of team-building, education, and the project into the meetings? Build the meeting around the answers. As the team gains experience, agendas will be developed during the prior meeting. A sample agenda for the first meeting is described in the next section.

• Plan for improving meetings

Monitor meeting activities to determine which ones help build the team and aid progress towards improvement. How will you know when something goes wrong? How can you help the group develop plans for working through problems? (See Chapters 6 and 7.)

V. Conducting the First Meeting

We have found the following sequence of activities to be very useful for the first meeting. It incorporates elements seen in later meetings (such as the warm-up activity), but is arranged to introduce members to various aspects of the project. These instructions will guide a team leader or other facilitator through the first meeting. They follow the accompanying sample agenda (p. 4-28) very closely; the corresponding agenda item numbers are indicated below.

1. Before Members Arrive

Arrive early. Write the meeting agenda on a flipchart page and tape it to the wall so it is visible to all; you may want to type it up and distribute copies to members as they arrive. On another flipchart page, write the name of the process and the improvement goals that have been developed. (You may want to save this page for re-use at later meetings.) Write down the mission statement on a third flipchart page. Check to make sure all the supplies are ready.

2. Greet Arrivals

Greet members by name or introduce yourself as they enter the room. Welcome each one personally.

3. Get Started

Establish a precedent for a prompt start. We suggest you begin at the announced starting time, even if some members have not yet arrived. If members know that a meeting won't wait for them, they will have an incentive to show up on time. If people are talking, get their attention by meeting their eyes and simply saying (loud enough to be heard), "It's time to get started." Introduce yourself and explain your role: to facilitate the meetings, plan meetings and other team activities, and serve as a focus person. Review the agenda to orient the team to this meeting. (Agenda Item 1.)

4. Warm-up (Optional)

At the first meeting (and all other meetings, for that matter) it works well to incorporate a five- to ten-minute warm-up activity to do while stragglers arrive. Some warm-ups focus people's attention on the task at hand, but at the first meeting you might want to stick to one that helps team members get better acquainted. (You can use a warm-up that serves as an introduction as Agenda Item 2, or use it in addition to the next step.) This activity differs from the warm-up described on p. 4-30: This one is briefer, and is focused on starting up the meeting rather than getting acquainted. This warm-up is optional.

5. Have Members Introduce Themselves

If the warm-up you choose does not include introductions, make time for that here. Simply go around the table and have members introduce themselves and perhaps say a few words about what they do. (Agenda Item 2.)

6. Review the Team's Purpose

State the mission; this is the team's purpose. From the previously prepared flipchart, read the name of the process being studied and the improvement goals. Say a few words about why you are excited about this project. Indicate how the educational system, its customers, each team member, and all the staff who participate in this work process will benefit. (Agenda Item 3.)

Chapter 4

Model Agenda for a Project Team's First Meeting

Instructions: Use this agenda as a model for your first meeting. On your form, enter the name of the team (if you have already decided on one), and its main goals or objectives. We have included time estimates for each item (for a total meeting length of about 3½ hours). Keep track of the actual times so you can get good at predicting how long your meetings will have to last. If you think you will not have enough time to finish all the items, indicate which are "musts" for this meeting. **Be sure to schedule regular breaks in meetings of this length**. The format differs slightly from that for regular meetings.

Project Team _____   **Meeting Date** _____

Goals for Improvement:
Note: Have your team goals listed on the agenda. They can be retyped onto the master form before it is copied.

1. **Review this agenda** (5 mins.)
   Add items, delete items, estimate the time needed for each item. Rank the item: must do today/should do today. Note item types: announcement, discussion, decision, action.

2. **Brief self-introductions by team members** (10 mins.)

3. **Review the mission statement from the leadership team** (15 mins.)

4. **Explain the goals of this meeting** (10 mins.)

5. **Get acquainted with each other** (35 mins. total)
   - An icebreaker in pairs followed by a group activity. (20 mins.)
   - A more detailed discussion of the process assigned to us for study. A description by all members of their roles in that process. (15 mins.)

6. **Define the roles of team leader, quality advisor, and team members** (10 mins.)

7. **Set ground rules and housekeeping rules** (10 mins.)

8. **An introduction to basic concepts** (60-90 mins.)
   - Deming's 14 Points/Joiner Triangle
   - The scientific approach
   - What is a process?
   - Customers and suppliers
   - The 85/15 Rule
   - How this project fits into our school district's larger effort
   - Our partnership with the leadership team

9. **An assignment for the next meeting: data, time** (10 mins.)
   Discuss possible readings or activities that team members can undertake before the next meeting.

10. **Meeting evaluation; questions and discussion**

7. Explain the Meeting Goals

Briefly outline the plan for the first few meetings: to build the team, explore quality issues, clarify the task, and further develop the improvement plan. As part of this orientation, you might place this project in the context of the educational system's quality improvement effort, and mention that the team has support from leadership and others resources available. Keep this portion brief as these topics can be discussed in detail later in the meeting. (Agenda Item 4.)

8. Get Acquainted with Each Other

In the first hour of a team's life, it is important for members to begin learning about task and about each other. People are embarking on a new experience, stretching old patterns of work and long-standing assumptions that things will never change. That's why it is critical to emphasize from the start that "we as team members are going to work together to reach our goals."

At this stage, then, spend 20 to 30 minutes on activities that focus on how team members will relate to each other and work together. We suggest using a warm-up activity done first in pairs and then as a group. (See "Warm-Ups," next page, and Chapter 7.) Follow this with a more in-depth discussion of the process; have team members describe where they fit into the process. (Agenda Item 5.)

9. Define Roles

After team members have described where they fit into the process, discuss how the team will operate. Describe your role as team leader in more depth. Explain the other roles: The quality advisor is a consultant for the team; team members contribute to understanding the process and carry out some of the data collection and

Warm-Ups

Warm-ups are quick activities to use at the beginning of meetings. They signal the start of the team activities, preparing the group to work together. There are many different warm-ups described in Chapter 7. Here is one that is easy to use and re-use, and is almost always appropriate.

The "Check-In"

Going around the room, have each member say a few words about how they are and what concerns or distractions they brought into the meeting. The purpose is to let the team know what may influence the participation of each member. For example: "The baby was up all night with an ear infection and I'm exhausted"; "We're trying to get grades out and everyone in my department is giving me the business about cutting out for this meeting, so I'm kind of distracted"; "I'm fine today"; "Glad to be here. It's a zoo down the hall today!"

analysis. Discuss how the team will draw conclusions from the data and develop proposed improvements, and make links to other educators and staff in this system. Briefly describe the leadership team, who is on it, and its purpose. (Agenda Item 6.)

10. Set Ground Rules

Have team members discuss ground rules for what the group will expect in terms of general courtesy (such as not interrupting conversations) and team members' responsibility for their behavior (such as promptness, carrying out assignments). Review the list given previously in this chapter (p. 4-16) for more detail. (Agenda Item 7.)

11. Complete the Agenda

In the model agenda (p. 4-28), we encourage lengthy discussions of the concepts underlying the team and its improvement goals, and what it means for the educational system. However, the team leader and quality advisor can adjust this agenda as they see fit. Whatever activity they choose should deepen the team's understanding of the continuous quality movement or its project. Ideally, this activity will combine both the team-building and process aspects of improvement. (Agenda Item 8.)

There are several suitable alternatives to a discussion of quality improvement theories and concepts, such as the team-building exercise shown (right). Other team-building exercises are given in Chapter 7. Always end with a meeting evaluation, described next. (Agenda Items 9 and 10.)

VI. Evaluations

In many respects, evaluation is the most important and difficult activity the teams will undertake. Self-critique is a team's main source of feedback, and the only way it can avoid letting problems go unnoticed for too long.

Because the team's work gets done or is presented at meetings, one logical way to evaluate the project is to evaluate the meetings.

The most convenient setting for evaluation is at the end of meetings, but that is sometimes difficult because people are often tired and don't feel like challenging themselves. One way around this is to evaluate the meeting at the mid-point rather than the end. While mid-meeting evaluation is not incorporated into our model agendas, we encourage team leaders to experiment with it.

Structure any evaluation around two points:

- **Effectiveness: Are we doing the right things?** Asking the right questions? Tackling the right problems? Working on issues related to the project?

- **Efficiency: Are we doing things right?** Are we taking unnecessary steps? Repeating ourselves? Spinning our wheels? Are we looking for processes?

When specifically applied to a meeting, a team should do both a general evaluation and a focused evaluation on how well the group discussed specific topics.

Team-Building Exercises

Certain activities are designed to help members learn to work better as a team. Several of these team-building activities are described in Chapter 7.

Here is one of the most common.

Touring Each Other's Classrooms, Schools, or Offices

Each team member can use part of a weekly meeting (or a session between regular meetings) to guide other members through her or his classroom or part of the building. That way team members get a first-hand look at how different parts of the organization function.

Each tour typically takes about 45 to 60 minutes.

The host member:

- Explains the main processes involved, perhaps providing a flowchart or lesson plan.

- Describes the part of the process that is related to the team's project.

- Introduces the team to other people working in this area.

- Allows time for questions from the team members.

One type of meeting evaluation format

To use this format, the team leader or other facilitator asks team members to rate the meeting on criteria important to the team. Often team members work individually at first, then share and discuss answers with their teammates. Other evaluation formats are less structured.

Our meeting today was:

Wonderful	1	2	3	4	5	6	A Waste of Time
Very Focused	1	2	3	4	5	6	Rambling
Energetic	1	2	3	4	5	6	Lethargic

•
•
•

I would characterize our methods as:

The Scientific Approach	1	2	3	4	5	6	Shooting from the Hip
Cooperative	1	2	3	4	5	6	Divisive

•
•
•

General evaluation

- How did this meeting go? What didn't we like?
- How was the pace, flow, and tone of the meeting? Did we handle items in a reasonable sequence? Did we get stuck?
- What might we do differently? What should we do that we didn't do? Do more of? Do less of? Not do at all? What was just right and should continue as is?
- Any other comments, observations, recommendations?

Focused evaluation

- How well did we stay on this (any specified) subject?
- Did we look for problems in the system rather than blame individuals?
- How well did we discuss the information? How clearly? How accurately?
- How well did we respond to each other's questions? How satisfied are we with answers to our questions?

One useful approach to evaluation is to monitor weak spots. For example, one project team noticed that meetings were frequently sluggish at the beginning. So for the next several meetings they evaluated themselves on how quickly they got started. They also discussed reasons for slow starts, and steps they could take to prevent slow starts. Another useful approach is to provide a short list of evaluation items, and rate each on a six-point scale (see top of page).

At evaluation time, each member rates the group on whatever items the team has selected. Then the group compares answers and discusses differences in ratings. The numbers themselves are not important; the discussion they provoke is important.

VII. Regular Meetings

Once past the hurdle of the first meeting or two, team members will become more comfortable with the meeting process and the project. Discussing all the issues described previously in "Goals for the First Meetings" will probably take you at least two or three meetings, and some of the items will carry through the entire project. Filling agendas for these meetings will therefore pose little difficulty.

By the end of that time, you should have an improvement plan and be able to structure agendas around the team's activities. Your meetings should settle into a routine of planning and carrying out meetings and between-meeting activities. (See "The Meeting Cycle," p. 4-35.)

Each agenda should include the items we've already pointed out: warm-ups, evaluations, item type, person responsible, and estimates of time. Keep track of the type of reports you usually have at your meetings, and make space for them on your standard meeting agenda, as we have indicated in the sample format (next page).

The bulk of your regular agenda—discussion of activities and problems, planning data collection, etc.—should relate to the improvement goals. You should also schedule periodic team-building activities.

Every team member should from time to time contribute items for the agenda and suggest ways to modify the overall improvement plan. Overall, the flow of your meetings, and the project itself, will be determined largely by this improvement plan you develop (see Chapter 5). In general, though, you can expect the following phases (depicted also in the figure on page 4-37):

1. Clarify goals
Discuss your mission, create an improvement plan.

Model Agenda for a Project Team's Regular Meetings

Instructions: We suggest using this format for several meetings until you become comfortable with the way agendas should be constructed. After that, feel free to modify this form to better suit your team's needs.

Project Team_____   **Meeting Date**_____

Goals for Improvement:
(Note: Have your team goals listed on the agenda.
They can be typed onto the master before it is copied.)

Item type (decision, discussion, action)	Must do/should do?	Time estimate
	Total Time	

1. **Icebreaker**

2. **Review the agenda**
   Add items, delete items, estimate the time for each item: must do today/ should do today

3. **Status reports on individual assignments**
   (List all assigments here.)

4. **Other reports, presentations, activities, or discussions**
   (List here.)

5. **Review of the status of our project: Where are we now relative to our plan?**

6. **Assignments for follow-up activities (what? by whom? due date?)**

7. **Upcoming events, presentations, special meetings, etc.**

8. **Review of items on the "Action List"**

9. **Review of items on the "Future Action List"**

10. **Agenda items for our next regular meeting**
    (List here.)

11. **Special activity scheduled for this meeting**

12. **Meeting evaluation**

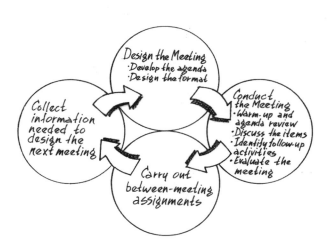

The Meeting Cycle

After the initial flurry of activity dies down, a project team's meetings will settle into an effective, comfortable routine where agendas are set ahead of time and incorporate work that members will do between meetings.

2. Educate and build the team

Set ground rules, discuss the quality improvement philosophy and tools, build relationships in the group.

3. Study the process or problem

Define the process (including who are its customers and suppliers), gather data to localize and identify root causes of problems.

4. Analyze data and look for solutions

Look for patterns in data, ask what they reveal about real causes of problems you are investigating and what solutions you should try.

5. Take appropriate action

Do what the data tell you to do—fine-tune procedures, add focus, correct problems, gather more data, make obvious changes, dig deeper for root causes, plan next steps, and so forth.

6. Repeat the improvement loop (Steps 3 to 5)

Keep going through Steps 3 to 5 until you have pinpointed the problems and found out what you need to know.

7. Closure

Wrap up the project, evaluate the results and the team's effectiveness, complete documentation, recommend follow-up actions and next steps.

Your improvement plan, of course, will be much more specific, and you should use it to keep the focus in the project. Another way to track your progress is to use the Progress Checklist (p. 4-38) to identify tasks completed or not completed. See also the Closure Checksheet (p. 4-42).

Chapter 4

VIII. Meetings Between Project Teams and Leadership Teams

It is very important for a project team and its leadership team to avoid being isolated from one another. Positive interactions between them can increase the chance of success. Typical encounters include discussing problems the project team encounters, revising the improvement plan, celebrating progress, and jointly working to improve a process.

The first contact between the project team and leadership team will probably come as the project team works through its mission statement (ordinarily written by the leadership team). Often this contact will be through the project team leader, but other times the teams meet together.

At first, these joint meetings will probably focus on ironing out controversial or unclear portions of the mission statement. After that, the two teams should hold meetings regularly; we recommend every four to six weeks. You may call additional meetings to address urgent issues, something that happens a lot in a project's early stages.

Joint meetings serve three purposes: to update the leadership team on progress made since the last joint meeting, to give them an opportunity to help the project team identify and overcome barriers to the project's success, and to give both teams a chance to clarify ambiguous issues.

Keep these joint meetings informal, with the emphasis on discussion and questions and answers rather than formal presentations. Hold them at a regular time and place. Do not change them except in case of emergencies. A team leader may be tempted to cancel or postpone this meeting when "we have nothing to report," but these meetings are

Model of Progress

This is a top-down flowchart showing the general progression of events in a project team. In the early part of an improvement project, team members clarify what it means to be on the team: what process they will work on, and what kinds of improvements are expected. From these goals and expectations, they draft an improvement plan. The first few meetings are typically devoted largely to team building and education. After team members have been exposed to quality and scientific principles, they are ready to begin work in earnest on the process. Usually, they study the process to learn more about how it operates and to identify problems. All theories are checked by collecting data, and appropriate actions are determined after analysis. The loop of problem analysis and data collection continues until the team is satisfied that it has identified and eliminated the root causes of problems.

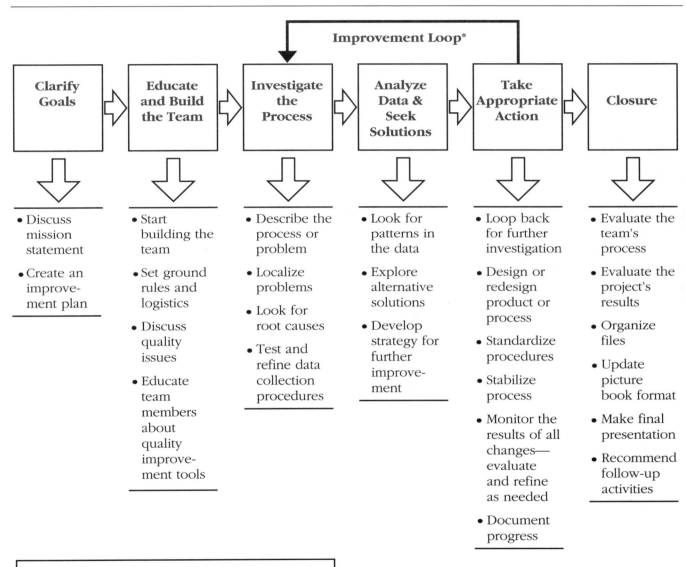

Improvement Loop*

Clarify Goals	Educate and Build the Team	Investigate the Process	Analyze Data & Seek Solutions	Take Appropriate Action	Closure
• Discuss mission statement • Create an improvement plan	• Start building the team • Set ground rules and logistics • Discuss quality issues • Educate team members about quality improvement tools	• Describe the process or problem • Localize problems • Look for root causes • Test and refine data collection procedures	• Look for patterns in the data • Explore alternative solutions • Develop strategy for further improvement	• Loop back for further investigation • Design or redesign product or process • Standardize procedures • Stabilize process • Monitor the results of all changes— evaluate and refine as needed • Document progress	• Evaluate the team's process • Evaluate the project's results • Organize files • Update picture book format • Make final presentation • Recommend follow-up activities

> * Details about the activities occurring in the improvement loop are given in Chapter 5, "Building an Improvement Plan."

Chapter 4

Progress Checklist

Instructions: Refer to this list occasionally to monitor the team's progress. This list can also give you clues of what to do if your team gets stuck between phases of the project. Some of these items may not pertain to your team—or you may be able to identify other milestones that are not listed here that you want to add.

Mission statement

___ Receive from leadership

___ Clarify; modify if necessary

___ Get leadership approval for mission revisions

___ Define goals and objectives related to mission

Planning

___ Select team members

___ Develop logistical system for team meetings

___ Create an improvement plan

___ Develop a top-down flowchart of project stages

Education/team-building activities

___ Introduce team members

___ Explain roles and expectations

___ Orient to group's process

___ Introduce basics of new approach:
14 Points, Joiner Triangle, key quality management concepts

___ Provide training in needed scientific tools

___ Develop ownership in project

Study the process

___ Construct top-down flowchart of process

___ Interview customers to identify needs

___ Design data-gathering procedures

___ Gather data on process

___ Analyze data to see if process is stable

___ Identify problems with process

Localize problems

___ Identify possible causes of problems

___ Select likely causes

___ Gather data to establish root causes

___ Analyze data

___ Rank causes

___ Develop appropriate, permanent solutions

Make changes/document improvement

___ Develop a strategic plan to test changes

___ Implement test

___ Gather data on new process

___ Analyze data, critique changes in light of data

___ Redesign improvements in process, and repeat this step if necessary

___ Implement further changes, or refer matter to appropriate person or group

___ Monitor results of changes

___ Establish a system to monitor in the future

Closure

___ Prepare presentation on project

___ Deliver presentation

___ Evaluate team's progress

___ Evaluate team's product

___ Document

intended to educate leaders, not impress them, and to keep communication lines open. So hold the joint meeting (though it might be briefer than usual) even when there has been little apparent progress.

Joint meetings will run more smoothly if

- They are held in a special location, one not associated with either leadership team meetings or project team meetings.

- The project team leader prepares a meeting agenda after checking with fellow team members and the leadership team to see whether there are specific issues to include.

- The project team prepares a brief update (using the picture book format, p. 4-13) as a reminder of what the team has accomplished. (The project team leader should guide team members in preparing the picture book format.)

SUMMARY

If you have followed along this far, your team is now up and running, busy examining its assigned process or problem and trying to find new ways to make the system work better for the customer. The team is actively supported by a leadership team that understands the time and work required for the project and that keeps in regular communication. Effective meetings are crucial to insure steady progress of the team. Each meeting should balance project content (what the team does) with meeting process (how the team works together). The more productive the meetings, the less chance a team has of getting sidetracked. To have effective meetings, use agendas, warm-ups, and team-building exercises; practice constructive feedback skills; and maintain complete records. In the next chapter, we describe specific strategies for improvement that teams can mold into a complete improvement plan. Each strategy is a sequence of activities that constitutes the core of the project team's work.

Team Presentations

Every team, sooner or later, will be asked to make a presentation to mark key milestones in its project. Some examples are when the team has documented the causes of a major quality or productivity problem, when a remedy has been tested and proven successful, or at the conclusion of a project.

These presentations usually take about 30 minutes. They should be self-contained, covering the context, purpose, key activities, and results of the project in a way that is understandable to anyone unfamiliar with the project. Involve every team member in the presentation.

While a leadership team is ordinarily the first audience for such presentations, potential audiences include other staff, the board of education, other schools, local businesses, and professional organizations.

Here's one recommended outline for these presentations:

1. Introduction
    1.1 Purpose of the project (mission).
    1.2 Achievements or major findings.
    1.3 Suggested next steps.

2. Description
    2.1 Main conditions found at outset of project.
    2.2 Major research studies or experiments done. Emphasize the purpose rather than detailed descriptions.
    2.3 Outcomes of research studies or experiments. Show results and charts. Describe impact and implications of outcomes/problems.
    2.4 Repeat steps 2.2 and 2.3 as many times as necessary to get final results. Keep these to a minimum to prevent confusion. Stick to "punch lines."
    2.5 Achievements or major findings (a repeat of step 1.2). Describe the anticipated outcomes for the project and the specific improvements that can be realistically expected.

3. Conclusions
    3.1 Impact of findings on system being studied.
    3.2 Suggestions for future work.
    3.3 Suggestions for leadership.
    3.4 Other recommendations.
    3.5 Acknowledgments.

Chapter 4

Closure Checklist

Instructions: Teams often have problems bringing their projects to an end. This checklist will help you determine when you have accomplished your tasks and help you plan activities that will signal the end of the project. Sometime before the end of the project, you can also use this list to spur discussion among team members using the topic, "How will we know when we're finished?" Add any items the team agrees to that are not already on this list.

___ **Avoid needless continuation**
  - Is your team's mission completed? Have you met your goals? Is your work done?

___ **Evaluate the team's process**
  - Nostalgia—what was it like working with this team early on?
  - What have you learned from this experience?
  - System-wide learnings form this experience—what advice would you give to other teams?
  - How well did you work with your leadership team?

___ **Evaluate the team's product**
  - Did you accomplish your mission? What helped your team? What hindered it?
  - What were your technical accomplishments?
  - Have the improvements been standardized and error-proofed? How will the improvements be maintained? How were these communicated among and between groups?
  - What other discoveries did you make? How were these communicated among and between groups?
  - Have you used the P-D-C-A cycle on the changes you made?

___ **Document the team's improvement**
  - Is your picture book format up to date? Does it contain your final results and conclusions?
  - Is your document file completed?
  - Final report to the leadership team

___ **Communicating the ending**
  - A joint task for the project team and leadership team
  - How will the team's improvements be communicated to the rest of the educational system?
  - How can the end of this project sow the seeds for future projects?
  - How will this team's learnings be communicated to the administration?
  - What recommendations will the team make for follow-up after the project is over?

___ **The celebration!**
  - What is the appropriate way to celebrate this closure? (Lunch/dinner/dessert?)
  - How will you say goodbye?

Chapter 5
Building An Improvement Plan

Teams that proceed with an improvement project without careful planning and appropriate staff development are probably headed for disaster. Without planning, teams often collect the wrong kind of data, invest in unnecessary though fashionable solutions, or ignore the needs of students and the community. As a result, their solutions may not be solutions at all. They end up with a process no better than at the start, an expensive investment that has done little good, or a service the staff, learners, and others in the community don't want. Perhaps worst of all, these winless projects create a crowd of once-hopeful administrators and teachers who now conclude "improvement projects don't work here."

Effective, permanent solutions and improvements result only from careful forethought and planning. Teams must envision how projects are likely to unfold, anticipate data collection and resource needs through different stages, and plan how to deal with these needs. They must pay close attention to the sequence in which actions will occur. And they must attend to people issues: how to involve people affected by the project; what to do if you run into people opposed to the project; how to open communication lines.

With experience, knowing what to do about these issues becomes second nature. But when you are just starting out, it's easy to be confused about what to expect or where a project might lead. Some direction is helpful. By comparing teams that flounder or get sidetracked with those that steadily progress towards their goals, we have discovered common threads in successful teams. This, in turn, let us develop a series of strategies, steps to follow, guidelines to consider, and questions to ask when planning for different stages in a project. The strategies will help you build an improvement plan by identifying the information and resources you will need during a project. Using the plan will let you avoid the most common pitfalls and dramatically enhance your school improvement team's chance of success.

Notes. . .

I. How to Use This Chapter

Goal of This Chapter

Our goal for this chapter is to provide you with information that will help your team create a plan for improvement.

How We Propose to Get You There

One of the best ways to build an improvement plan is to look at a project as a collection of distinct pieces. Each piece has specific goals and needs. Though these specific goals are different from project to project, there are usually common themes that apply to all projects. We have captured these common themes in a series of *improvement strategies*. Each improvement strategy guides you step-by-step through activities that will help you meet your project needs. We provide general questions that indicate in which direction your team should head, and your team provides specific answers for your project. By working through these questions and guidelines, you can develop action plans and allocate tasks to various team members.

To get the most out of this chapter, we recommend that you:

1. Glance through the strategies at the end of this chapter.
A quick scan of the strategies will help you see how they are constructed. Remember that these strategies are the building blocks of an improvement plan.

2. Review the basic strategies of the scientific approach.
These are four strategies that will be used frequently by every team, so they make a good starting point for any project. Read through the general instructions (p. 5-32) before you begin working with

these strategies. That way your team will know when and how to incorporate the strategies (which appear at the end of this chapter) during your project.

3. Determine which other sections of this chapter best apply to your team.

Your next steps after scanning the strategies of the scientific approach depend on your team's situation. Here are our suggestions:

- If members of your team don't understand your mission statement, or think it is too broad, you can work through the exercise on "Discussing Your Mission," p. 7-29. After you clarify your mission, review the criteria below to determine which other sections of this chapter apply to your team.

- If your team has not been told specifically what process or problem to address, you must start by identifying improvement needs. Instructions for this activity are given in "Defining a Project," which starts on p. 5-10.

- If you have an inexperienced team but understand your mission, stick to the sequence of strategies in the "Five-Stage Plan for Process Improvement" (p. 5-16). This five-stage plan provides a general framework suitable for improving school processes. It is also useful for experienced teams that are studying processes not previously studied.

- An experienced team with a clear mission can build its own plans from the strategies at the end of this chapter, following the guidelines in "Customized Improvement Plans" (p. 5-24). We advise going this route under two circumstances: when your team is studying a problem not easily associated with a single process, or when you understand the process well enough to know specifically which strategies will be useful.

Structure of this Chapter

The rest of this chapter describes how to use the various strategies we have put together.

- **Sections II & III**
  Describe activities that every team needs to conduct successful projects.

- **Section IV**
  Is aimed at teams that need to select or narrow down their project before they can construct an improvement plan. Teams that have well-defined mission statements need not read this section.

- **Section V**
  Describes the general approach to school process improvement that we have found useful. Most teams—and especially those just starting out—will benefit from these activities.

- **Section VI**
  Is aimed at teams whose goals do not fit into the general scheme we outline. These teams can custom-fit our strategies to suit the needs of their projects.

- **Section VII**
  Contains the strategies themselves, arranged in the order they are discussed in earlier sections (that is, the strategies that apply to all teams come first, then the strategies used to identify improvement needs, then the general strategies used by most teams).

Chapter 5

CREATE A TOP DOWN FLOWCHART

4. Read the pertinent sections more closely.

When your team is ready to begin planning, discuss the instructions you think apply to your team. (This will be either the Five-Stage Plan for Process Improvement, or a Customized Improvement Plan.) To fully understand these discussions, you will have to occasionally refer back to specific strategies in the second half of this chapter. To make this easier, we provide page numbers each time a strategy is referenced.

5. Create a top-down flowchart and work through the plan.

Put major activities in the strategy into a top-down flowchart format (p. 2-23), using terminology that applies to your team. Refer to this flowchart as you work through each step, determining what actions, resources, training, and so forth you will need throughout the project. Assign responsibilities where possible. Try to figure out milestones that will let you judge your progress. You will not be able to work through everything in detail the first time through because later project stages depend on the results of your initial efforts. Instructions for working through the plans are given later in this chapter.

6. Periodically recheck and modify the plan.

The usefulness of the plan is most apparent when your team is stuck or sidetracked. Checking the plan periodically can help prevent these unwanted events. Sometimes you will need to revise the plan to reflect changes in your strategy. Revising the plan forces your team to develop clarity and agreement on the path ahead.

II. What Every Team Needs to Know, Part 1: *Five Crucial Improvement Effort Activities*

The following five activities must be incorporated into every step of every project. Teams that forget to use them will be more likely to run into barriers, such as opposition from people who feel ignored or misused. Teams who follow these suggestions will travel a smoother road to long-lasting improvements.

1. Maintain Communications

A project's success depends on how well team members communicate what they are doing not only among themselves but also to anyone likely to be affected by or interested in their activities. For example, if a team was about to collect data from a classroom, team members should notify the principal and supervisors in advance and tell them exactly why, how, and when the data will be collected. Similarly, a team studying how staff use their time should explain that the goal is to identify how the system operates, not to blame individuals for problems within it (see 85/15 Rule).

This kind of communication is simply being considerate to colleagues and other employees in the system. It encourages cooperation and often leads to suggestions for improving the data collection process. Therefore, the strategies in this chapter may not always mention "notify principals and supervisors" or "explain to the people working with the process what you are about to do" as specific steps. But you should include these activities throughout your project.

Five Crucial Improvement Activities

1. **Maintain Communications**
2. **Fix Obvious Problems**
3. **Look Upstream**
4. **Document Progress and Problems**
5. **Monitor Changes**

Chapter 5

2. Fix Obvious Problems

The better you get at studying processes, the more problems you will find that need fixing. Generally, we recommend exploring problems in depth, collecting data to make sure you have developed appropriate solutions. But there are times when a problem is easily fixed, and in those cases we urge you to go ahead and make the change. Do not wait until the end of a project to fix obvious problems.

Before making any change, however, ask yourselves these questions: "What's the worst that could happen if this solution associated with the process change doesn't work? How easy will it be to undo the change? Will this delay other actions? How expensive will this change be in terms of money, time, and the disruption and inconvenience to colleagues?" If it looks like the solution you propose could have substantial negative effects if it doesn't work, take the time to explore other options. If it is simple to put in place and easily undone, go ahead and try it out.

3. Look at Earlier Phases

Most problems we see are only symptoms of other problems in earlier activities in the process. For example, variation in learning outcomes may be the result of variation in curriculum content; mistakes in the delivery of the curriculum may be the result of mistakes in the planning process or its implementation or any activities in between. To make long-lasting improvements, you must seek out these causes and find ways to prevent them. Whenever your team is faced with a problem, mentally walk through the entire process and see if you can identify conditions in earlier phases that may be the cause of lack of improvement.

4. *Document Progress and Problems*

In every educational system, there are problems that get "solved" over and over again, problems you hear about every week, month, or year. You try something once; it doesn't do much good, so somebody else tries something different the next time (with little idea of what has gone before), and so on. If you're lucky, the problem will decrease or disappear for a while, but it always returns because the solutions tried are aimed at symptoms rather than at causes of the problem.

For example, one school district experienced low assessment results at the third grade level in mathematics: the number of students mastering the learning outcomes for the math assessment was low. Teachers and administrators experimented with various drills and test practice materials. When the assessment was readministered later that school year, the number of students mastering the learning outcomes increased appreciably. The next school year the problem reappeared. However, the teachers were not sure what they had done to the learning process that had eliminated the problem. Now, the school district knows that the process is capable of better results, but has no record of what was done when the better results were achieved.

The simple way to get out of this trap is to keep and use good records of everything tried on the process. They are valuable data for future efforts. (See the discussion in Chapter 4 about team records and documentation.)

5. *Monitor Changes*

Rarely does something turn out exactly the way you planned. Changes made to a process or system are no exception. Though careful planning reduces the chances of unanticipated problems, there is no guarantee

Chapter 5

that everything will work perfectly. The only sensible plan of action, therefore, is to monitor actions so you can quickly catch mistakes and prevent them from becoming major problems.

III. What Every Team Needs to Know, Part 2: *Basic Strategies of the Scientific Approach*

Earlier in this handbook, we described a scientific approach as making decisions based on data, looking for root causes of problems, and seeking permanent solutions instead of relying on quick fixes. Teams new to quality improvement may not know how to put these statements into action, so we have developed four strategies to help. These four strategies, "Collect Meaningful Data," "Identify Root Causes of Problems," "Develop Appropriate Solutions," and "Plan and Make Changes," should be a part of every team's activities.

1. **Collect Meaningful Data** (p. 5-36) is the foundation of the scientific approach. Every team needs data it can rely on, data it knows are free from measurement errors or mistakes in procedures, data suited to its purpose. Too often, teams collect inappropriate data or devise poor collection procedures. Since they have never been shown how to recognize such mistakes, they base decisions on unreliable data, and end up failing to bring about the desired improvement. They collect more data (probably repeating the same mistakes), act on the results, see they still haven't made the improvement they need, collect more data . . . and on and on. This cycle will continue until teams learn correct data collection methods.

   Every strategy in this text and almost every activity a project team undertakes rely on the data the team collects, and it pays to do it

right. Consequently, "Collect Meaningful Data" may be the single most important strategy your team will use. It emphasizes basic tactics such as knowing exactly why you want to collect data, using operational definitions so everyone will take measurements in the same way, and periodically checking the stability of your measurement systems.

2. **Identify Root Causes of Problems** (p. 5-39) is necessary for developing permanent solutions to problems; failure to identify root causes associated with the problem is another reason why so many "solutions" tried today turn out next week to be no solution at all. People more often react to visible symptoms of a problem than look for the underlying cause. One trick used in this strategy is having you explore many potential sources of problems instead of zeroing in on one cause early in the game.

3. **Develop Appropriate Solutions** (p. 5-41) asks you to define your goals and gather data on a variety of alternatives. Often people think they know the cause of a problem before they even start the project, and probably are convinced they have a perfect solution. And maybe they do. But if all team members are committed to a scientific approach, hunches must be supported by data. If the hunch turns out to be right, you still benefit from this exercise by learning a lot about how to make the change. More often, though, the solution turns out to be something entirely different from what you suspected.

4. **Plan and Make Changes** (p. 5-44) runs a close second in importance to "Collect Meaningful Data" in determining a project's success. As the Japanese and other pioneers in this approach have learned, there is no substitute for careful planning. Unfortunately, leaders in this country have been raised on a "ready, fire, aim!" attitude instead of "ready, aim, fire!" This encourages people to act even if it isn't the right thing to do. The essence of this strategy is having teams look ahead, anticipate resources and training

necessary for a successful project, and think about what to do if they run into problems. Though these steps add time up front, the careful planning and execution increase the chances of success, and save time in the long run.

IV. Defining a Project

Sometimes administrators or leadership teams commission a project team to study specific process problems associated with a readily identified process, or about which they already have data. These teams are lucky: They have well-defined missions. People whose teams fit this category can skip this section and move to Section V or some other appropriate section. Other teams are less fortunate, and have to spend several meetings choosing a project. The information here on identifying improvement needs is directed towards these latter teams, specifically:

- Teams with a mission statement that is too broad ("reduce complaints")

- Teams with an unclear or undefined mission ("get a team together to work in the curriculum department")

- Teams who need to describe the nature and severity of a process problem before they can decide how to proceed with their project ("is tardiness really a big problem?")

- Teams whose sole mission is to identify and describe process problems so that more focused projects can be designed, probably involving different teams (school bus runs are too long)

- Teams who have the leeway to select their own project (overdue books in the media center)

Teams in these situations who plunge into a project without first narrowing the focus are likely to end up with nothing but headaches. They need to define a project that is reasonable: neither so large that they will never make a dent, nor so small that no one will care.

Refining a Mission Statement

A project team that either does not understand its mission statement or thinks the statement is inappropriate in some way should first review the advice given to administrators in Chapter 3 on "Selecting a Project" (p. 3-1) and "Common Errors in Selecting Projects" (p. 3-2). The lessons stressed there also appear in the "Project Selection Checklist" (p. 3-4). Four of the most important criteria we discuss are:

- Refuse to select or work on a project that no one really cares about.

- Avoid a process that may be changing (for example, computerizing the library/media center), unless your work is preparation for the change.

- Recognize that when you have chosen to study a system ("hiring new employees"), you should narrow it to a single process ("recruiting candidates for entry-level teaching positions").

- Define the project as a process or problem ("study the textbook selection process") rather than as a solution ("justify the replacement of all textbooks").

The first point is especially important: Projects are more likely to succeed if a team works on a problem or process important to its members, even if the scope or direction is different from what a principal or supervisor might have chosen. At the same time, successful projects typically have the interest and support of the principal and supervisor. Success depends on a balance between the needs of the leadership team and the project team. Therefore, it is important for the two teams to work together in defining the project.

Another critical point is to always work on only one process at a time. The exceptions to this rule are rare, and occur only when there is a group of processes that are closely related. If your team thinks that your mission statement disobeys one or more of these rules, you should discuss the statement in depth at one of your first team meetings.

We describe one procedure for doing this in the team-building exercise "Discussing Your Mission" (p. 7-29). You need not use the format given there, but you may find some helpful ideas for structuring your team's discussion.

Once the team is satisfied with its mission statement and goals, you can start developing your own improvement plan, as described later in this chapter (Section VI).

Five Ways to Identify Improvement Needs

If a team is faced with either having to select its own mission or narrowing the goals given to it by the leadership team, there are five ways to see which areas need improving the most. Two methods, "multivoting" and "nominal group technique" (both described in Chapter 2), are simple ways to reach consensus on what problem should be attacked. The other three methods are strategies (described in detail at the end of this chapter) that lead teams through plans for identifying potential projects.

1. & 2. Multivoting and Nominal Group Technique

Multivoting and nominal group technique are the least formal ways to select a project because the results are based on team members' opinions rather than on hard data.

The term "multivoting" derives from the process of taking multiple votes to determine what problem is most important to team members. You can use brainstorming or some other method to generate a list of possible projects. Then team members vote for the ones they consider most important. At the end of the first round of voting, drop the items with the fewest votes from the list, and then vote again on the remaining items. Continue until only one or two items are left. (See p. 2-43 for detailed instructions.)

Nominal group technique is a group process with restricted interaction between participants. Like multivoting, nominal group is a multiround voting process, but here team members individually assign point values to items they think are important; in this setting, those would be potential projects. Whether an item is kept or dropped from the list during each round depends on the total points it accumulates. (See p. 2-45 for more detailed instructions.)

The real advantage of using multivoting or nominal group technique is that they reflect a consensus among members about what is important. The final project choice will therefore have the support of the team. These methods also allow teams to start making improvements faster than if they used one of the strategies described below.

To decide whether to use these methods, you must weigh your knowledge about suggested project topics against the possibility of making a wrong choice. Sometimes problems are so obvious that it wastes time to follow one of these elaborate decision-making strategies. Yet if you make decisions based on team members' opinions, you could end up with a project with a smaller payoff than other projects you might identify through data collection.

Five Ways to Identify Improvement Needs

- **Multivoting** and **Nominal Group Technique**
- **Identify Customer Needs and Concerns**
- **Study the Use of Time**
- **Localize Recurring Problems**

Chapter 5

IDENTIFY CUSTOMER
NEEDS & CONCERNS...

3. Identify Customer Needs and Concerns

Under Quality Leadership, an educational system's goal is always to satisfy and delight the learner and the community that needs educational services. What better way to choose a project, then, than by finding out what is important to the members of the school community? The strategy "Identify Customer Needs and Concerns" (p. 5-46) leads a team through steps designed to get reliable and useful information about the community's concerns. This strategy is especially effective in departments or entire schools that have not been in close contact with their customers. For example, the librarian might use this strategy to get to know the needs of those who rely on his or her services.

4. Study the Use of Time

Most educational systems spend a great deal of time working around problems or trying to remedy past failures. Knowing how teachers and administrators use their time can expose these problems. The strategy "Study the Use of Time" (p. 5-48) helps you plan a project to get the necessary information. Most often a time study simply shows where resources are spent or inefficiencies exist. Further study will be needed to identify causes and solutions for these inefficiencies.

A note of caution: Expect to encounter some distrust from the people involved in the time study, particularly the first few times you use this strategy. People have grown used to the idea that someone keeps track of their time only in order to catch them making mistakes. If teachers or others fear that the results will be used against them, the team will never collect accurate data. Assure all subjects that you are only looking for faults in a system, not judging individual performance, and carry through with this pledge.

If potential time study subjects cannot be reassured and still distrust your team's intentions, don't do it. Wait for the environment to change. The time study recommended here is an amazingly useful tool in helping people find ways to improve their effectiveness, but only when used correctly, when the atmosphere is right.

5. Localize Recurring Problems

Principals and teachers usually know, in a general sense, what problems surface regularly in the schools and classrooms. To make long-lasting improvements, however, project teams need precise information, including accurate definitions of problems and data on their occurrence (such as like curriculum framework, administrative policies and practices, and assessment methods). Pinpointing where and when a process problem occurs is called "localizing." You will use your energies best if you localize a problem before plunging deep into a project. The more information you have, the better you will be able to focus on the real source of problems. Gathering information on where and when a problem occurs and doesn't occur is well worth the effort.

Sometimes it is easy to tell where a problem is first observed, but hard to know where it first occurs. For example, mistakes may appear when a teacher tries to recall a computer record, but the mistakes could be caused upstream where information is gathered and entered into the computer. Localizing the problem first directs a team towards the part of the process that really needs improvement.

At other times, staff may think a problem is widespread—that it happens "all the time"—when in fact it only appears in one type situation. For example, a team thought much of the attendance data was full of errors. After data collection, they discovered that the pattern of errors occurred frequently in only two situations (bus-delay days and substitute teacher days). By localizing the problem before going into more detailed study, they saved time and effort they would have otherwise wasted on the wrong parts of the process. (See "Localize Recurring Problems," p. 5-50.)

Localizing Problems

Five elementary schools send their students to one middle school. Sixth-grade teachers repeatedly have claimed that some students are not prepared to deal with an element of the curriculum. Subsequent analysis, however, revealed that most of the students who lacked the particular skill came from only two of the five schools.

Teachers and administrators from these two schools met, formed teams, and analyzed why their students lacked the skill while those from other schools did not. They identified several areas of needed change and were able to raise their students' skill levels. Not only was the skill level improved, but the effort was accomplished cooperatively and amicably.

Chapter 5

Before continuing on to the improvement stages of a project, your team should know what process you are going to study and what kinds of improvements you need to make. Your team may need to go through several rounds of using the strategies just described before you feel confident about the project's definition and scope.

V. Five-Stage Plan for Process Improvement

Once a team is ready to make improvements, team members have to flesh out their plans. While processes differ widely from one educational system to the next, there is a general approach that applies in almost all situations. We have divided this approach into five stages, each composed of one or more strategies.

The sequence of stages is based on recognizing that most process problems arise from six sources:

1. Inadequate knowledge of how a process does work.

2. Inadequate knowledge of how a process should work.

3. Errors and mistakes in executing the procedures.

4. Current practices that fail to recognize the need for preventive measures such as controlling the process for ordering supplies, preventing the circumstances that contribute to unruly behavior, maintaining machines, etc.

Five-Stage Plan for Process Improvement

It is natural for inexperienced project teams to have difficulty planning their first projects. Typically, they are faced with many problems clamoring for their attention. Our Five-Stage-Plan, depicted in the top-down flowchart below, is a general improvement framework useful for all kinds of processes. It has teams tackling common problems in an order that increases the likelihood of success—peeling off layers of problems as you peel layers from an onion. Each stage is made up of one or more strategies, described at the end of this chapter, that indicate the kinds of questions teams will have to answer during that stage of the plan.

The first step in any project is to understand the process—how it currently operates, what it is supposed to accomplish, who its customers are, and what they expect. When teams know what the process should be doing, they can often find simple ways to standardize procedures, which usually makes a process run more smoothly.

With one layer of problems stripped away, others will be exposed, and teams will have a clearer picture of what further changes are appropriate. As the process is studied, it will gradually show less waste and complexity. At that point, the team will be able to see where it can cut down on unnecessary activities. Then comes the difficult task of removing and controlling variation.

As the project begins to wind down, teams must find ways to perpetuate their progress. They must put in place systems for continuous improvement.

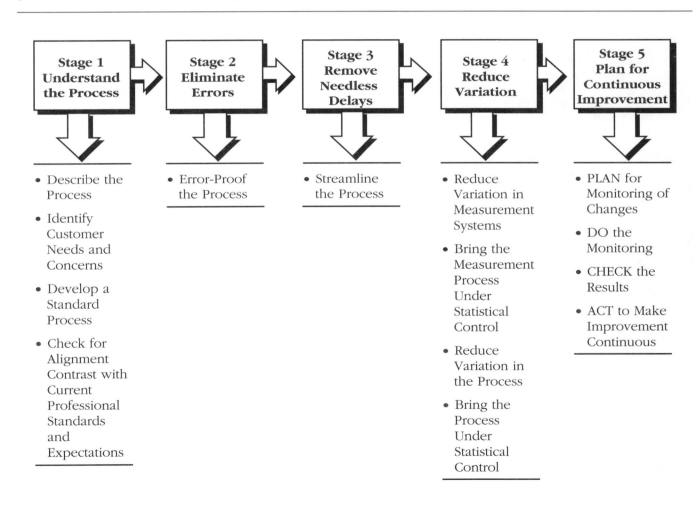

Stage 1 Understand the Process	Stage 2 Eliminate Errors	Stage 3 Remove Needless Delays	Stage 4 Reduce Variation	Stage 5 Plan for Continuous Improvement
• Describe the Process	• Error-Proof the Process	• Streamline the Process	• Reduce Variation in Measurement Systems	• PLAN for Monitoring of Changes
• Identify Customer Needs and Concerns			• Bring the Measurement Process Under Statistical Control	• DO the Monitoring
• Develop a Standard Process			• Reduce Variation in the Process	• CHECK the Results
• Check for Alignment Contrast with Current Professional Standards and Expectations			• Bring the Process Under Statistical Control	• ACT to Make Improvement Continuous

Chapter 5

Six Sources of Problems in a Process

1. **Inadequate knowledge of how a process does work.**

2. **Inadequate knowledge of how a process should work.**

3. **Errors and mistakes in executing the procedures.**

4. **Current practices that fail to recognize the need for preventative measures.**

5. **Unnecessary steps, inappropriate measures.**

6. **Variation in inputs and outputs.**

5. Attitudes that encourage unnecessary activities, needless barriers in the process, and other wasteful measures.

6. Variation in prior experiences, teaching methods, curricula, and so on, and in learner outcomes.

Most likely, a process will have problems arising from each source. Each type demands a different approach to finding solutions. A team can increase its effectiveness by focusing on one type of process problem at a time, an idea we have incorporated in the five-stage improvement plan described here. This plan attacks the process problems in the order listed above, allowing a team to gradually expose problems and tailor solutions to each situation.

The following improvement plan works equally well on instructional and noninstructional processes. Sometimes you will follow the sequence straight through; other times you will loop through some steps several times as you learn from your data.

Stage 1: Understand the Process

Before your team can make improvements, each member must thoroughly understand the process. What are the process activities and in what sequence are they used to achieve the desired outcome? To really know what is right and what is wrong with a process, you must answer three questions: How does the process currently work? What is it supposed to accomplish (that is, how does the desired outcome relate to student and community needs)? What is the current best-known way to carry out the process?

Investigating these questions is the best way for your team to gather information that will let you set goals and objectives for the rest of the improvement project.

Obvious benefits include:

- **Arriving at a common understanding**

    When project team members work through the recommended steps and questions of a strategy, they gain a common understanding of the process. They will start using the same terminology, and won't waste time pulling in different directions or gathering irrelevant information.

- **Eliminating inconsistencies**

    These strategies lead you systematically through a process and have you compare how various people associated with the process carry out their work or activities. You are bound to find inconsistencies, many of which can be traced to a lack of documentation and inadequate training about the best-known way to run the process. The uniformity of services and processes often increases dramatically once people performing certain administrative activities start using the same procedures to do their work.

- **Highlighting obvious problems**

    Looking closely at a process almost always highlights glaring problems that have gone unnoticed but can be fixed easily. This is particularly true of paperwork processes.

Our recommended strategies for understanding a process:

1.1 Describe the Process (p. 5-52)

    This strategy leads your team through the process activity-by-activity. When you complete the process, you will know who does what and when.

Benefits of Studying a Process

- **Arriving at a common understanding**
- **Eliminating inconsistencies**
- **Highlighting obvious problems**

Chapter 5

Why Streamline?

Doing work in large batches is like driving down the road with a dirty windshield. As long as you can't see the road ahead, you think you're in good shape. Streamlining a process—removing delays and unnecessary steps—lets you clean off that windshield and avoid potential disasters.

1.2 Identify Customer Needs and Concerns (p. 5-46)

This strategy focuses your team on the purpose of its work: for example, doing something to benefit the students. Skip this step if you have found glaring problems that do not directly affect the learning outcomes of students.

1.3 Develop a Standard Process (p. 5-54)

Armed with the knowledge of how the process currently works and what it is supposed to do, your team will almost always be able to devise better procedures to implement the process. Get everyone who works with the process to use and contribute to the curriculum framework, instructional strategies, management and assessment methods and practices. You will be amazed by the dramatic improvements brought about by less rework and remedial activities, better quality, and greater job satisfaction.

Stage 2: Eliminate Errors

Everyone makes mistakes. Yet we fail to realize that many mistakes can be prevented by making simple changes to a process. For instance, there may be a checklist of paperwork necessary for admitting a transfer student from another district, or a checklist of requirements for application to a college, or a checklist of procedures required in a fire drill. Such activities can reduce the occurrence of mistakes and omissions. These are examples of "error proofing" a process.

Stage 3: Remove Needless Delays

Increasing numbers of educational systems are realizing that traditional practices of instruction and administration no longer meet the needs of

an ever-changing educational population, e.g., lecturing most of the time with no consideration to learner involvement. These traditional activities or practices mask problems instead of solving them. In addition, processes tend to grow or become more complex over the years, many steps losing whatever value they once had.

To get out of this trap, move towards "a system analysis approach" of staff development that examines each process activity to see if it is necessary and adds value to the teaching/learning process. The result of this critical examination is often a reduction in wasted time and effort and dramatically improved instruction. The resulting improvements increase quality, too.

The strategy we have developed, "Streamline a Process" (p. 5-57), lets team members eliminate unnecessary work. We saved this strategy for the third stage because few people can recognize unnecessary work until the most glaring process problems are eliminated. The process should already be in relatively good shape by the time your team gets to this stage.

Stage 4: Reduce Variation

As discussed in Chapter 2, the sources of variation come in two flavors: common causes and special causes. The trick is to tell them apart. Common causes typically come from numerous, ever-present sources of slight variation. Special causes, in contrast, are not always present, and usually cause greater fluctuations in the process. Eliminating common causes requires fundamental changes in how a process is operated; special causes can often be taken care of through relatively simple changes. The strategies here are targeted primarily at eliminating special causes of variation.

Getting rid of variation usually happens in two stages: taking it out of measurement processes, then looking at learning or administrative processes. Reducing measurement variation must come first because it obscures the performance of a teaching/learning process and masks the effects of changes to it.

Example: There must be a common way to define and measure "Drop-out" before you can determine how big a problem it is now and whether, later on, you have been able to improve it.

The techniques for reducing measurement variation are almost identical to those for reducing process variation. Thus, the following recommended sequence has some repetition.

To reduce variation:

4.1 Use "Reduce Sources of Variation" (p. 5-59) on measurement systems.
> If you can't measure precisely, you will miss important improvement opportunities, or worse, waste your time chasing ghosts.

4.2 Then use "Bring a Process Under Statistical Control" (p. 5-61) on your measurement processes.
> Repeatedly measuring one item will help you identify and eliminate special causes of variation in your measurement processes. Omitting this step is, in our experience, a false saving; whatever time or money you save by skipping this step you will lose later in remediation.

4.3 After the measurement process is in control, return to "Reduce Sources of Variation" (p. 5-59), but this time use it on the targeted process.

With measurements that are in control, you will be in a much better position to detect real changes in your process.

4.4 Finally, use "Bring a Process Under Statistical Control" (p. 5-61) on the targeted process.

Here, every person working on the process is a detective tracking down special causes. Keep monitoring the process until there are no signs of special causes.

Stage 5: Plan for Continuous Improvement

By this stage, the most obvious sources of problems will have been eliminated from a process. Now your team must look for ways to make improvement a constant, never-ending part of the process. Use the strategy "Plan and Make Changes" (p. 5-44) to monitor the effectiveness of changes you made in the process. Ongoing training and education in areas related to the process and instruction in the skills associated with statistical tools are critical. Active experimental studies can be helpful (see, for example, "Improve the Design of a Process," p. 5-63). Before bringing the project to a close, discuss ways to keep the improvement philosophy alive. Keep records about the process and procedures up to date; make sure they are used. Write out the team's recommendations and next steps for continued improvement.

Chapter 5

VI. Customized Improvement Plans

Most teams will be able to use the five-stage improvement plan just described, particularly if they are working on a process that has not been studied previously. However, experienced teams or teams working on a well-studied process may not need to use the entire five-stage plan. Such teams can select appropriate strategies to custom fit improvement plans to their situations. We caution, though, that only teams with experienced members or quality advisors, or those studying a process that has already been studied, should consider this option.

You can venture into customized improvement plans if (a) you have a clear mission statement and know in some detail what your goals are, and (b) you have prior experience in continuous quality improvement projects and know how to plan. You might also be able to use them if the process problem you are working on has already been studied and improved to the point where parts of the five-stage plan are no longer pertinent.

As you study the strategies we present here, keep in mind that every team needs to use the four basic strategies of the scientific approach throughout the project no matter what other strategies are used.

Creating a Customized Improvement Plan

No two projects will be the same. Ever. For that reason, we can only describe in the most general terms a process for creating a customized improvement plan. Please read the general guidelines BEFORE your team begins to build your plan. This process will probably take you several meetings to complete.

Creating a Customized Improvement Plan

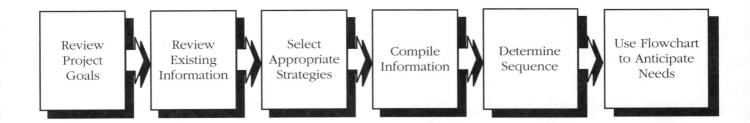

As you work through the steps, try to remember these guidelines:

- The key to choosing appropriate strategies is to ask what you want to accomplish and what information you need. For example, if you want to study the problem of parent complaints, you will need to ask questions such as, "Are we providing what the parents want?" and "Do all parents report the same problem, or is it confined to one group? What is different about the parents who have the problem and those who don't?" The answers to these questions can be found with "Identify Customer Needs and Concerns" (p. 5-46) and "Localize Recurring Problems" (p. 5-50). The results of these preliminary investigations will point to further actions or strategies.

- There is no single strategy that is the right starting point for all projects. Deciding what strategies to use, where to start, and what sequence to use depends on the type of project. Most project teams skip back and forth between strategies, sometimes working through two or more concurrently.

- Think carefully about the sequence. Do not omit steps of a strategy merely to save time. The order in which you use the strategies has great impact on the team's ultimate success. Trying to develop solutions before isolating root causes of a problem would obviously be a waste of time. Likewise, isolating root causes would be inappropriate before localizing the problem.

Step 1: Review your project goals.

As a team, write down your project goals in detail. Be as specific as possible. Remind yourselves how these goals relate to the needs of your community and your learners. Talk about what your goals mean in terms of changing or improving the quality characteristics of the process or service you are studying. (For example, will the

Chapter 5

improved process be "free of errors" or "more stable" or "result in different specific learning outcomes"?)

Step 2: Review existing information, determine gaps that need to be filled.

Worksheet #1 (right) will help you keep track of the information you generate for this step and Step 3. Make enough copies of this worksheet so you have one for each project goal.

2.1 Start by filling in the upper left-hand box with a brief description of one goal.

2.2 Next, discuss what information or data already exist that might help you understand how to reach this goal. ***Unless you know where, when, and how the data were collected, be suspicious.*** If you know of existing data that you think will help, but you don't know who collected the data or what conditions existed when they were collected, and have no way of finding out, then plan to repeat the study. There are just too many ways that data can be inaccurate for you to trust data that you know nothing about. Jot notes in the appropriate space about where to get these data.

2.3 After you've identified potential sources of existing data or information, compare this with the goal and improvement needs. What gaps are there between what you already know and what you need to find out or accomplish in relation to the goal? Enter this in the upper right-hand box.

2.4 Repeat Steps 2.1 to 2.3 for each project goal.

Customized Improvement Plan

Worksheet #1—Describing the Project Needs

Instructions: Fill out one sheet for each goal the team identifies.

Describe one project goal	What other data or information do you need?
	Circle the strategies you think will help you meet this need.

Are there existing data that apply?	Scientific Approach	Identifying Improvement Needs	Improving a Process
	Collect Data	Brainstorming or Multivoting	Describe a Process
	Identify Root Causes of Problems	Identify Customer Needs and Concerns	Standardize a Process
	Develop Appropriate Solutions	Study the Use of Time	Error-Proof a Process
	Plan and Make Changes	Localize Recurring Problems	Streamline a Process
			Reduce Sources of Variation
			Bring a Process Under Statistical Control
			Improve the Design of a Product or Process
			Check for Alignment

Chapter 5

Step 3: Select appropriate strategies.

Compare these needs with the strategies at the end of this chapter, and decide which ones provide the closest match. One way to keep track of this information is to complete the rest of Worksheet #1 (p. 5-27) that we began in Step 2. If none of the strategies seems to match, we recommend that you use the Plan-Do-Check-Act cycle described in "Plan and Make Changes" (p. 5-44).

HINT: The four strategies of the Scientific Approach are usually used in combination with at least one other strategy. For example, you may have to "Collect Meaningful Data" in order to "Identify Customer Needs and Concerns." Before moving to Step 3, check the sheets you have filled out. If the only item or items circled fall under the category of the Scientific Approach, this usually indicates that you are focusing on an intermediate goal rather than a true goal of the project.

Step 4: Compile the information for all the goals.

After you have completed Worksheet #1 for each goal, combine the information and determine a proper sequence of strategies. An easy way to see which strategies you have picked out is to complete Worksheet #2 (page 5-30).

Step 5: Determine an appropriate sequence. Create a top-down flowchart showing this sequence.

Once you have a complete list, try to place each item in a logical order. (HINT: We recommend using the strategies in an order close to the sequence used in this book.) You can summarize this information in the form of a top-down flowchart like the one shown on page 5-17. If your team can't agree on a particular sequence, sketch out top-down flowcharts for the most likely sequences, and have your team discuss each one until you reach consensus on which one to try.

What to Do If You Get Stuck Between Steps

Inexperienced project teams often have difficulty moving from one step to the next. Starting a new strategy, or even moving from one step to the next step, can be almost as overwhelming as starting a whole new project. We suggest you use a P-D-C-A (Plan-Do-Check-Act) approach:

Plan:

Refer to your improvement plan; have team members discuss their readiness to begin the next stage or step. What have you learned so far? What should you do next? What understanding or skills will your team need in the next stage? How will you learn what you need to know? If the team is reluctant to move to the next step, read through the discussion of "Floundering" (p. 6-32). If you have no improvement plan, create one.

Do:

Make some early attempts at the next steps in the strategy or plan you are following. Allow yourselves to make mistakes.

Check:

Reflect on your trial efforts and identify ways to improve them. What worked or went well? What didn't work well? What resources, training, or knowledge do you need to do a better job? Can the leadership team help you fulfill these needs?

Act:

Have the team discuss how to incorporate the lessons learned from your trial runs. Repeat the early steps including these improvements.

P-D-C-A or P-D-S-A?

As Dr. Deming often points out, when the Plan-Do-Check-Act (P-D-C-A) cycle was being used years ago by Walter Shewhart, it was known as the "Plan-Do-Study-Act" cycle (or even the "Shewhart Cycle"). Here's how Dr. Deming drew it for us:

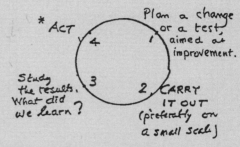

Though it may be more properly called P-D-S-A, we chose to stick with the terminology of P-D-C-A because it is so firmly rooted in quality improvement language.

Still another version of this cycle is known as S-D-C-A, or "*Standardize*-Do-Check-Act." This reference is used particularly when people are improving the methods used on a process. The goal, as we have pointed out, is to have all employees involved with a process use the same procedures. In this case, the S-D-C-A Cycle is used to check how well the standardization process is going, and also indicates that the work of improving methods is never done.

Chapter 5

Customized Improvement Plan
Worksheet #2—Compiling the Information

Instructions: Write a key word or two for each project goal along the top of the columns where indicated. Under each goal, check the strategies you decided were appropriate. Make sure your improvement plan includes all the strategies you identify, and try to find ways to combine goals and strategies wherever possible.

Enter key words identifying each goal across the top ⟶			Goal 1	Goal 2	Goal 3	Goal 4	Goal 5
Scientific Approach		Collect Meaningful Data					
		Identify Root Causes of Problems					
		Develop Appropriate Solutions					
	Plan and Make Changes						
Identifying Improvement Needs	Brainstorming or Multivoting						
	Identify Customer Needs and Concerns						
	Study the Use of Time						
	Localize Recurring Problems						
Improving a Process	Describe a Process						
	Standardize a Process						
	Error-Proof a Process						
	Streamline a Process						
	Reduce Sources of Variation						
	Bring a Process Under Statistical Control						
	Improve the Design of a Product or Process						
	Check for Alignment						

Step 6: Use the flowchart and descriptions of the strategies to help you anticipate training and resources you will need.

For example: What people will you need to involve? What communication challenges will you face? What project management skills are needed? How long will the project take to complete?

If you find that the procedure we recommend fails to meet your team's needs, or you run into obstacles or are unable to determine a best path, it is all right to just "do something" **as long as you use a Plan-Do-Check-Act strategy.** Use the consensus-building models in Chapter 2 to decide on a course of action that everyone can accept. Then build a Plan-Do-Check-Act cycle into that course of action. This will insure that you plan the actions you intend to take rather than plunging ahead blindly. It will also provide you with the means to check the effectiveness of any actions you take, so you can make improvements as the project goes along.

Chapter 5

Tailoring the Strategies

Each strategy is written in very general terms, so teams will have to tailor the language to suit their projects. For example, almost all teams—instructional and noninstructional alike—will have to deal with measurement issues. Their members have to agree on operational definitions for problems and for data collection procedures. (For instance, "How do we define late?")

VII. The Strategies

There are 15 strategies all told (see list p. 5-35). Each embodies a logical, scientific approach to quality improvement, and reflects activities common to tasks associated with these issues. Together, they simplify the planning process by providing a framework around which project teams can create improvement plans. As mentioned earlier in the chapter, we divide them into three categories depending on their use: those forming the basis of the scientific approach, those for identifying improvement needs (selecting an improvement project), and those for improving processes.

Detailed instructions start on page 5-36. Before you get there, though, take a look at the items on the next three pages: The first (on facing page) gives some general background on how to approach use of the strategies. The second (p. 5-34) describes how several teams have used the ideas represented by the strategies. The third (p. 5-35) is a list and summary of the strategies.

Common Questions About Using the Strategies*

1. Do we have to do every step?

For beginning teams, the answer is "YES!" Each strategy is organized to automatically incorporate a scientific approach. To skip any step is to risk missing data that you may need later on down the road. The truth is that you may find some of the steps won't help very much. But there is no way for inexperienced people to know ahead of time which ones will ultimately be useful and which won't.

However, note that we ask a series of questions with each step. These questions are there to spur your own thinking. You may not need to answer absolutely every question listed, and you may come up with other questions pertinent to your project that we have not included.

Experienced teams—those with at least a year or two under their belts—will be able to use these strategies as planning guides rather than scripts they must strictly follow. They may find that some steps do not apply to their teams. Though we strongly recommend that they stick as close as possible to the sequence we have outlined, there may be times when it is all right to modify or skip one of the steps. Be careful though. In most cases, we have you using information you gather in one step for something else later in the strategy.

2. Do we have to follow these steps in order?

Again, the answer is "yes." We have carefully chosen a sequence that makes it easiest for you to answer questions, gather appropriate data, and so forth.

You can, however, feel free to return to any step if at a later stage you find that you need more details.

3. Should we be able to answer each question at the meetings?

Each strategy will be a mixture of questions you can resolve right at the meeting (such as taking a vote on a particular issue), and goals that you must work on outside the meeting (such as collecting data). Even for the activities you will pursue outside of the team meeting, you must discuss them first in the meeting. For instance, if there are assignments to be done outside the meeting, be clear about what is expected of any team member involved—when the person or people will be expected to report back to the team, what it is they will have to report (conclusions, recommendations, charts or graphs of data, items for further discussion, and so forth), what resources they have access to, and their limits of authority or responsibility.

4. Are there any time limits set on when we should finish?

No. Work through each of the strategies when it is appropriate. Work at a comfortable pace: Don't try to do everything at once, but plan well enough in advance of any activity so that you have adequate time to prepare. The level of detail you need will change from step to step, however. Typically, at first you will spend too much time on some steps and not enough on others. With experience, you will learn how much detail is appropriate for your situation.

5. Can we use tools other than those mentioned here?

Yes. Feel free to use whatever scientific tools are appropriate for your project. We have just listed the tools used commonly in the steps we outline. You may find that you need others.

---

* We are indebted to Cindy Butler, a statistician with much practical experience in implementing quality improvement, for showing us how to structure this discussion.

Chapter 5

Using Process Improvement Ideas

A principal received an inordinate number of complaints from a bus driver, students, and parents about the conduct of bus riders on the "purple bus." After speaking to some of the students on board the bus with no results, the principal decided to call the "purple bus" riders together to collect data regarding conduct on the bus. The students suggested ways to improve conduct, which included assigned seats, children sitting in pairs, and older children being responsible for younger ones. There were fewer complaints—fewer problems.

#   #   #

A middle school became concerned about placing identified handicapped students in regular classrooms. The principal, teachers, and a statistician identified ways to collect and analyze data regarding the performance of these students. The result of the experience was that identified handicapped students were performing better in the regular classroom than expected. A team was established to analyze the process and standardize it.

The team explored the issues of student placement and training of the regular classroom teachers in the process of improving the system.

#   #   #

A school district needed to make sure the number of school dropouts reported to the state department of education was accurate. They used control charts to make sure the numbers remained in statistical control. They then formed teams of school staff members, students, parents, and community members to study the problem.

#   #   #

An elementary school staff believed that there were too many classroom interruptions during the course of a day, which limited instructional time. A team of teachers and the school principal, working with a quality facilitator, carefully defined the problem. They decided to ask the entire staff to record all classroom interruptions for several days.

After collecting and analyzing the data, the team identified the school's administrative use of the public address system as being the greatest contributor to class interruptions. Teachers using students to deliver notes was the second greatest contributor to interruptions. The team recommended to the staff several ways to cut down on interruptions. After discussing these suggestions at a faculty meeting, the staff selected several suggestions to implement in order to cut down on interruptions.

The 15 Improvement Strategies

Strategies of the Scientific Approach

Collect Meaningful Data
Used to point out common sources of inaccurate data and indicate how they can be combated.

Identify Root Causes of Problems
Used to identify and verify actual causes of a problem.

Develop Appropriate Solutions
Used to identify changes that attack the root causes of problems.

Plan and Make Changes
Used to implement changes smoothly and effectively.

Strategies for Identifying Improvement Needs

Identify Customer Needs and Concerns
Used to describe useful ways to get information from customers.

Study the Use of Time
Used to identify which activities consume people's time and to highlight opportunities for improvement.

Localize Recurring Problems
Used to identify where and when problems occur and don't occur.

Strategies for Improving a Process

Describe a Process
Used to identify obvious improvements or to begin a more detailed study.

Develop a Standard Process
Used to increase the uniformity of a product or service by developing standard procedures that everyone follows.

Error-Proof a Process
Used to eliminate and prevent the most common mistakes made in the execution of a process.

Streamline a Process
Used to eliminate waste from a process.

Reduce Sources of Variation
Used to eliminate the most obvious causes of variation.

Bring a Process Under Statistical Control
Used to make a process more predictable by bringing variation under control.

Improve the Design of a Product or Process
Used to identify and control factors that have the most impact on the quality of a product or process.

Check for Alignment
Used to remove inconsistencies and conflicting standards and expectations from inside and outside the system.

Chapter 5

Strategy 1: Collect Meaningful Data

Purpose:

Collecting meaningful data is one of the most important things to do well no matter where you work. There are just too many ways in which data can be in error: They may be the wrong kind of data for what you need; it's easy to combine data that should not be mixed; data collectors often use different procedures unless they are specifically taught what to do; there may be some bias in the process of data collection you don't know about. The possibilities for error are almost endless. Thus, it always pays to be suspicious of data and data collection procedures until they are proven reliable. This strategy is one of four basic strategies of the scientific approach.

1. Clarify Data Collection Goals

It is easy to become swamped with useless data, especially when data collection is done without a clear purpose.

- Why are you collecting data?

- What data are you going to collect?

- How will the data help you meet customer needs—the needs of learners, staff, administrators, and the community? To improve administrative or clerical operations?

- Imagine you have the data in hand: What could these data tell you? What will you do with the data? What will you do after that? Would another kind of data be more helpful?

2. Develop Operational Definitions and Procedures

Most people approach data collection with a concept they would like to understand—measuring "interruptions," parents' perception of a "successful learner," "timeliness," for example. An operational definition translates the concept into procedures that everyone can follow when measuring or discussing it.

- What is the concept you are trying to study or evaluate?
  Examples: mastery of adding two digits, multiplication, the concepts of up, down, and over.

- What data will allow you to attach a value to this concept? By what standards will you judge it? How far off from perfect does the measurement have to be to count as a defect or problem?
  Examples: Does "on-time to class" mean within minutes? What constitutes a quality essay? Do you have samples of the quality essay to show people? Think of different ways to operationally define the concept you are studying and see which comes closest to what you mean.

Strategy 1: Collect Meaningful Data

• What is your plan for collecting these data? What procedures will be used? Will the data collectors have to take samples? How often? How many? Can you get the measurement/data immediately or will there be a delay?

Write down clear descriptions of how to measure the process characteristic. Be specific. Compare possible procedures with an eye towards places where the data collectors could easily make mistakes. Look for procedures that are less error-prone. Procedures that give faster results are generally a better choice, even if they are a little less reliable than other alternatives. NOTE: When asking teachers to collect data on classroom absence, use random samples, e.g., on what days and during what classroom periods will the teachers collect the data.

• How will the data be recorded?

Practice using whatever checksheet or questionnaires you design. Modify them as needed.

• Are your definitions, guidelines, and procedures comparable to those used by other educators or administrators? Do you define some characteristic (e.g., "sufficient homework") the way parents or other teachers do?

The data will probably not be comparable if different methods or definitions are used.

3. Plan for Data Consistency and Stability

Meaningful data must be both consistent and stable. Data are consistent if any two people who measure the same things arrive at essentially the same answer. Data are stable when they do not show signs of special causes of variation over time. Ignoring these issues usually leads to wasted effort.

• What are some factors that might cause measurements of the same item to vary?

Each situation is unique, with a unique set of factors that are important. Brainstorming a list of factors and arranging them on a cause-and-effect diagram is a good way to identify possible sources of variability in your measurement process. For example, if everyone does not follow the exact procedure, how might that affect the data?

• How can you reduce the impact of these factors? For example, work to eliminate the differences in measurements taken on the process. You can reduce variability among data collected by classroom teachers by having them all use the same methods for measuring or categorizing items. Get all the classroom teachers to walk through the processes and reach consensus on procedures.

Chapter 5

4. Begin Data Collection

Explain the procedures to all data collectors, especially if there are some who are not on the team. Have all data collectors follow the procedures you developed. Have someone who knows what to do watch and instruct beginning data collectors.

> When gathering data over time or from different units, make sure they are standardized so you can compare data collected at different points. This is important when comparing standardized test and when differentiating between common and special causes.

5. Continue Improving Measurement Consistency and Stability

Continuing to check data consistency and stability often exposes problems that, if left uncorrected, could lead to incorrect conclusions.

- Are measurements stable over time?

  If practical, evaluate measurement stability by repeatedly measuring the same item periodically. Plot the results on a control chart; take action if measurements are out of control. More elaborate procedures may be needed if the measurements are dependent upon the exact time you take them.

- Are measurements consistent?

  Periodically check consistency by having data collectors measure an identical item (if the tests are time dependent, have a pool of items from which to randomly draw samples). How much variability is there? Can you reduce the variability?

- Do dot plots of the data show any strange features?

  Many strange patterns can appear in plots. For example, do the data stop abruptly at a specified value? If so, data collectors may be reluctant to record points above or below a certain level (often at specification limits). At first, have a statistician, quality advisor, or someone with equivalent experience evaluate your plots.

Strategy 2: Identify Root Causes of Problems

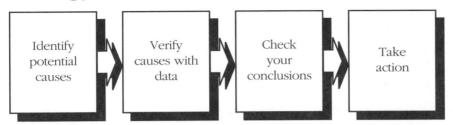

Identify potential causes → Verify causes with data → Check your conclusions → Take action

Purpose:

Jumping to conclusions without understanding the root causes of problems often leads to wasted time and resources. Usually it's best to have localized the occurrence of a problem before attempting to identify its root causes. Before starting, be sure everyone agrees on the definitions of the problems. You may also need to resolve issues concerning methods of measurement, assessment, procedures, and so forth. This strategy is one of four basic strategies of the scientific approach.

1. Identify Potential Causes

Consider inviting people not on the team to a meeting to discuss these issues. The more areas of the process that are represented, the more likely you are to identify the real causes.

- What are possible causes of the problem you are studying?

  Use brainstorming and cause-and-effect diagrams to bring out ideas. Write down all possibilities at first; later you can discuss and eliminate some. One way to get at root causes is to think of what might be the cause of each possible cause you list. Example: If you have pupils late to class, figure out what causes the lateness. Continue exploring the "causes of the causes" until you run into a question you can't answer; figure out what kind of data you will need to answer that question. When you're done, generate a list of the most likely causes.

- How could you detect the influence of these potential causes? What patterns would you expect to see in data?

2. Verify Causes with Data

- Do you have any existing data that could help you decide which are the actual causes of problems? Are you sure the existing data are relevant to the problem being studied?

  Data on administrative areas are generally, but not always, more reliable than existing data on instructional processes. Carefully consider the logic that supports existing data.

- Does the problem always appear when any of the possible causes you identified are active?

- What additional information or data do you need? How can you get it?

  This is usually the meat of the project—observing the process, counting, measuring, plotting data, and so forth. Check "Collect Meaningful Data" (p. 5-36) to help you get the data you need.

- Who will collect the data?

- When will they be collected?

- Where will they be collected?

- How will they be analyzed?

  Use graphs, charts, and other visual summaries whenever possible.

3. Check Your Conclusions about Causes

After you collect the data, show your summaries to people knowledgeable about the process.

- Do people with knowledge of the process agree with your conclusions? If not, what additional data could you get that might support or contradict your conclusions?

4. Take Action

- Are there obvious changes that would eliminate the root causes of problems?
  Fix obvious problems immediately; monitor your solutions to make sure they work.

- What steps should be taken next?
  You may want to "Develop Appropriate Solutions" (p. 5-41) next.

Strategy 3: Develop Appropriate Solutions

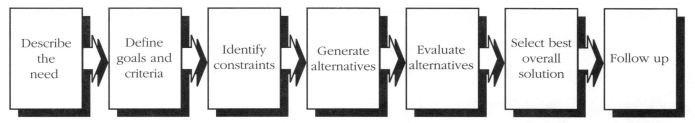

Purpose:

The crux of the scientific approach is to develop solutions that really *solve* problems. Throughout a project, you should make obvious changes that are easy to implement and have few, if any, possible negative side effects. But it will require substantial changes to solve most problems, and the only way to really solve problems—now and forever—is to eliminate their causes. The strategy "Identify Root Causes of Problems" (p. 5-39) will let you locate the cause if you haven't already done so; then you can use this strategy to develop ways to eliminate these causes. This strategy also works when the underlying causes of a problem are unknown or unknowable. For instance, you may not know all the causes of tardiness, but you can still improve the process. Be patient and collect data on a variety of alternatives. Do not simply charge ahead with the first reasonable idea that comes to mind. This strategy is one of four basic strategies of the scientific approach.

1. Describe the Need

- Precisely what problem, need, or opportunity for improvement are you addressing?

- What people or classrooms or departments or schools are involved?

- What problems are customers (internal and external) having because of this situation?

- What operational definition best fits this problem, need, or opportunity?
  Example: What is an "excessively long waiting period"?

2. Define Goals and Criteria

- Given the need, problem, or opportunity, what are the goals of your solution? What are your desired outcomes?
  Develop a statement that describes these outcomes or goals.

- What are the criteria or characteristics of an "ideal" solution?
  Example: Inexpensive, easy to implement, understood by all being affected, and solves the problem.

Refer to "Developing Criteria for Ideal Solutions" (p. 5-43) for more details.

- Which criteria MUST a solution meet to be seriously considered?
  Proposed solutions that fail to meet MUST criteria are automatically rejected.

- Which criteria are only WANTS?
  WANTS are criteria that are desirable, but not necessary. You might give weight to the WANTS to reflect their importance, for example, 3 points if very important, 2 points if moderately important, 1 point if less important.

3. Identify Constraints

Constraints are unchangeable factors that will limit the options you can realistically consider (e.g., regarding state-mandated staffing and curriculum requirements). Do not be overly pessimistic or overly optimistic. Before accepting the factor as unchangeable, do some trial tests. "Unchangeable" factors are commonly more flexible than people think; but paying attention to real constraints will help you avoid naive solutions and wasted time.

Chapter 5

Strategy 3: Develop Appropriate Solutions

- How much money will you realistically be able to use? At what level of expense will the budget-watchers start to get nervous?

- What written or unwritten rules—sacred cows or taboos—might make a solution easier or more difficult to carry off?

- What limits are there on the present technical ability of team members and other involved parties? How might these change in the foreseeable future?

- Are there factions, rivalries, or historic issues between individuals or groups to be considered?

4. Generate Alternatives

Use brainstorming techniques to stimulate people's imaginations.

- What are minor (not very disruptive) solutions that you could put in place right away?

- What are the most conventional solutions?

- What are some workable solutions that would be a substantial change to the present system?

- What are some unconventional solutions?
  Listen to and build on team members' wild ideas. Even if they seem totally impractical at first, you might find later that you can use pieces of them.

5. Evaluate the Alternatives

Develop a list of the final candidates. Keep it varied. Look for ways to combine the ideas generated in the previous step. Allow for at least two or three basic approaches, each with some slight variations. Often the options include features borrowed from the wild or unconventional ideas proposed in the brainstorm.

- Which solutions deal directly with the root causes of the problem?

- Which solutions are easiest to introduce, implement, and maintain?

- Could major changes be phased in?

- Which solutions increase work in the system the least? The most?

- What are possible disadvantages, negative consequences, or other weakness of each alternative? What would make each alternative misunderstood, unwelcome, unsupported, or unsuccessful? How likely are these to happen? How might you revise the proposed solution to avoid or minimize these factors?
  This evaluation is important because it can open your eyes to ways for turning a mediocre solution into a highly desirable one.

- How does each candidate solution measure up to the goals, criteria, and constraints you identified?
  Eliminate any that do not satisfy the goal and the MUST criteria, or see if they can be changed to conform. Rank others according to how many WANTS they meet in addition to the MUSTS.

- Can the best solutions be blended or used simultaneously?
  If possible, develop a workable network of solutions.

Strategy 3: Develop Appropriate Solutions

Developing Criteria for Ideal Solutions

To guide any major decision, you must have the right goals in mind and know what criteria an appropriate action needs to meet. There are four categories of criteria to assess and weigh carefully:

- **Organizational/Cultural**
  § Do you have systems in place to support changes?
  § Will the environment and culture of your school system support such changes?
  § Are there champions for the changes? Is there leadership support of the changes?

- **Safety/Health**
  § What factors in the decision are likely to affect the safety and health of staff and students?

- **Developmental/Educational**
  § What skills, training, and education do the teachers and other involved personnel have? Will this limit your options in any way?
  § Do you have capable supervisors with additional skills and training?
  § Do you have the resources to provide training or education if necessary?

- **System/Operational**
  § Into what process does the solution have to fit?
  § How will changes affect the current process? Will you be able to change your procedures or curriculum or instruction if you need to?
  § What processes for supplying materials and information will be affected?
  § What processes for disseminating services are involved?
  § What aspects of these processes are unchangeable? Are you sure?

6. Select the Best Overall Solution

Compare the proposed solutions, and choose several of the most likely alternatives. Get feedback from anyone involved in or affected by the proposed changes. The changes should be as simple as possible to make and maintain. Aim for changes that address the root causes of problems. If practical, avoid changes that increase the amount of work or that add unnecessary activities or steps to the process.

7. Follow Up

- What changes should be implemented right away?
  Document how you make your choice. If your team is authorized to take action, proceed immediately to the strategy "Plan and Make Changes" (p. 5-44), which will lead you through careful planning and execution of the solution(s) you decide to try. Success will depend on how well you anticipate the resources needed to carry off the change, how much training and preparation everyone receives, whether key leaders lend their support, and so forth. If your team is not authorized to take immediate action, write up your recommendations for how the change should be made and give it to your leadership team or other appropriate group.

- What possible solutions need further improvement?
  Ideally, you are looking for permanent, upstream changes that prevent a problem from recurring. However, it may be necessary to use temporary or downstream "Band-Aids" while long-term approaches are being developed.

- What other groups or people need to be involved in further action?

Chapter 5

Strategy 4: Plan and Make Changes

(Plan-Do-Check-Act)

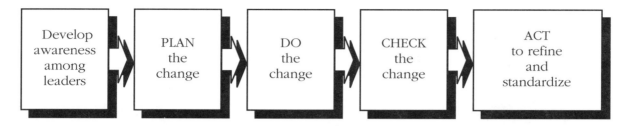

Purpose:

The goal is to implement changes smoothly and learn how to make future changes go even more smoothly. A planning tool that can help you keep track of the information you generate is the Planning Grid, described in Appendix 3. This is one of four basic strategies of the scientific approach.

1. Develop Awareness among Key Leaders

Very little will happen with your solutions unless the leadership of your educational system cares about the problem.

- Who should be alerted to the existence of the process problem? How should it be brought to their attention?

- Which leaders are likely to support efforts to solve the problem or address the need? What must be done to develop a group of leaders who will stand behind the effort and give it support and guidance?

2. Plan the Change

- Precisely what change is to be made?

- How do you know the planned change is appropriate? Have other alternatives been explored?
  If no other alternatives have been explored, you may want to first work through the strategy "Develop Appropriate Solutions" (p. 5-41).

- What sequence of steps are needed for this change? What are the major substeps of each step?
  Map out the new process on a flowchart. (See pp. 2-22 to 2-28 for more details.)

- Who will be directly involved in carrying out each step and substep? Who will need to be consulted?

- Whom will the change affect? Who will need to change the way they do their jobs? How will they be trained? How will you get qualified trainers? How will the effects of the training be checked?
  Do not surprise people with the change. Get information to everyone before they hear rumors. Seek input from people who will be affected by the change. Explain the change and explain how it will affect them and how they will be kept informed. Ask them what they need to know to be comfortable with the change. Incorporate suggestions from them into the plan, if reasonable.

- How long will the change take? How long will each step and substep take?

- How will you know when each activity is completed? What milestones of progress will there be? What will be the product of each step or substep?

- How will you monitor the change's effectiveness? What might go wrong in implementing the plan? What side effects might there be? How can you check or avoid these side effects?
  Imagine that it is a year from now and the change has not been fully successful. What were the most likely causes of problems? Pay particular attention to the people involved, their understanding, their buy-

Strategy 4: Plan and Make Changes

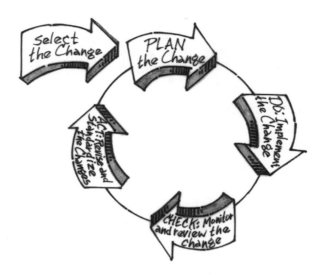

in, their training, and how their time will have to be allocated. Imagine what a successful change would look like one year from now: What made it successful? What constitutes a reasonable amount of success after one year?

- What will you do about unexpected problems? Who will have the authority to take action?

- Taking all these factors into account, what can be done to increase the likelihood of success?

- How will you monitor and check the progress of the change? The effectiveness of the change? How will you measure the benefits of the change? What are the key points to monitor to determine if the change is proceeding as expected?

- How will you collect, review, and act on this information?

3. Do the Change

It is often best to carry out a small-scale study of the change before making it widespread. Train those whose jobs will change. Personally supervise execution of the change.

4. Check the Change

Monitor the progress and effectiveness of the change according to your plan. Gather data from key points. Check for side effects and backsliding.

5. Refine and Standardize the Change

- What did the information you collected tell you about the effectiveness of the change?

- What can be done to error-proof the process? (See "Error-Proof A Process," p. 5-56, for hints.)

- How can the change be refined? Do another Plan-Do-Check-Act cycle if refinements are substantial. Standardize the new procedures. Transfer responsibility for ongoing monitoring and improvement to all the appropriate teachers and administrators.

- What do you need to do to complete the documentation of the change?

- What lessons learned here about the new procedure and implementing change apply elsewhere? How can these lessons be communicated?

Chapter 5

Strategy 5: Identify Customer Needs and Concerns

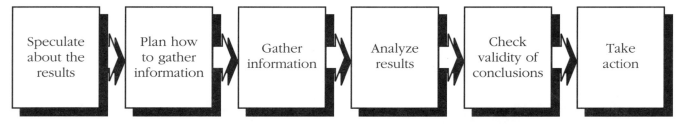

Purpose:

The goal should be to exceed customer expectations, not merely meet them. Learners and the community should boast about how much they benefit from what you do for them. To attain this goal, you must collect reliable information on what they need and want from your service. In doing so, you will find out whether your processes are on target and effective. This strategy can be used to identify potential improvement projects or just to clarify a project's goals.

1. Speculate about the Results

Checking your initial guesses against what you learn is a good way to keep track of how well you know your learners and your community.

- What do you think your learners and the community will say about your instructional process?

- What do you think you will find out about their needs?

2. Plan How to Gather Information

- From which learners and community members will you seek information? From which potential learners and community members? What kinds of information will you seek?

- How will you allow the learner or community member to tell you what is needed?
  Plan to have some time with learners or community members when they can just talk about their concerns and not simply answer specific questions. A useful question to ask people is, "What are three things we can do to improve the quality of educational services?" Personal discussions with customers, singly and in groups, are best. Questionnaires with fixed categories of response are seldom as useful.

- What problems do learners or community members have even when your service seems to have worked well? (This can help you think outside the conventional bounds of curriculum and teaching methods.)
  There may be changes you can make in your process that will solve problems caused by something else in society.

- How will the information of the process and its outcomes be collected? By whom? How will the information be analyzed? By whom?
  Review suggestions given under "Collect Meaningful Data" (p. 5-36).

3. Gather Information

A pilot study is often useful. Gather information from a few learners or community members, then review your plan before gathering more information.

4. Analyze the Results

- What improvements did learners and community members suggest? How did these compare with what you guessed?

- What problems did these customers have? How many had each kind of problem?
  If appropriate, develop graphs and other summaries to aid communication.

- What problems did the learner have when carrying out the activities of the process?

- How do these customer needs relate to your service?

5. Check the Validity of Your Conclusions

- Are learning outcomes, curricula, and instructional strategies aligned with learner and community needs?

- Do the learners and the community agree with your summaries?

6. Take Action

Make obvious changes immediately. Plan ways to address longer-term issues. Plan for regular contact with learners and community members so you can keep in touch with their problems and ideas. Tell these customers what you have heard and what you plan to do. Follow up.

Chapter 5

Strategy 6: Study the Use of Time

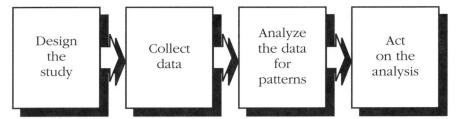

Purpose:

Use this strategy to find out which activities consume people's time and which of those add no value to your service. This knowledge will highlight opportunities for improvement, making this strategy useful in the early stages of projects. It is particularly effective for administrative and service processes as well as instructional processes. Note: The more that people fear the results will be used against them, the less your chances of getting accurate data. Work hard to eliminate fear. Focus on improving processes and systems and eliminating unnecessary work and hassles—not on judging people! Work only with groups that are receptive: Don't force the study on any group that remains unconvinced of its purpose. Success and improvement with receptive groups will go a long way towards convincing cautious groups to give it a try. This strategy is used to identify improvement needs.

1. Design the Study

- What do you hope to accomplish?
  Explain this to the people involved in the study. Have them participate in planning the study.

- How many people will be involved?

- How will the data be collected?
  There are several kinds of data that reflect how people spend their time. Often, people program a watch to beep regularly, and mark down what they are doing when it goes off. For example, the watch beeps every 47 minutes, and people record what they are doing. Have someone with statistical training help you look at several possible data collection schemes and decide which suits your purpose best.

- What data collection forms will be used?
  Open-ended forms (ones without fixed categories) are best at the beginning. Later on, forms or checksheets with fixed categories can be used.

- Who will need to be trained to do the study? How will they be trained?

- What do you think will turn out to be the biggest time-consumer?

2. Collect Data

Review suggestions given under "Collect Meaningful Data" (p. 5-36). Reminder: A pilot study is often useful.

- What problems do people have when collecting data?

- Do people understand the procedures? The forms?
  Make refinements as needed.

- Are the results giving you the information you want? Do they have content validity? If not, what changes are needed?

3. Analyze the Data

- Are people spending time on the right things? Have they been told what activities they *should* be spending time on?

- Which activities would be unnecessary if the process worked flawlessly?

- Are there problems in your classroom or school that are inherited from other classrooms or schools? How can these be addressed?

- Are there problems that arise from other processes in your classroom or school? What can you do about them?

- What categories do the observations fall into?

- How many observations are there in each category? Where is the most time spent?
  Order the categories from most frequent to least frequent; display them with a Pareto chart (p. 2-29).

4. Take Action

- Which problems associated with the most time-consuming activities can you solve right away?

- Which problems need further study?

- What other recommendations can you make?

Strategy 7: Localize Recurring Problems

| Define recurring problems | → | Assess impact of each problem | → | Localize each major problem | → | Discuss conclusions with key players | → | Take action |

Purpose:

To clearly define recurring problems, you must learn precisely when and where they occur. This knowledge is essential in finding causes underlying these problems. This strategy can be used in two contexts: (1) in the first project stages to find out where to focus the effort, and (2) later on to further pinpoint the occurrence of a problem. This strategy is used both to identify a general improvement need within a process and to further pinpoint a problem within a general area.

1. Define Recurring Problems

Often people will have an idea of what problems they want to solve, but in order to make improvements, they need very clear, precise definitions.

2. Assess the Impact of Each Problem

- How often does this problem occur?

- How severe is it when it occurs?

- Do you already have any data on its impact?

- Would other data be useful to determine its impact? How can you get it?
  Focus data collection efforts here on determining the impact of the problem.

3. Localize Each Major Problem

Collect data on the occurrence of the problem. Use the following questions to help focus data-gathering.

- When does the problem occur? When doesn't it occur?
  If you haven't done so, determine what process or processes are associated with the problem.

- Where does it occur or where is it first observed? Where doesn't it occur? Where is it not observed?

- Which process, curriculum, instructional, administrative, or assessment, has the problem most often? Least often?

- Are there other problems that always or often occur together with this problem? Could these be related somehow? Are there problems that you might ordinarily expect to see but don't?

- Who tends to have the problem most often?
  NOTE: Be careful to avoid finger-pointing. Look for problems to solve in the system, not individuals to blame!

- Do you have any data already?

- What other data would be useful? How can you get them?
  Use the suggestions under "Collect Meaningful Data" (see p. 5-36).

- What do the data tell you about the occurrence of this problem?
  Prepare graphs and other summaries to aid communication. Pareto charts (p. 2-29) are often used here.

Strategy 7: Localize Recurring Problems

4. Discuss Conclusions with Key Players

- Do the results of your data collection seem logical to the people involved?

- Do they agree with the conclusions you reached about the occurrence of this problem? If not, what other data do you need?

5. Take Action

Determine what actions to take next. Typically, this means moving on to another strategy, which is often "Identify Root Causes of Problems" (p. 5-39).

- Are there obvious changes that would eliminate the problem? Are there obvious ways to prevent similar problems in the future?
  Fix the obvious problems immediately; monitor your solutions to make sure they work.

- What steps should be taken next?
  It is often desirable to "Identify Root Causes of Problems" next.

Chapter 5

Strategy 8: Describe a Process

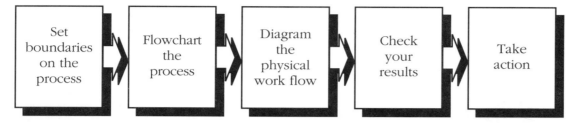

Purpose:

The goal is to develop a useful description of your process as it currently works. This often leads to discovery of obvious improvements. It also becomes a solid basis for more detailed study of the process. This strategy is part of a general process improvement approach.

1. Set Boundaries on the Process

- Precisely where does the process you are going to study start and stop?
  Example: In studying the inclusion or mainstreaming process, does it start when the student arrives in the classroom? In the placement conference?

- What inputs and supplies are part of this process?

- What are its outputs (the service or desired learning outcomes)?

- Who are the internal customers of this output?

- Who benefits from this process? Who will use the service? (These are not always the same people.)

2. Flowchart the Process

- What kind of flowchart is most helpful in this situation?
  There are several kinds of flowcharts, ranging from the very detailed, complete form to a much simpler top-down version. (See Chapter 2 for examples of different flowcharts, pp. 2-22 to 2-24.) In many cases, it works best to first draw the process as it would work if everything in the process went perfectly. Then, if necessary, notations can be made where adjustments, remediation, supervision, and delays occur.

- How much detail in the chart will be useful at this point?
  Start with just the major activities, then add details later if necessary.

- Who are the participants in this process? Which of them should be involved in constructing the chart? Who should be consulted after drawing the chart?

- Who does what? When? Where? Why? How?

- What activities are a part of this process? Does everyone agree?

3. Diagram the Physical Flow of Work

Having pictures of how people or information actually moves in the process helps to highlight wasted motion. Trace the movement of students, teachers, or office staff on a diagram of the floor plan (see the work-flow diagram on p. 2-26). Living Flowcharts are particularly useful here, too (see p. 7-16).

4. Check Your Results

Get the reactions of others to the flowchart or work-flow diagram. Improve the diagrams as appropriate.

5. Take Action

- Are there obvious changes that would improve the process?
  Fix obvious problems immediately. Monitor your solutions to make sure they work. Watch for side effects.

Chapter 5

Strategy 9: Develop a Standard Process

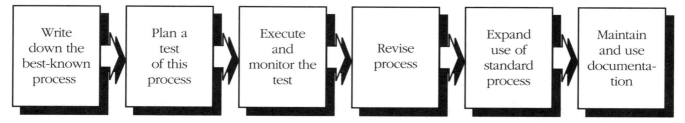

| Write down the best-known process | Plan a test of this process | Execute and monitor the test | Revise process | Expand use of standard process | Maintain and use documentation |

Purpose:

The goal is to increase the uniformity of a service by developing a standard process, starting from today's best-known process. Simply getting everyone to consistently use the set of activities that result in quality outcomes is a major step forward because it provides a basis for further study and improvement. This strategy is part of a general process improvement approach.

1. Write Down the Current Best-Known Process

The current best-known process describes the method of work that gets the best results for this particular process. Sometimes it may be best to have one person write it out; at other times, it might be more effective to involve the whole work group. The participants might, for instance, discuss how they do each activity, then choose a best method. Alternatively, they might start by observing the person who everyone agrees is the best at this particular activity. Use flowcharts and pictures when describing the process.

2. Plan a Test of This Process

Get a small group of people to try out the best-known process.

- How many people will be involved in the test? If there are only a few people who work with the process, consider involving all of them in the pilot. If there are many people, select a few to try out the best-known process.

- How will the participants be trained? Who will train them? How will the trainers be trained?

- How will they keep track of their progress? How will you know what works and what doesn't work?

- How will the process and any changes be documented? How will documentation be kept up to date?

3. Implement and Monitor the Test

Actively collect information and gather ideas for improvement from those trying to use the best-known process.

- Are any of the instructions unclear?

- What process problems occur?

- What problems or actions come up that aren't covered in the description of the best-known process?

- Has variation in the process been reduced to a desired range? Could it be reduced any further?

- Have mistakes or waste of time or materials been reduced? Can they be reduced even more?

4. Revise the Process

Use the information you gathered to improve the process.

5. Expand Use of the Standard Process

If only a few people were involved in the pilot, expand use of the revised process to the others. Use the strategy "Plan and Make Changes" (p. 5-44) to help carry off this expansion.

6. Maintain Documentation

Have everyone use the newest, most improved process; challenge them to develop further refinements. Ask them to routinely use the best-known process until suggested improvements have been tested and taught to everyone. Keep records up to date and make sure they are used, particularly to train new staff members.

Strategy 10: Error-Proof a Process

Purpose:

Many errors in processes can be prevented through simple measures once educators know what to look for and how to combat common oversights. Be sure to monitor all changes. This strategy is part of a general approach to process improvement.

1. Identify Mistakes

- What mistakes occur in each process activity?
  Use the process flowchart as a guide to think through each activity. Picture each activity and think of what goes wrong in its process. Begin to collect data on mistakes.

2. Identify Less Error-Prone Activities

- Would changing the order of activities prevent mistakes?

- If an activity is often forgotten, consider revising the sequence to make it more prominent.

- Would changing a form prevent mistakes?
  Use shading, different type sizes and looks, color coding, a different layout, or an altered sequence of information to make forms easier to read, understand, and follow.

- Would using a checklist prevent mistakes?
  Checklists are a simple way to make sure everything that is supposed to happen does happen, and in the proper sequence. Use them in almost any situation.

- Would clear directions, graphically illustrated and prominently displayed, prevent mistakes?
  The less frequently an activity is used, the more likely it is that staff will need easy-to-understand in-

structions to remind them how to perform the task. Even frequent activities need instructions displayed for the benefit of new or substitute staff members.

- Can you think of entirely new procedures that are less error-prone?
  Be creative. Pretend you were designing this process from the beginning: What could you do to prevent the kinds of errors that appear in the current process? What can be done to incorporate these ideas into your current activities?

3. Restructure the Learning Environment

With enough ingenuity, you can prevent most mistakes. When a mistake is discovered, immediately stop the process. This is a useful way to highlight problems and foster solutions.

- Would changing the process prevent any of the mistakes you found? What would an ideal process look like?

- Would a technology that checks for errors or completeness be useful?
  Simple, inexpensive technology can eliminate many costly mistakes. For example, word processing technology can catch many spelling and punctuation mistakes.

Strategy 11: Streamline a Process

Purpose:

The administrative processes of the educational system must be aligned with what is taught, how it is taught, and how the desired learning outcomes are assessed. Activities should not be designed to merely patch problems; they should support a balanced alignment of curriculum, instruction, and assessment. This strategy is part of a general approach to process improvement.

1. Examine the Value of Each Process Step

- Which steps merely undo or patch problems caused upstream? Can upstream problems be solved?

- Are some steps a result of excessive caution or mistrust? Can something be done to remove the mistrust?
  For example, forms should require no more than one signature to be approved. Getting multiple signatures is a waste of time and indicates that people do not trust one another's judgment. Perhaps creating consensus around operational definitions of "completed" or "acceptable" forms would reduce this mistrust.

- Do all steps add value to the service, or can you eliminate some?

2. Reduce Barriers to Learning

- Are there learning barriers associated with the process?

- What are the current learning barriers related to the process? How much do they vary?

- How much can the barriers be reduced without changing the process?

3. Reduce Batch Sizes

- Do a certain number of forms or orders accumulate before they are handled?

- How can batch sizes be sharply reduced? How much efficiency would be lost with a much smaller batch size?
  Work towards batch sizes of one.

4. Reduce Change-over and Cycle Times

- When there are multiple services, how much time does it take to change from one to another at each step in the process?

- How can you reduce change-over times?
  The goal is rapid transitions from one activity to the next. The easy accessibility of materials and equipment may be a key to rapid transitions. Changing the work area layout may help in adminsitrative processes.

- What is the current cycle time? How long does it take for a request for information or some form or written notice to get through the entire process?
  Identify the steps in the process and estimate how long each step should take. Gather data on how long each step actually takes. Attack first those steps that consume the most time.

Chapter 5

5. Monitor Improvements

As changes are made, continue to gather data on their effect on total cycle time. Constantly look for ways to improve any of these process characteristics.

Strategy 12: Reduce Sources of Variation

Evaluate sources of variation → Eliminate or reduce variation → Use knowledge in further studies

Purpose:

This strategy provides a way to eliminate the most obvious sources of variability in a service, or a measurement process. To evaluate a measurement process, measure the same item repeatedly, if possible. If the measurement is destructive, get a set of items as close to identical as possible, and select from this pool randomly. This strategy is part of a general approach to process improvement.

1. Evaluate Sources of Variation

Look for when and where in your process different conditions or methods lead to differences in desired outcomes. Stratification analysis is a useful tool here (see p. 2-34). Prepare graphs and other summaries of the analysis of the data collected to aid teamwork and communication and encourage action.

For example, color code data elements and data points on dot plots, histograms, and control charts. Do you see differences between:

WHO
- Different people (such as new teachers versus experienced teachers)?

- Different learners? Different supervisors?

WHAT
- Different measurement instruments? Alternative ways to assess?
- Different curriculum materials? Different curriculum materials of varying learning styles?

WHERE
- Different parts of school building (gym, art class, auditorium, boiler room, cafeteria)?

WHEN
- Different times of the day, different days of the week? The beginning or end of the week or month? Nearness of a holiday? Different class periods? Different time intervals within the class period?

2. Eliminate or Reduce Variation

- Which of the sources you identified previously can be eliminated?
  For example, in-service training and professional development and feedback might help educators reach common and agreed-upon methods.

- Can the impact of other sources on the teaching-learning process be reduced?
  Examples: Sometimes activities of the process can be redesigned to be less sensitive to variation of other sources, i.e., materials, equipment, or facilities. Working with publishers could improve the desired outcomes.

- Which sources cannot be eliminated or reduced? Are you sure? Could you conduct pilot studies to make sure?

3. Use Knowledge in Further Studies

If you are uncertain that data have been collected with comparable methods and under comparable conditions, avoid mixing them. Mixing data from different collection methods can be dangerous. Guard against the possibility of combining data that should be kept separate.

Chapter 5

- Is there any way the results can be standardized to eliminate consistent differences you've identified?
  Example: If classroom A has more students than classroom B, measure the number of interruptions per student per day rather than the number of total interruptions per day in each classroom.

- Can you tell whether the variation arises from special or common causes?

- For example, is there a particular day that classroom interruptions are excessive, and why? How would that affect your future actions?

- Another example: in bringing a process under statistical control, separate control charts may be needed for different sets of classrooms in a building unless you have shown that there is no appreciable difference between those classrooms.

Strategy 13: Bring a Process Under Statistical Control

| Plan the chart | Start the chart | Eliminate special causes | Plan for continuous improvement | Evaluate the chart's usefulness |

Purpose:

You can get rid of many obvious sources of variation through the use of stratification analysis, as described in "Reduce Sources of Variation" (p. 5-59). But you need more sophisticated tools for tracking down less obvious sources of variation, so you can bring the process under statistical control. When a process is under statistical control, its performance is more predictable, and you have a good starting point for making more fundamental improvements. Control charts are the best way to bring a process under statistical control. Processes can speak to us through these charts, telling us when to track down and eliminate special causes of variation. When this is done, the performance of the system will be predictable within certain limits. Everyone involved in the charting or analysis should have some training on the nature and use of control charts. Such training is critical for administrators, superintendents, board of education members, teachers, and supervisors. It is also important to have the guidance of someone with statistical knowledge. That person needs to understand how to construct the various types of control charts and know when each is appropriate. This strategy is part of a general approach to process improvement.

1. Plan the Chart

Involve the control chart quality facilitator in the planning stage and throughout the effort; this guidance is necessary each time you use control charts during the first year or two of the quality effort.

- What should you measure and plot? For educational outcomes, what key quality characteristics of the outcome are related to what the learner and the community need? For measurement processes, what content should you measure?

- How, when, and where will the data be collected? How will accuracy be checked? How will you select samples?

- What kind of chart and scales are appropriate?

- Who will collect the data? Who will plot the data?
  Typically, classroom teachers or administrators collect the data and plot the chart. They then work on identifying and removing special causes of variation.

It is extremely useful to have places on the chart where the data plotters can make notations about process conditions.

- What will happen when there is a signal of a special cause? Who will have the authority to take action?
  Administrators need to actively support corrective actions, but many times the classroom teachers or others plotting the data are themselves in the best position to know what actions are most appropriate.

2. Start the Chart

Begin taking data and charting. Develop appropriate control limits when sufficient data have been collected. On the charts, note process conditions, describe special causes you find and eliminate, and mark down any other useful information.

- Are sampling procedures appropriate?

- Is the chart revealing the kind of information you need in order to track down special causes? If not, should it be modified or discontinued?

3. Eliminate Special Causes

Seek out special causes of variation in response to signals from the chart. Evaluate process capability, i.e., the range of the outcomes of the current process is within the desired range of process outcomes.

- Is action being taken when there are signals of special causes? Are root causes of key problems being identified and removed? When the process is not capable of producing the desired outcomes, can you reduce the impact of known sources of variation?
Example: Variability in learner outcomes may be related to variability in the curriculum materials. Working collaboratively with a publisher is a way to seek another answer to the problem.

4. Plan for Continuous Improvement

As you get nearer to statistical control, you can start making fundamental improvements to the process. Once special cause variation starts to disappear, other problems may start to surface. Plan ways to deal with the process problems and to make obvious improvements. The strategy "Improve the Design of a Service or Process" (p. 5-63) may be useful.

- How will changes you recommend be implemented? Who will be responsible for monitoring these changes?

5. Evaluate the Chart's Usefulness

There should eventually come a time when the control chart is no longer useful because most special causes have been eliminated. When that happens, the chart should be discontinued, but possibly revived periodically just to make sure nothing in the process has changed.

Strategy 14: Improve the Design of a Process

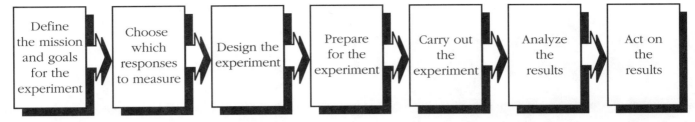

| Define the mission and goals for the experiment | Choose which responses to measure | Design the experiment | Prepare for the experiment | Carry out the experiment | Analyze the results | Act on the results |

Purpose:

To make fundamental improvements in the design of processes, you may need to develop an active program of experimentation. This strategy leads you through the job of planning and executing an effective experiment to test many factors at the same time (see the discussion of designed experiments in Chapter 2). Most likely, it will take several rounds of experiments for you to pinpoint the changes that will lead to the biggest improvement. (see "A Simple Designed Experiment," p. 5-64; another example is given in Chapter 2, p. 2-20.)

1. Define the Mission and Goals for the Experiment

Be precise. If you are not precise, chances are you will not meet your goals.

- Which key quality characteristics of your outcome or process would you most like to improve?
  Examples: learning outcomes, flexible scheduling, classroom interruptions, improved behavior.

- What questions would you most like to answer?
  Examples: How does the availability of many library/media resources influence learning? What factors have the most effect on desired learning outcomes?

- How general do you want your results to be? What subjects or age levels or conditions of learning are you going to use in the experiment?
  Should the results be applicable to all grade levels in the school? To only certain subject areas? Are you investigating all learning conditions or only certain ones (such as when the topic is introduced or when you reach a certain level of discussion)?

- Which of these goals are musts, and which may be put aside if time or resources are limited?

2. Choose Which Responses to Measure

- What key process or service characteristic(s) are you going to study?
  For example, will you establish and describe proficiency levels? Rate of mastery? Retention characteristics? Transferability of the skill?

- How will you measure this quality characteristic? What data will you collect?
  See "Collect Meaningful Data" (p. 5-36) for hints.

- How will you analyze and use the data set you collect? See "Collect Meaningful Data" (p. 5-36) for hints.

- Will the data really tell you what you need to know?
  Pretend the data are in hand and think of possible questions the data would reveal. Would you have the information you need to take action?

- How will the data be collected? How will the data be recorded? By whom? What training do the data collectors need?

- What can you do to ensure the consistency and stability of these measurements?
  See "Collect Meaningful Data" (p. 5-36) for suggestions.

Chapter 5

A Simple Designed Experiment

As a simple example, suppose you wanted to find the best way to operate a hot-air popcorn popper. First, you define "success" as the least number of unpopped kernels in each batch. You think the following factors would affect the number of unpopped kernels: how much popcorn you start out with, the type of popcorn, the age of the popcorn, whether it was refrigerated or not, the brand of popcorn popper, and whether the machine is pre-warmed. You will test these factors at the following levels:

amt. of popcorn	1/3 cup (low)	1/2 cup (high)
type of popcorn	yellow	white
age of popcorn months	<6 months	>6
refrigeration	no	yes
brand of popper	A	B
Prewarming	no	yes

To run a designed experiment on these factors, you would determine which combinations of these factors and levels to test.

Some possible combinations are:

(1) 1/3 c. corn—yellow—less than 6 months—refrigerated—popper B—no prewarming

(2) 1/2 c. corn—white—less than 6 months—not refrigerated—popper B—prewarmed

There are many other combinations, and the key to designed experiments lies in choosing the combinations, or runs, that will give you the most information. There are rules and guidelines to follow when choosing these runs, but you will need assistance from someone experienced in using designed experiments.

After you have selected and performed the runs that fit your needs, the results of all the runs are compared and examined for patterns that reveal significant information. Learning to detect and interpret these patterns is another skill that can only come with experience.

In an experiment similar to the one we've just described, the best combination of factors depended on which popper was used. In all cases, using less corn, making sure it was refrigerated and not too old worked best, but with popper A the yellow corn was better and with popper B the white corn was better.

- How will the data be analyzed?

- What training would you provide those who process and prepare the data files for analysis?

3. Design the Experiment

- What process factors are likely to affect outcomes and characteristics you have identified?
  Gather together a diverse group of people knowledgeable about this process and have them brainstorm a list of factors that might affect the outcomes. Group the process characteristics using categories such as materials, technology, classroom teachers, administrators, etc. For example, an outcome such as mastery of a mathematical concept might be affected by the amount of time, the type of materials, the method of teaching, and so forth.

- What are efficient ways to pilot various combinations of these process characteristics?
  Multiple process characteristics are best handled through designed experiments. If no one on your team is trained in the use of design experiments, seek the help of people who are. Ask them to help you decide on an appropriate number of factors and levels for each factor. Ask them to show you what combinations of factors and levels to pilot, in what sequence, on what days, and so forth. See previous example to see how these factor combinations work.

- How can you minimize disruption to other educational activities (such as ongoing learning)?

Strategy 14: Improve the Design of a Process

- How much time will be needed to run the entire research study? Each trial?

- Can all of your goals be met in this time period? If not, would it be worthwhile to invest in additional resources so you could reach all the goals or decrease the time needed for the experiment?

  Note: Inevitably, you will have to perform these experiments within certain budgetary or time restraints. However, since it usually takes several rounds of the study to pinpoint the desired outcome you want, a good rule is never to use more than 25 percent of your resources on the initial study .

4. Prepare for the Experiment

- Will anyone need to learn data collection techniques or alter their roles while the experiment is in progress? Is training needed?

  If there are people not on the team who will be collecting data, be there personally to help them take data, answer their questions, and ensure that the plan is followed and that unforeseen problems are handled reasonably.

- How will you communicate your plan?

  Create a table showing the experiment, which factors will be tested when, in what combinations, and at what levels. Post this prominently in the school, or wherever the study is taking place, in advance of the experiment.

- What can go wrong with the experiment? How can you reduce the likelihood of these problems?

  Rehearse data collection procedures with anyone involved in data collection. Are the data collection forms and procedures clear?

5. Carry Out the Experiment

Implement your plan. Monitor each step so you will catch problems early if they arise. Modify your plans as needed.

6. Analyze the Results

Plot the data in time order, by process characteristic levels, or by whatever approaches you find helpful. Look for interactions and determine the main effects of each process characteristic. Perform other statistical analyses if necessary.

- What have you learned? Which key process characteristics are important; which have little or no effect on the process outcome you studied?

  Process characteristics with little impact can be set at their most convenient or most economic levels.

- What patterns appear in the data? What do they tell you about your outcome or process?

7. Act on the Results

- How can you change your process to incorporate what you have just learned?

- What are appropriate next steps? More studies? Immediate action?

- Who will be responsible for seeing that changes are made?

Strategy 15: Check for Alignment: Contrast the Current Actual Process and Methods with Professional Standards and Expectations

Identify the standards that pertain to the process under study	Identify other parts of the system that interact with this process	Analyze the current level of alignment and interaction	Align those standards and practices which are important to align

Purpose:

Both the educational processes and various administrative processes should ordinarily be conducted in a manner which conforms to prescribed professional standards. For instance, does the curriculum reflect national or professional standards? Are accounting procedures performed in accordance with professional accounting practices? Furthermore, there should be consistency within and between various functions and activities of your educational system. For example, is the assessment of learning outcomes aligned with what is taught and how it is taught? Is the system aligned both within itself and with key outside standard setters?

1. Identify the standards that pertain to the process under study

- What is the purpose of this process?

- What principles and values are important to maintain in this process?

- Who are the "standard setters"? What is the source of pertinent standards?

- What are the relevant standards?

2. Identify Other Parts of the System That Interact with This Process

- What are the parts of the system that must be aligned and integrated with this part?

- What are the items of dependency and expectation?

3. Analyze the Current Level of Alignment and Interaction

- What is working well? What strengths in the current process should be preserved?

- With which standards or expectations is the current process *not* in alignment?

- List any inconsistency in standards. What internal/external standards and expectations are contradictory to each other?

- Sort and prioritize the areas of non-alignment. What are the consequences of the process remaining unaligned with any standard or expectation? What are the priorities for alignment?

4. Align Those Standards and Practices Which Are Important to Align

- Use PDCA for a successful effort.

SUMMARY

A main difference between projects operated under previous styles of management and those run under quality leadership can be summed up in one word: planning. Teams must spend time in the early stages of their projects planning how the project will unfold. Planning is the heart of using the scientific approach to quality improvement. Only then can teams study correct process problems, gather data that will prove useful, and learn from experience.

This chapter provides planning guides in the form of 15 quality improvement strategies. Each strategy is designed to guide teams through specific activities that form part of their plans—such as gathering information from learners and the community, standardizing a process, or bringing processes under statistical control. Teams can use these strategies to create a map or improvement plan for their project.

Chapter 5

Chapter 6
Learning to Work Together

The ordinary project team is a complicated creature. Members must work out personal differences, find strengths on which to build, balance commitments to the project against the demands of their everyday work, and learn how to improve quality.

Dealing with internal group needs that arise from these pressures is as important as the group's external task of making improvements. Yet even teams that grasp the importance of improving quality often underestimate the need for developing themselves as teams. When a team runs smoothly, members can concentrate on their primary goal of improving a process. In contrast, a team that fails to build relationships among its members will waste time on struggles for control and endless discussions that lead nowhere.

The more you know about what to expect as your group progresses, the better equipped you will be to handle difficulties. You will be able to recognize and avoid many disruptions, and together work through those that cannot be avoided. To build the group skills needed to achieve these goals, you must start by understanding what lies behind most troubles.

I. Undercurrents in Team Dynamics

To outside observers, the only obvious team efforts are associated with the *task* of improving a process: having meetings, gathering data, planning improvements, making changes, writing reports, and so forth. If, indeed, these were the team's only concerns, progress would be very fast. But when people form into groups, something always seems to get in the way of efficient progress.

The problem is that there are hidden concerns that, like undercurrents, pull team members away from their obvious tasks. When they walk through the door into a meeting, team members are beset by conflicting emotions: excitement and anxiety about being on the team, loyalty

Notes. . .

to their departments or schools, nervous anticipation about the project's success.

If left unattended, these undercurrents can inhibit a group's chance of becoming an effective team. Every group must therefore spend time on activities not directly related to a task, activities that build understanding and support in the group. You need to resolve issues that fall into what one author, William Schutz, calls the "interpersonal underworld."

These are issues not often spoken about, but common to us all, and they fall into three categories:

1. Personal identity in the team

It is natural for team members to wonder how they will fit into the team. The most common worries are those associated with:

- *Membership, Inclusion:* "Do I feel like an insider or outsider? Do I belong? Do I want to belong? What can I do to fit in?"

- *Influence, Control, Mutual Trust:* "Who's calling the shots here? Who will have the most influence? Will I have influence? Will I be listened to? Will I be able to contribute? Will I be allowed to contribute?"

- *Getting Along, Mutual Loyalty:* "How will I get along with other team members? Will we be able to develop any cooperative spirit?"

2. Relationships between team members

With few exceptions, team members want the team to succeed, to make improvements, and to work cooperatively with each other.

They extend personal concerns to the team: "What kind of relationships will characterize this team? How will members of different ranks interact? Will we be friendly and informal or will it be strictly business? Will we be open or guarded in what we say? Will we be able to work together, or will we argue and disagree all the time? Will people like or dislike me? Will I like or dislike them?"

3. Identity with the educational system

Team members usually identify strongly with their departments or schools, and they will need to know how membership in the team will affect those roles and responsibilities: "Will my loyalty to the team conflict with loyalty to my colleagues? Will my responsibilities as a team member conflict with my everyday duties?" Usually, it is the project that suffers if the two compete.

Just as team members must reach outside the group to maintain ties with their departments or schools, so must the team as a whole build relationships throughout the entire educational system. Political astuteness is crucial. Finding influential people to champion the team and its project can make a big difference in the support your team receives from the educational system. The more people you convince that quality improvement projects are worthwhile, the better off your team and the entire educational system will be. A team's relationship with its leadership team is one avenue for creating such support within the educational system.

II. Stages of Team Growth

As the team matures, members gradually learn to cope with the emotional and group pressures they face. As a result, the team goes through fairly predictable stages:

Forming:
Stage 1 of Team Growth

When a team forms, team members are like hesitant swimmers standing by the side of the pool and dabbling their toes in the water.

Stage 1: Forming

When a team is forming, members cautiously explore the boundaries of acceptable group behavior. Like hesitant swimmers, they stand by the pool, dabbling their toes in the water. This is a stage of transition from individual to member status, and of testing the leader's guidance both formally and informally.

Forming includes these feelings . . .
- Excitement, anticipation, and optimism
- Pride in being chosen for the school improvement project
- Initial, tentative attachment to the team
- Suspicion, fear, and anxiety about the job ahead

. . . and these behaviors.
- Attempts to define the process and decide how it will be accomplished
- Attempts to determine acceptable group behavior and how to deal with group problems
- Decisions on what information needs to be gathered
- Lofty, abstract discussions of concepts and issues; or, for some members, impatience with these discussions
- Discussion of symptoms or problems not relevant to the task; difficulty in identifying relevant problems
- Complaints about the educational system and barriers to the project

Because there is so much going on to distract members' attention in the beginning, the team accomplishes little, if anything, that concerns its project goals. This is perfectly normal.

Storming:
Stage 2 of Team Growth

As team members start to realize the amount of work that lies ahead, it is normal for them to almost panic. Now they are like swimmers who have jumped into the water, think they are about to drown, and start thrashing about.

Stage 2: Storming

Storming is probably the most difficult stage for the team. It is as if team members jump in the water, and, thinking they are about to drown, start thrashing about. They begin to realize the project is different and more difficult than they imagined, becoming testy, blameful, or overzealous.

Impatient about the lack of progress, but still too inexperienced to know much about decision making or the scientific approach, members argue about just what actions the team should take. They try to rely solely on their personal and professional experience, resisting any need for collaborating with other team members.

Storming includes these feelings . . .
- Resistance to the project task and to quality improvement approaches different from what each individual member is comfortable using
- Sharp fluctuations in attitude about the team and the project's chance of success

. . . and these behaviors.
- Arguing among members even when they agree on the real issue
- Defensiveness and competition; factions and "choosing sides"
- Questioning the wisdom of those who selected this project and appointed the other members of the team
- Establishing unrealistic goals; concern about excessive work
- A perceived "pecking order"; disunity, increased tension, and jealousy

Footnote: Much of this material was inspired by Bruce W. Tuckman's "Development Sequence in Small Groups," in *Psychological Bulletin*, 1965.

Norming:
Stage 3 of Team Growth

As team members get used to working together, their initial resistance fades away. They start helping each other stay afloat rather than competing with one another.

Again, these many pressures mean team members have little energy to spend on progressing towards the team's goal. But they are beginning to understand one another.

Stage 3: Norming

During this stage, members reconcile competing loyalties and responsibilities. They accept the team, team ground rules (or "norms"), their roles in the team, and the individuality of fellow members. Emotional conflict is reduced as previously competitive relationships become more cooperative. In other words, as team members realize they are not going to drown, they stop thrashing about and start helping each other stay afloat.

Norming includes these feelings . . .
- A new ability to express criticism constructively
- Acceptance of membership in the team
- Relief that it seems everything is going to work out

. . . and these behaviors.
- An attempt to achieve harmony by avoiding conflict
- More friendliness, confiding in each other, and sharing of personal problems; discussing the team's dynamics
- A sense of team cohesion, a common spirit and goals
- Establishing and maintaining team ground rules and boundaries (the "norms")

As team members begin to work out their differences, they now have more time and energy to spend on the school improvement project. Thus, they are able to at last start making significant progress.

Performing: Stage 4 of Team Growth

As team members become more comfortable with each other, and better understand the project and what is expected of them, they become a more effective unit with everyone working in concert.

Stage 4: Performing

By this stage, the team has settled its relationships and expectations. They can begin performing, diagnosing and solving problems, and choosing and implementing changes. At last team members have discovered and accepted each other's strengths and weakness, and learned what their roles are. Now they can swim in concert.

Performing includes these feelings . . .
* Members having insights into personal and group processes, and better understanding of each other's strengths and weakness
* Satisfaction at the team's progress

. . . and these behaviors.
* Constructive self-change
* Ability to prevent or work through group problems
* Close attachment to the team

The team is now an effective, cohesive unit. You can tell when your team has reached this stage because you start getting a lot of work done. The duration and intensity of these stages vary from team to team. Sometimes Stage 4, *performing,* is achieved in a meeting or two; other times it may take months. Use the descriptions here to compare your team with the normal pattern for maturing groups. Understanding these stages of growth will keep you from overreacting to normal problems and setting unrealistic expectations that only add to frustration. Don't panic. With patience and effort this assembly of independent individuals will grow into a team.

Chapter 6

Roller Coaster of Highs and Lows

Every team goes through cycles of good times and bad times. The duration of these highs and lows will vary for each team, depending on how quickly they progress, work through obstacles or problems, and so forth. Team members should know that such cycles are normal and do not indicate whether the team will ultimately be successful.

- Excited, Proud
- Satisfied, Pleased
- Optimistic
- So-So, Bored
- Impatient, Discouraged
- Frustrated

First 3-4 wks. "The Honeymoon" Early Planning & Training

III. Roller Coaster of Highs and Lows

Knowing about the typical stages a team passes through—forming, storming, norming, and performing—should relieve much of the fear team members have about the project's success. It is also helpful to be aware of the roller coaster of highs and lows every team experiences.

A team's mood usually reflects its fortune: With every step forward, the future looks bright and team members are optimistic. But no matter how well a team works together, progress is never smooth. As progress swings from forward to stalled, and then from stalled to backward, the team mood will swing, too. These swings are only partly linked to the stages of growth, and usually the changes are unpredictable.

As shown (above), the team begins with hopefulness and optimism. These positive feelings may last a while, but usually change to boredom and impatience as the project gets underway and members feel overwhelmed when they realize just how much they have to learn about quality improvement. Somewhere in here the storming starts.

When they finally begin collecting data, team members again feel encouraged—at last they are making progress! Rarely does this elation last: Since few people are experts in scientific methods the first time out, team members almost always uncover mistakes in data collection procedures, and realize they must go back and do it again. The mood swings down. Recovery comes as the team learns from experience, makes another attempt, and gathers good, reliable data.

The pattern is different for each team. Team members' attitudes depend on both the speed of progress and the resistance or encouragement they receive from the leadership team and their department or school.

The best way to deal with this cycle is to understand and accept it with a "this too shall pass" attitude. Changes in attitude, just like growth stages, are normal. The team must cultivate patience, and pass it on to

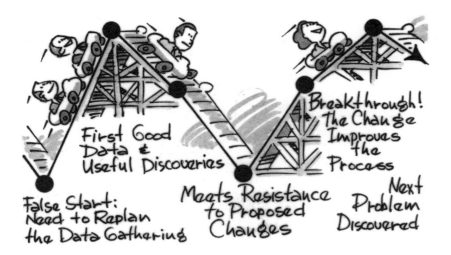

First Good Data & Useful Discoveries

False Start: Need to Replan the Data Gathering

Meets Resistance to Proposed Changes

Breakthrough! The Change Improves the Process

Next Problem Discovered

its leadership team. Eventually, everyone will better understand how projects unfold, and will be able to set a realistic pace for the project.

Teams can also take a more active approach to dealing with the stages and cycles they experience by learning when and how to avoid or work through group problems. The rest of this chapter describes approaches for improving the group's ability to solve and prevent problems.

IV. Recipe for a Successful Team

No team exists without problems. But some teams, particularly those who have learned to counter the negative team dynamics, seem to be especially good at preventing many typical group problems. How close a team comes to this ideal depends on the following ten essential ingredients:

1. Clarity in Team Goals

A team works best when everyone understands its purpose and goals. If there is confusion or disagreement, they work to resolve the issues.

Ideally, the team . . .
- agrees on its mission, or works together to resolve disagreement;
- sees the mission as workable or, if necessary, narrows the mission to a workable size;
- has a clear vision and can progress steadily towards its goals;
- is clear about the larger project goals and about the purpose of individual steps, meetings, discussion, and decisions.

Chapter 6

Indicators of potential trouble
- Frequent switches in directions
- Frequent arguments about what the team should do next
- Feelings that the project is too big or inappropriate
- Frustration at lack of progress
- Excessive questioning of each decision or action taken
- Floundering

Recommendations
If team members feel they don't understand the mission, try working through the exercise "Discussing Your Mission" (p. 7-29). Emphasize the right of each team member to ask questions about a decision or event until satisfied with the answers. If you find the mission is too broad, work with the leadership team to find something workable.

2. An Improvement Plan

Improvement plans help the team determine what advice, assistance, training, materials, and other resources it may need. They guide the team in determining schedules and identifying mileposts. The improvement plans we recommend in Chapter 5 are built from strategies that incorporate the scientific approach, a task that can be difficult for early teams.

Ideally, the team . . .
- has created an improvement plan, revising it as needed during the project;
- has a flowchart or similar document describing the steps of the project;
- refers to these documents when discussing what directions to take next;
- knows what resources, schedules, and training are needed throughout the project, and plans accordingly.

Indicators of potential trouble
- Uncertainty about the team's direction (the team muddles through each activity without a clear idea of how to get the information it needs)
- Being "lost in the woods" (when one activity is completed there is little or no idea of what to do next)
- "Fishing expeditions" (the team plunges ahead, hoping to stumble across improvement ideas)
- "Filling the sky with lead" (launching many improvement activities without thinking about what each is supposed to do or what the precise mission is, hoping at least one will hit the target)

Recommendations

Seek assistance from a competent technical advisor. Work through the improvement plans in Chapter 5; ask yourselves what you need in order to fulfill your mission. Ask your leadership team to review or, if necessary, help formulate your plan.

3. Clearly Defined Roles

Teams operate most efficiently if they tap everyone's talents, and all members understand their duties and know who is responsible for what issues and tasks.

Ideally, the team . . .
- has formally designated roles (all members know what is expected of everyone, especially the leader, facilitator, and quality advisor);
- understands which roles belong to one person and which are shared, and how the shared roles are switched (for instance, using an agreed-upon procedure to rotate the job of meeting facilitator);

Ten Ingredients for a Successful Team

1. **Clarity in Team Goals**
2. **An Improvement Plan**
3. **Clearly Defined Goals**
4. **Clear Communication**
5. **Beneficial Team Behaviors**
6. **Well-defined Decision Procedures**
7. **Balanced Participation**
8. **Established Ground Rules**
9. **Awareness of Group Processes**
10. **Use of the Scientific Approach**

Chapter 6

- uses each member's talents, and involves everyone in team activities so no one feels left out or taken advantage of (for example, not always having women take the notes or the men take the lead).

Indicators of potential trouble
- Roles and duty assignments that result from a pecking order
- Confusion over who is responsible for what
- People getting stuck with the same tedious chores

Recommendations
The team must decide on how roles will be assigned and changed. Review the role descriptions in Chapter 3 (pp. 3-4 to 3-15). Have the team leader and quality advisor discuss their responsibilities and those of any other designated roles. The team leader might facilitate discussions on what duties must be assigned, how they will be assigned, and how they can be changed. Reach consensus about roles within the team.

4. Clear Communication

Good discussions depend on how well information is passed between team members.

Ideally, team members should . . .
- speak with clarity and directness (for example, avoid using questions to disguise statements);
- be succinct, avoiding long anecdotes and examples;
- listen actively, explore rather than debate each speaker's ideas;
- avoid interrupting and talking when others are speaking;
- share information on many levels, for example:

§ *sensing statements* ("I don't hear any disagreements with John's point. Do we all agree?")

§ *thinking statements* ("There seems to be a correlation between the number of errors and the volume of work.")

§ *feeling statements* ("I'm disappointed that no one has taken care of this yet.")

§ *statements of intentions* ("My question was not a criticism. I simply wanted more information.")

§ *statements of actions* ("Let's set up a pilot program to test the new science curriculum.")

Indicators of potential trouble

- Poor speaking skills (mumbling, rambling, speaking too softly, little eye contact)
- Members are unable to say what they really feel; cautiousness; lots of tentative, conditional statements ("Do you think, maybe, that sometimes it might be that . . .")
- Everyone senses there is more going on than meets the eye; people's words do not match their tone of voice or mannerisms
- Opinions expressed as facts or phrased as questions
- Plops: statements that receive no acknowledgment or response
- Bullying statements ("What you don't understand is . . .")
- Discounts ("That's not important. What's worse is . . .")

Recommendations

Develop communication skills, and learn to recognize problems that result from poor communication. Use the meeting evaluation to discuss how well team members communicate. Have observers (team members or outsiders) watch the group and give honest feedback on communication dynamics (see "Observing Group Process," p. 7-31). Videotape a discussion; review and critique it.

Chapter 6

5. Beneficial Team Behaviors

Teams should encourage all members to use the skills and practices that make discussions and meetings more effective (see pp. 4-2 to 4-7).

Ideally, team members should . . .
- initiate discussions;
- seek information and opinions;
- suggest procedures for reaching a goal;
- clarify or elaborate on ideas;
- summarize;
- test for consensus;
- act as gatekeepers: direct conversational traffic, avoid simultaneous conversations, throttle dominant talkers, make room for reserved talkers;
- keep the discussion from digressing;
- compromise and be creative in resolving differences;
- try to ease tension in the group and work through difficult matters;
- express the group's feeling and ask others to check that impression;
- get the group to agree on standards ("Do we all agree to discuss this for 15 minutes and no more?");
- refer to documentation and data;
- praise and correct others with equal fairness; accept both praise and complaints.

Indicators of potential trouble
- Failure to use discussion skills
- Reliance on one person (the leader) to manage the discussion; no shared responsibility
- People repeating points, unsure whether anyone heard them the first time

- Discussions that are stuck; wheel-spinning; inability to let go of one topic and move onto the next
- Discussions in the hallway after the meeting are more free and more candid than those during the meeting

Recommendations

Refer to our three-part discussion on "Working Through Group Problems" that appears later in this chapter (Constructive Feedback, p. 6-20; General Guidelines, p. 6-29; Ten Common Problems and What to do about Them, p. 6-32). The team leader can also create an exercise out of effective discussion skills (p. 4-5). For example, team members could pick two or three skills for the entire team to practice at a meeting, reviewing their performance during the meeting evaluation.

6. Well-defined Decision Procedures

You can tell a lot about how well a team is run by watching its decision-making process. A team should always be aware of the different ways it reaches decisions.

Ideally, the team should . . .
- discuss how decisions will be made, such as when to take a poll, when to decide by consensus (are there times when a decision by only a few people is acceptable?);
- explore important issues by polling (each member is asked to state an opinion verbally or in writing);
- decide important issues by consensus;
- test for consensus ("This seems to be our agreement. Is there anyone who feels unsure about the choice?");
- use data as the basis of decisions.

Indicators of potential trouble
- Conceding to opinions that are presented as facts with no supporting data
- Decisions by one or two people in the group, without team members agreeing to defer to their expertise
- Decision by a minority
- Too-frequent recourse to "majority rules" or other easy approaches that bypass strong disagreement
- Decision by default; people do not respond to a statement (the "plop"); silence interpreted as consent

Recommendations

Have the team leader (or, if necessary, the quality advisor) lead a discussion on decision making in the team. Occasionally, designate a member or outsider to watch and give feedback on how decisions are made so the group can talk about necessary changes in the group (see "Observing Group Process," p. 7-31).

7. Balanced Participation

Since every team member has a stake in the group's achievements, everyone should participate in discussions and decisions, share commitment to the project's success, and contribute their talents.

Ideally, the team should . . .
- have reasonably balanced participation, with all members contributing to most discussions;
- build on members' natural styles of participation.

Indicators of potential trouble
- Some team members have too much influence, others, too little

- Participation depends on the subject being discussed (for example, only those who know the most about a subject are actively involved; others do not even ask questions)
- Members too often contribute only at certain times to a conversation or meeting
- Some members speak only about a certain topic ("hot buttons," participation only when the subject touches, for example, budget, staffing, or training)

Recommendations

Use brainstorming (p. 2-41) to elicit input from all team members during discussions. If problems persist, adapt the "Disruptive Group Behavior" exercise (p. 7-9) to your group (for example, incorporate "Overbearing Participants," p. 6-34; "Dominating Participants," p. 6-35; or "Reluctant Participants," p. 6-36).

8. Established Ground Rules

Groups invariably establish ground rules (or "norms") for what will and will not be tolerated in the group. A complete list of typical issues included in ground rules is given in Chapter 4 (p. 4-16).

Ideally, the team should . . .

- have open discussions regarding ground rules, where the group discusses what behaviors are acceptable and unacceptable;
- openly state or acknowledge norms ("We all agreed to decide the issue this way").

Indicators of potential trouble

- Certain important topics are avoided; too many subjects are taboo; conversations recur that are irrelevant to the project and harmful to the group

- No one acknowledges the norms; everyone acts as they think the group wants them to act; no one is able to say exactly what ground rules the team follows (for example, no one cracks jokes even though it was never stated that jokes would be out of place)
- Recurring differences about what is or is not acceptable behavior
- Behavior that signifies irritation; for example, repeated disregard for starting and ending times
- Conflict over assumed norms or conflicting expectation

Recommendations
Groups must take time at the beginning of the group to discuss and agree on obvious ground rules. From time to time, review the ground rules, adding, deleting, or revising them as needed. Particularly pay attention to current and possible ground rules during times of conflict and antagonism.

9. Awareness of the Group Process

Ideally, all team members should be aware of the group process, how the team works together, along with paying attention to the content of the meeting.

Ideally, team members should . . .
- be sensitive to nonverbal communication, for example, be aware that silence may indicate disagreement, or knowing that physical signs of agitation might indicate someone is uncomfortable with a discussion;
- see, hear, and feel the group dynamics;
- comment and intervene to correct a group process problem;
- contribute equally to group process and meeting content;
- choose to work on group process issues and occasionally designate a team member or outsider to officially observe and report on group interactions at a meeting.

Indicators of potential trouble

- Lack of reference to undercurrent issues, particularly when the group is having difficulty
- Pushing ahead on the project when there are nonverbal signs of resistance, confusion, or disappointment
- Inattention to obvious nonverbal clues and shifts in the group mood
- Members attributing motives to nonverbal behavior ("You've been quiet during the last 30 minutes. You must not be interested in what's being said.")
- Remarks that discount someone's behavior or contribution, or group process issues ("Let's get on with the task and stop talking about that stuff.")

Recommendations

Use the series of observation formats described in "Observing Group Process" (starting on p. 7-31) to work through pertinent group issues before they become a problem. Use the quality advisor as an observer to evaluate how well the group handles problems, confusion, discussions, and so forth. Encourage the team to have several "process checks," times when members can say how they think the meeting is going or express thoughts for which there were no appropriate times in the meeting. Routinely include group process issues in meeting evaluations.

10. Use of the Scientific Approach

Teams that use a scientific approach, the reliance on good data for problem solving and decision making, have a much easier time arriving at permanent solutions to problems. Failure to use a scientific approach seriously compromises a basic principle of quality improvement and can ruin the team's chance for success. The scientific approach helps avoid many group problems and disagreements. Many arguments are

between individuals with strong opinions. The scientific approach insists that opinions be supported by, or at least defer to, data.

Ideally, the team should . . .
- demand to see data before making decisions and question anyone who tries to act on hunches alone;
- use basic statistical tools to investigate problems and to gather and analyze data;
- dig for root causes of problems;
- seek permanent solutions rather than rely on quick fixes.

Indicators of potential trouble
- Team members insist they don't need data because their intelligence and experience are enough to tell them what the problems and solutions are
- Wild stabs at supposed solutions: jumping to conclusions, too many inferences and assumptions, shooting from the hip
- Hasty action, a "ready, *fire*, aim!" approach

Recommendations
Make sure the team has access to an expert for training and assistance (usually this is the quality advisor). Every team should talk about the importance of enforcing a scientific approach, especially when decisions or actions are needed.

V. Working through Group Problems, Part 1: *Constructive Feedback*

No matter what pressures a team encounters, a fundamental message of this handbook is that it can work hard at its project and support members' needs. The single most important skill to have in working through any problem is the ability to give constructive feedback.

Why? Because most often problems are expressed as criticism of someone's action. When you are criticized by someone, it is difficult to know what to do. A common reaction is to feel critical of them: "What right do they have to criticize *me?*" Suppose it is you reacting negatively to behavior that truly disrupts the group's progress. Do you sit on your negative feelings for the sake of group harmony? Is there a way to express dissatisfaction without provoking a confrontation that might disrupt the group even more?

There are proven methods for giving and receiving criticism, methods that work equally well for giving and receiving praise. The goals are to give constructive feedback, whether positive or negative, and to make sure that any feedback you receive is constructive. While there is no guarantee, following the guidelines below will minimize the possibility of provoking a bad scene. Use them to help you decide when to give feedback, how to tell a person or group what you think, and how to listen to their feedback.

Guidelines for Constructive Feedback

Useful feedback comes in several forms. *Statistical data* provide feedback from a process, measurements that tell you how well a process is running, whether changes you tried were effective, and so forth. *Parent and community feedback* tells you how your educational system is doing and whether your service meets their needs. The most common form of feedback (and our focus here) is simply *one person talking to another.*

Many people know that to get good data or useful information you must plan carefully and follow established rules and guidelines. Few

Footnote—Five authors have made significant contributions to the formulation of these rules: Norman Berkowitz, a professor of psychology at Boston College with insight into what happens when simple disagreement turns into hostility; Chris Argyris, a well-known author in the field of organizational change; Eric Berne, the founder of Transactional Analysis; Virginia Satir, a eminent family therapist; and Thomas Gordon, psychologist and author of *Leader Effectiveness Training.*

Chapter 6

Guidelines for Constructive Feedback

- **Acknowledge the need for feedback**

- **Give both positive and negative feedback**

- **Understand the context**

- **Know when to give feedback**

- **Know how to give feedback**
  - § Be descriptive.
  - § Don't use labels.
  - § Don't exaggerate.
  - § Don't be judgmental.
  - § Speak for yourself.
  - § Talk first about yourself, not about the other person.
  - § Phrase the issue as a statement, not a question.
  - § Restrict your feedback to things you know for certain.
  - § Help peple hear and accept your compliments when giving positive feedback.

- **Know how to receive feedback**
  - § Breathe.
  - § Listen carefully.
  - § Ask questions for clarity.
  - § Acknowledge the feedback.
  - § Acknowledge valid points.
  - § Take time to sort out what you heard.

people know that the same ideas apply to person-to-person feedback. Thinking ahead of time about what you are going to say and how you are going to say it, and following the guidelines given below, will increase the value of what you say to another person.

To make personal feedback constructive, you must:

• **Acknowledge the need for feedback**

The first thing to recognize is the value of giving feedback, both positive and negative. Feedback is vital to any educational system committed to improving itself, for it is the only way to know what needs to be improved. Giving and receiving feedback should be more than just a part of a team member's behavior; it should be part of the entire educational system's culture.

You will need good feedback skills to improve your team meetings, and, more generally, interactions between team members. These skills will also help you communicate more effectively with other members of the school system, including parents and students, the community at large, and the people who supply products and goods to the system. In fact, you will find many opportunities to apply these skills in your work. First, however, your team should agree that giving and receiving feedback is an acceptable part of how you will improve the way you work together. This agreement is necessary so that no one is surprised when he or she receives feedback.

• **Give both positive and negative feedback**

Many people take good work for granted and give feedback only when there are problems. This is a bad policy: People will more likely pay attention to your complaints if they have also received your compliments. It is important to remember to tell people when they have done something well.

• **Understand the context**

The most important characteristic of feedback is that it always has a context: where it happened, why it happened, what led up to the activity of the process that is not effective. You never simply walk up to a person, deliver a feedback statement, and then leave. Before you give feedback, review the actions and decisions that led up to the moment.

• **Know when to give feedback**

Before giving feedback, determine whether the moment is right. You must consider more than your own need to give feedback. Constructive feedback can happen only within a context of listening to and caring about the person.

Do not give feedback when:

§ You don't know much about the circumstances of the behavior.
§ You don't care about the person or will not be around long enough to follow up on the aftermath of your feedback. Hit-and-run feedback is not fair.
§ The feedback, positive or negative, is about something the person has no power to change.
§ The other person seems low in self-esteem.
§ You are low in self-esteem.
§ Your purpose is not really improvement, but to put someone on the spot ("gotcha!"), to punish or blame, or demonstrate how smart or how much more responsible you are.
§ The time, place, or circumstances are inappropriate (for example, in the presence of outsiders).

Chapter 6

An Easy-to-Remember Guide for Constructive Feedback

Sequence	Explanation
1. "When you . . ."	Start with a "When you . . ." statement that describes the behavior without judgment, exaggeration, labeling, attribution, or motives. Just state the facts as specifically as possible.
2. "I feel . . ."	Tell how their behavior affects you. If you need more than a word or two to describe the feeling, it's probably just some variation of joy, sorrow, anger, or fear.
3. "Because I . . ."	Now say why you are affected that way. Describe the connection between the facts you observed and the feelings they provoke in you.
(4. Pause for discussion)	Let the other person respond.
5. "I would like . . ."	Describe the change you want the other person to consider . . .
6. "Because . . ."	. . . and why you think the change will alleviate the problem.
7. "What do you think?"	Listen to the other person's response. Be prepared to discuss options and compromise on a solution.

How the feedback will work:

When you [do this], I feel [this way], because [of such and such]. What I would like you to consider is [doing X], because I think it will [accomplish Y]. What do you think?

Example:

"When you are late for faculty meetings, I get angry because I think it is wasting the time of all the faculty and we are never able to get through our agenda items. I would like you to consider finding some way of planning your schedule that lets you get to these meetings on time. That way we can be more productive at the meetings, and we can all keep our tight schedules."

• **Know how to give feedback**

If the circumstances are appropriate for giving feedback, use the following guidelines for compliments as well as complaints. Use the "Easy-to-Remember Guide for Giving Constructive Feedback" (p. 6-24) the first few times; though it may feel awkward, you will soon get more comfortable and be able to give constructive feedback without having to refer to the guide.

§ *Be descriptive.*

Relate, as objectively as possible, what you saw the other person do or what you heard the other person say. Give specific examples, the more recent, the better. Examples from the distant past are more likely to lead to disagreement over "facts."

§ *Don't use labels.*

Be clear, specific, and unambiguous. Words like "immature," "unprofessional," "irresponsible," and "prejudiced" are labels we attach to sets of behaviors. Describe the behavior and drop the labels. For example, say, "You missed the deadline we had all agreed to meet" rather than "You're being irresponsible and I want to know what you're going to do about it!"

§ *Don't exaggerate.*

Be exact: To say "You're always late" is probably untrue and, therefore, unfair. It invites the feedback receiver to argue with the exaggeration rather than respond to the real issue.

§ *Don't be judgmental.*

Or at least don't use the rhetoric of judgment. Words like "good," "better," "bad," "worst," and "should" place you in the role of a controlling parent. This invites the person receiving your comments to respond as a child. When that happens, and it will most of the time, the possibility of constructive feedback is lost.

§ *Speak for yourself.*
Don't refer to absent, anonymous people. Avoid such references as "A lot of people here don't like it when you. . . ." Don't allow yourself to be a conduit for other peoples' complaints. Instead, encourage others to speak for themselves.

§ *Talk first about yourself, not about the other person.*
Use a statement with the word "I" as the subject, not the word "you." This guideline is one of the most important and one of the most surprising. Consider the following examples regarding lateness:

1. "You are frequently late for faculty meetings."
2. "You are very prompt for faculty meetings."
3. "I feel annoyed when you are late for faculty meetings."
4. "I appreciate your coming to faculty meetings on time."

Statements 1 and 2 are "you" statements. People become defensive around "you" statements and are less likely to hear what you say when it is phrased this way. Statements 3 and 4 are "I" messages and create an adult/peer relationship. People are more likely to remain open to your message when an "I" statement is used. Even if your rank is higher than the feedback recipient, strive for an adult/peer relationship. Use "I" statements so the effectiveness of your comments is not lost.

§ *Phrase the issue as a statement, not a question.*
Contrast "When are you going to stop being late for faculty meetings?" with "I feel annoyed when you are late for faculty meetings." The question is controlling and manipulative because it implies "You, the responder, are expected to

adjust your behavior to accommodate me, the questioner." Most people become defensive and angry when spoken to this way. On the other hand, the "I" statement implies "I think we have an issue we must resolve together." The "I" statement allows the receiver to see what effect the behavior had on you.

§ *Restrict your feedback to things you know for certain.*
Don't present your opinions as facts. Speak only of what you saw and heard and what you feel and want.

§ *Help people hear and accept your compliments when giving positive feedback.*
Many people feel awkward when told good things about themselves and will fend off the compliment ("Oh, it wasn't that big a deal. Others worked on it as much as I did."). Sometimes they will change the subject. It may be important to reinforce the positive feedback and help the person hear it, acknowledge it, and accept it.

• **Know how to receive feedback**
There may be a time when you receive feedback from someone who does not know feedback guidelines. In these cases, **help your critic refashion the criticism** so that it conforms to the rules for constructive feedback ("What did I say or do to dissatisfy you?"). When reacting to feedback:

§ *Breathe.*
This is simple but effective advice. Our bodies are conditioned to react to stressful situations as though they were physical assaults. Our muscles tense. We start breathing rapidly and shallowly. Taking full, deep breaths forces your body to relax and allows your brain to maintain greater alertness.

Chapter 6

§ *Listen carefully.*
Don't interrupt. Don't discourage the feedback-giver.

§ *Ask questions for clarity.*
You have a right to receive clear feedback. Ask for specific examples ("Can you describe what I do or say that makes me appear aggressive to you?").

§ *Acknowledge the feedback.*
Paraphrase the message in your own words to let the person know you have heard and understood what was said.

§ *Acknowledge valid points.*
Agree with what is true. Agree with what is possible. Acknowledge the other person's point of view ("I understand how you might get that impression") and try to understand their reaction.

Agreeing with what's true or possible does not mean you agree to change your behavior. You can agree, for instance, that sometimes you jump too quickly to a conclusion without implying that you will slow down your conclusion-making process. Agreeing with what's true or possible also does not mean agreeing with any value judgment about you. You can agree that your reports have been late without thereby agreeing that you are irresponsible.

§ *Take time to sort out what you heard.*
You may need time for sorting out or checking with others before responding to the feedback. It is reasonable to ask the feedback-giver for time to think about what was said and how you feel about it. Make a specific appointment for getting back to him or her. Don't use this time as an excuse to avoid the issue.

VI. Working through Group Problems, Part 2: *General Guidelines*

It would be nice to say that if you follow the advice in this handbook, you will never run into problems. But we all know that simply isn't true. Though severe problems are rare, occasionally an individual's behavior disrupts the group. You should be prepared to deal with disruptive situations.

Generally, your best strategy is to:

- **Anticipate and prevent group problems whenever possible**

    As noted previously, most problems can be anticipated or prevented if a group spends time developing itself into a team: getting to know each other, establishing ground rules, discussing norms for group behavior, agreeing to an improvement plan. If you do this when your team starts, you will save time, and prevent hassles, frustrations, and animosities.

- **Think of each problem as a group problem**

    A natural tendency is to blame individuals for causing problems. Remember the 85/15 Rule: Most problems are attributable to the system, not the individual (see p. 2-12). The truth is that many problems arise because the group lets them happen or even encourages them in some way. Examine each problem in light of what the group does to encourage or allow the behavior and what the group can do differently to encourage more constructive behavior. Assume the problem continues to exist because it somehow benefits the group: What could that hidden benefit be? How have group members contributed to the continuation of the problem?

Guidelines for Reacting to Group Problems

- **Anticipate and prevent group problems whenever possible.**

- **Think of each problem as a group problem.**

- **Neither over-react nor under-react. A leader's range of responses typically includes:**
  - § Do nothing (non-intervention)
  - § Out-of-meeting conversation (minimal intervention)
  - § Impersonal group time (low intervention)
  - § Out-of-meeting confrontation (medium intervention)
  - § In-group confrontation (high intervention)
  - § Expulsion from the group **(Do Not Use This Option)**

- **Neither over-react nor under-react**

  Some behaviors are only minor disruptions in the group's progress. These are usually not a problem and sometimes even give a needed break in the activity. Other behaviors are very disruptive and impede, halt, or reverse the team's progress towards its goals. Some behaviors are chronic, occurring over and over again. The team leader should respond appropriately to the seriousness of the problem, ignoring minor disruptions, confronting chronic or serious disruptions directly. Experienced leaders develop a range of responses to typical problems, each more direct than the previous one. This way they can "crank up" the response as a problem gets more disruptive and the team realizes the seriousness of the situation.

A leader's range of responses typically includes:

§ *Do nothing (non-intervention)*

Ignore the offensive behavior, particularly if it is not a chronic problem or doesn't seem to inhibit the group. Sometimes, the leader need not intervene because other group members will deal with the offending behavior. In such cases, the leader is available to facilitate the discussion provoked when one member confronts another.

§ *Out-of-meeting conversation (minimal intervention)*

Talk to the disruptive members outside the group meeting, asking them what would increase their satisfaction with the group. Give constructive feedback.

§ *Impersonal group time (low intervention)*

At the start of a meeting, talk about general group process concerns without pointing out individuals, perhaps by going through a list previously written on a flipchart. Include the disruptive behavior on the list. During the critique at the end of the meeting, the group evaluates itself on each item on the list. It is usually difficult to deal with problems without referring to the offenders. Sometimes not referring to the specific offenders is awkward and phony. One way to get around this is to describe the context of the problem (such as, "Every time we talk about subject X, we get side-tracked"). Focus attention on how the group encourages the problem and what the group can do to discourage it. This approach treats all problems as group process problems rather than offenses by individuals.

§ *Out-of-meeting confrontation (medium intervention)*
Out-of-meeting confrontation is the same as out-of-meeting conversation except the leader is more assertive. Use it when other attempts have failed, especially when the disruptive behavior continues even when the group has tried to change. Sometimes this confrontation may lead to an informal "contract" regarding agreed-upon changes in the leader's and member's behavior. (For example, "I know you don't get along with Joe and I will do everything I can to avoid pairing you on assignments. For your part I want you to stop being critical of him during team meetings.")

§ *In-group confrontation (high intervention)*
As a last resort, after other approaches have failed, the leader may deal with the offending behavior in the presence of the group. This disrupts the group's other business and exposes an individual's behavior to open critique in the group. This tactic can be effective; it can also be a disaster. The leader must prepare carefully for this intervention: how to word the confrontation, what reactions to anticipate, how to avoid defensiveness or hostility in the offending member. Use constructive feedback techniques, expressing feelings as "I statements" (p. 6-26). The purpose of high intervention is to change the offensive behavior, not to punish the offending member.

Chapter 6

§ *Expulsion from the group* (***do not use this option***)
We believe that you should never kick anyone off a project team and recommend against expulsion for the following reasons: It can create a stigma that remains with the group and with the expelled member for a long time. The costs of expelling a member are ill will, creating an adversary, and creating an unfavorable impression of the group among others in the educational system.

What can a team leader do when highly disruptive behavior continues? One of the best strategies is to talk privately with the offending team member, and point out that disruptive behavior seems inconsistent with a commitment to help the team succeed. If the person would rather not attend meetings, find other ways to allow his or her input into the project.

VII. Working Through Group Problems, Part 3: *Ten Common Problems and What to Do About Them*

One way to deal with group problems, particularly those arising from unspoken issues such as competing loyalties to the team and work groups, is to talk about them. Most problems, though, require a more structured solution. The following examples show how to use the guidelines for constructive feedback and working through common team problems.

1. Floundering

Teams commonly have trouble starting and ending a project or even different project stages. They flounder, wondering what actions to take next. At the beginning, they sometimes suffer through false starts and directionless discussions and activities. As the group progresses, team members sometimes resist moving from one phase or step to the next. At the end, teams may delay unnecessarily, postponing decisions or conclusions because "We need something else. We're not ready to finish this yet."

Problems at the beginning suggest the team is unclear or overwhelmed by its project. A few improvement teams have experienced difficulty in understanding what a process is and what key processes of the educational system are in need of improvement. Start-up problems may also indicate group members are not yet comfortable enough with each other to engage in real discussion and decision making.

Floundering when trying to make decisions may indicate that the group's work is not the product of consensus, but some members are reluctant to say they don't support the group's conclusions. Floundering after completing one phase of a project could mean the group does not have a clear vision, mission, or plan, and does not know what steps to take next. Floundering at the end of the project usually indicates that the team members have developed a bond and are reluctant to separate. Or, perhaps, they are reluctant to expose their work to review and possible criticism from outsiders.

How a team leader can deal with floundering

- Get the group to look critically at how the project is being run. Review your Improvement Plan (Chapter 5), using the hints for "What to Do if You Get Stuck Between Activities " (p. 5-29); or create a plan if you don't already have one. Use the "Progress Checklist" (p. 4-38) or the "Closure Checklist" (p. 4-42) to stimulate discussion.
- "Let's review our mission and make sure it's clear to everyone."
- "Let's go over our improvement plan and see what we have to do next."
- "What do we need to do so we can move on? What is holding us up?" (Data? Knowledge? Assurances? Support? Feelings?)

Ten Common Group Problems

1. **Floundering**
2. **Overbearing participants**
3. **Dominating participants**
4. **Reluctant participants**
5. **Unquestioned acceptance of opinions as facts**
6. **Rush to accomplishment**
7. **Attribution**
8. **Discounts and "plops"**
9. **Wanderlust: digression and tangents**
10. **Feuding members**

Chapter 6

Overbearing Participants . . .

seem to hold an unusual amount of influence in a group, often because they have a higher rank in the company or in-depth technical knowledge.

- "Are we getting stuck because we have previous business that is unfinished? Does anyone feel we have missed something or left something incomplete?"
- "Let's reserve time at the next meeting to discuss how we will proceed. Meanwhile, I suggest that each of us write down what we think is needed to move to the next stage."

2. Overbearing Participants

Some members wield a disproportionate amount of influence in a group. These people usually have a position of authority or an area of expertise on which they base their authority. Teams need authorities and experts because these are important resources. Most teams benefit from their participation. But the presence of an authority or an expert is detrimental when the person:

- Discourages or forbids discussion encroaching into his or her authority or expertise. ("You need not get involved in those technicalities. We are taking care of that. Let's move on to something else.")
- Signals the "sacredness" of an area by using jargon or referring to present state regulations or federal requirements, or local board of education policies as the ultimate determinants of future actions. ("What you don't understand is that PL94-142 requires a conference with parents to discuss a child's handicapping condition.")
- Regularly discounts any proposed activity by declaring that it won't work, or citing instances when it was tried unsuccessfully here or in the past. Other members soon get the message that their suggestions will be seen as trite or naive. ("We tried that curriculum approach in Lake Wood School in 1988. It was a disaster! Steer clear of that solution.")

Dominating Participants . . .

like to hear themselves talk, and rarely give others a chance to contribute.

How a team leader can deal with overbearing participants
- Reinforce the agreement that no area is sacred; team members have the right to explore any area that pertains to the project.
- Get the authority or expert participant to agree (before the project starts, if possible) that it is important for the group to make its own way, for all members to understand the process. The expert may occasionally be asked to instruct the group, to share knowledge or a broader perspective.
- Talk to the authority or expert out-of-meeting, and ask for cooperation and patience.
- Enforce the primacy of data and the scientific approach. ("In God we trust. All others must have data!")

3. Dominating Participants

Some members, with or without authority or expertise, consume a disproportionate amount of "air time." They talk too much. Instead of concise statements, they tell overlong anecdotes and dominate the meeting. Normal moments of silence that occasionally occur are an invitation for the dominator to talk. Their talk inhibits the group from building a sense of team accomplishment or momentum. Other members get discouraged and find excuses for missing meetings.

How a team leader can deal with dominating participants
- Structure discussion on key issues to encourage equal participation. For example, have members write down their thoughts and share them around the table. (See "Nominal Group Technique," p. 2-45.)
- List "balance of participation" as a general concern to critique during the meeting evaluation.
- Practice gatekeeping: "We've heard from you on this, Lee. I'd like to hear what others have to say."
- Get the team to agree on the need for limits and focus in discussions, and the value of balanced participation.

Chapter 6

Reluctant Participants . . .

feel shy or unsure of themselves in the group, and must be encouraged to contribute.

4. Reluctant Participants

Many groups have one or two members who rarely speak. They are the opposites of the dominators. When invited to speak, these "underbearing" members commonly say "I am participating; I listen to everything that's said. When I have something to say, I'll say it." Each of us has a different threshold of need to be part of a group ("tribal" instincts versus "loner" instincts) and a different level of comfort with speaking in a group (extrovert versus introvert). There is nothing right or wrong about being tribal or a loner, extroverted or introverted; these are just differences between people. Problems develop in a group when there are no built-in activities that encourage the introverts to participate and the extroverts to listen.

How a team leader can deal with reluctant participants
- Structure participation the same way as for dominating participants.
- When possible, divide the project task into individual assignments and reports.
- Act as a gatekeeper: "Does anyone else have ideas about this?" (said while looking at the reluctant participant); more directly, "Sam, what is your experience with this area?"

5. Unquestioned Acceptance of Opinions as Facts

Some team members express personal beliefs and assumptions with such confidence that listeners assume they are hearing a presentation of facts. This can be dangerous, leading to an unshakable acceptance of various "earth-is-flat" assertions. Most team members are reluctant to question self-assured statements from other members. Besides not wanting to be impolite, they think they need to have data before they

Rush to Accomplishment . . .

is common to teams being pushed by one or more members who are impatient for results and unwilling to work through the necessary steps of the scientific approach.

challenge someone else's assertions. Worse yet, the skeptic could be wrong and lose face with the team.

There is an ancient axiom of debate that says if a speaker presents something as fact without legitimate supporting evidence, the listener need not have evidence to respond with skepticism.

How a team leader can deal with unquestioned acceptance of opinions as facts
- "Is what you said an opinion or a fact? Do you have data?"
- "How do you know that is true?"
- "Let's accept what you say as possible, but let's also get some data to test it."
- Have the group agree on the primacy of the scientific approach.

6. Rush to Accomplishment

Many teams will have at least one "do something" member who is either impatient or sensitive to pressure from administrators or other influential people or groups. This type of person typically reaches an individual decision about a problem and its solution before the group has had time to consider different options. They urge the team to make hasty decisions and discourage any further efforts to analyze or discuss the matter. Their nonverbal behavior, direct statements, and "throw away" expressions constantly communicate impatience.

Too much of this pressure can lead a group in a series of random, unsystematic efforts to make improvements. Like hunters shooting blindly at silent birds in a heavy fog, they are satisfied that they're "doing something" and pray that at least one shot will hit the target.

Teams must realize that improvements do not come easily, and rarely can they make significant gains overnight. Quality takes patience.

Chapter 6

How a team leader can deal with a rush to accomplishment
- Remind team members of their prior agreement that the scientific approach will not be compromised or circumvented.
- Make sure he or she is not among those exerting the pressure.
- Confront the quick fixer, using the techniques of constructive feedback. Have examples of quick fixing and describe the effect of this impatience on the team's work.

7. Attribution

As individuals and groups, we tend to attribute or assign motives to people when we disagree with or don't understand their opinion or behavior. Through attribution, we try to bring order and meaning into apparent disorder and confusion.

However, attribution should not be a substitute for the hard work of seeking real explanations. It also creates resentment: It is perfectly normal to bristle when someone else tells you they know what makes you tick or tries to explain your motives.

Within a team, attribution can lead to hostility when aimed at another team member ("What you don't understand is . . ." or "He's/she's just trying to take the easy way out."). When aimed at individuals or groups outside of the team ("They won't want to get involved. They're just waiting till they can collect their pension.") it can lead to misguided efforts based on erroneous attributions.

How a team leader can deal with attribution
- Reaffirm prior agreement on the primacy of the scientific approach.
- "That may well explain why they behave the way they do. But how do we know? What has anyone seen or heard that indicates this? Can we confirm that with data?"

Discounts and "Plops" . . .

arise when team members fail to give credit to another's opinions. They are likely to ignore this person's contributions.

- If the attribution is from one member to another, don't let it go by without checking it out. "Jamie, I heard Sal describe your approach as 'catering to the other side.' How would you describe it?"

8. Discounts and "Plops"

We all have certain values or perspectives that are, consciously or unconsciously, important to us. When someone else ignores or ridicules these values, we feel discounted. This discounting can also cause hostility in a team, especially if it happens frequently.

For instance, there will be times in every team when someone makes a statement that "plops." No one acknowledges it, and the discussion picks up on a subject totally irrelevant to the statement, leaving the speaker to wonder why there was no response.

Discounts happen for many reasons. Perhaps the discounted member said something irrelevant to the team's discussion, or did not clearly state the idea. Perhaps the rest of the team missed the meaning in the statements. No matter what the reason, every member deserves the respect and attention of the team. Teams must help discounted members identify and articulate what is important to them.

How a team leader can deal with discounts and plops
- Include training in active listening and other constructive behaviors early in the team's life.
- Support the discounted person. "Nancy, it sounds like that is important to you and we aren't giving it enough consideration"; "I think what Jerry said is worthwhile, and we should spend time on it before we move on"; "Bill, before we move on, is there some part of what you said that you would like the group to discuss?"
- Talk out of the meeting with anyone who frequently discounts, puts down, or ignores previous speakers' statements. Use the guidelines for constructive feedback.

Chapter 6

Wanderlust . . .

happens when team members lose track of the meeting's purpose, or want to avoid a sensitive topic. Discussions then wander off in many directions at once.

9. Wanderlust: Digression and Tangents

The following scenario will probably sound familiar to anyone who has sat in on meetings: A group describing unsuccessful teaching practices is told of how one teacher solved the problem. This reminds someone of how that same teacher solved a problem in another school, which reminds someone else of an incident between that teacher and his/her supervisor, which leads to a discussion of whatever happened to that supervisor, which leads to a discussion of retirement condominiums in Florida, and on and on. When the meeting ends, the team wonders where the time went.

Such wide-ranging, unfocused conversations are an example of wanderlust, our natural tendency to stray from the subject. Sometimes these digressions are innocent tangents from the conversation. But they also happen when the team wants to avoid a subject that it needs to address. In either case, the meeting facilitator is responsible for bringing the conversation back to the meeting agenda.

How a team leader can deal with wanderlust
- Use a written agenda with time estimates for each item; refer to the topic and time when the discussion strays too far.
- Write topics or items on a flipchart and post the pages on the wall where all members can refer to them throughout the discussion.
- Direct the conversation back on track: "We've strayed from the topic, which was _____. The last few comments before we digressed were_____."
- "We've had trouble sticking to this point. Is there something about it that makes it so easy to avoid?"

Feuding Team Members . . .

can disrupt an entire team with their disagreements. Usually these feuds predate the team and are best dealt with outside the team meetings.

10. Feuding Team Members

Sometimes a group becomes a field of combat for members who are vying with each other. Usually, the issue is not the subject they are arguing about, but rather the contest itself. Other members feel like spectators at a sporting match, and fear that if they participate in any disagreement between the pair, they will be swept into the contest on one side or the other. Usually these feuds predate the team, and in all likelihood will outlast it, too. The best way to deal with this situation is to prevent it by carefully selecting team members so that adversaries are never on the same team. If that is impossible, then bring the combatants together before the first meeting to work out some agreement about their behavior.

How a team leader can deal with feuding team members

- When confrontations occur during a meeting, get the adversaries to discuss the issues out of the meeting. Offer to facilitate the discussion.
- Push them to some contract about their behavior (if you agree to G, I will agree to H) or ground rules for managing their differences without disrupting the group.

SUMMARY

For better or for worse, when people work together on an improvement project, more than the project occupies their energies. In this chapter we have discussed the diversity of nonproject issues and concerns, and suggested ways to deal with them. Frequently, mastery of these "people issues" makes the difference between teams that break *through* to fundamental improvements and those that break *down* before they get there. Structured activities presented in Chapter 7 will help teams prevent and avoid many common group problems. There we present activities that help teams start meetings ("warm-ups") or develop into a cohesive group ("team-building exercises").

Chapter 7
Team-Building Activities

Some educational leaders think the team-building dimension of a project is as important as process improvement. One educational system routinely devotes the first several team meetings to team-building activities, convinced there is a payoff in team enthusiasm and efficiency.

Another payoff appears when the project is over: The educational system has a group of teachers, staff, principals, and supervisors with a solid, trusting, working relationship that cuts across departments and roles.

In Chapter 6 we talked about the pressures and loyalties that shape team dynamics, and said there are activities that help teams work through the negative aspects. In this chapter we describe these activities. The chapter begins with a collection of warm-ups, brief 2- to 15-minute activities used at the beginning of meetings to free members from outside distractions so they can focus on the meeting. A selection of team-building exercises fills the remainder of the chapter. The exercises help teams work through common group issues, provide for team members' needs, prevent problems, explore dimensions of the project, and learn more about quality improvement. They require more time than warm-ups, hours rather than minutes, and are appropriate during the first months of a team's efforts.

The activities we present are meant to be guidelines, and perhaps inspire you to create variations more suited to your team. All instructions are written for the meeting facilitator, a role usually played by the team leader.

I. Warm-Ups

Team members come into meetings with a lot of distractions. Just as it is important to stretch muscles before physical exercise, people should stretch their minds before each meeting. A warm-up activity allows a

team to leave behind concerns and ease into the meeting, to gradually focus on its task.

Warm-ups are also just plain fun. They signal a lightening up and give members permission to talk to people they might not normally talk to about things they usually don't talk about. They also encourage a little spontaneity and a bit of adventure. For example, some warm-ups ask participants to talk about their childhood or something important to them. When team members begin talking about their youth or feelings, many facades and poses disappear. Members start letting go of their roles, and can meet each other as equals.

The warm-ups here have been used successfully in many types of groups, but that does not mean they are appropriate for every group. The facilitator, who should be involved in setting agendas, should ask two questions when choosing a warm-up: Does this warm-up challenge the group to a new experience without making them too uncomfortable? And, will I be reasonably comfortable leading this exercise?

When using a warm-up for the first time, you should describe the warm-up to the group and then be the first to do it. This shows team members how to do it and demonstrates that you are not asking them to do something you are unwilling to do yourself. After leading the warm-up, ask who is willing to go next. Then look around the team and wait for a volunteer to go next.

Team Member Introductions

Going around the table, have team members introduce themselves to the group. Everyone tells: name; role in my school system or school; the thing I like best about my role, a recent success in my work, or what I currently find most challenging in my role; and how I got to be on this team. This activity is especially appropriate at the first team meeting.

Paired Introductions

Pair up members who don't know each other well. Have them get acquainted by asking each other questions such as:

- What is your name?
- What is your role?
- How long have you been at the school (district)?
- What got you started here?
- What do you like best about your role?
- How did you become part of this team?
- Do you have a family? What does your spouse do? Children? How old?
- What is your favorite weekend recreation?

Before the meeting, the team leader and quality advisor choose which questions to present, write them on flipcharts, and post the pages where all members can see them. Optional: You can follow the paired introductions by having partners introduce each other to the rest of the group.

Flipchart Introductions

Some team members will have had experience writing on flipcharts in front of a group. But they will have to write on flipcharts during meetings, and will probably be asked to make presentations from time to time. This exercise gives members experience using a flipchart for discussing ideas, and helps them get better acquainted.

Each member takes a turn at the flipchart talking about and writing down the answers to one or more of the following directions (selected in advance by the team leader or quality advisor):

- Tell us the name of your hometown, and describe three or four of its characteristics that you find most memorable.
- List one or two occupations you learned about as a child, and three or four early impressions of each.

Chapter 7

- Draw a "picture" of either your childhood or present "family" (include neighbors, pets, and relatives).

First Job

Working in pairs or with the whole group, members talk about one of their first jobs. Since members are learning about quality, each of them may want to talk about:

- What parts of the job didn't make sense then (and still don't make sense).
- What impression I have of the principals, supervisors, and other administrators and what I learned from them.
- What I learned about the "working world" from that job.

Background

Have members list background information they would like to know about each other, such as age, marital status, years living in this area, hometown, etc. List these items on a flipchart. Then have team members take turns answering these questions.

Superlatives

Ask members to study the composition of the group and silently decide on a superlative adjective (youngest, tallest, baldest, grandmotherliest) that describes them in contrast to the others. Then go around the table sharing adjectives and testing the accuracy of people's perceptions.

Hopes and Concerns

Have team members reflect on their hopes for this project, and their concerns about the outcome. Encourage them to think as broadly as possible. They may write down their expectations if they want.

After individual reflection, divide the group into pairs, and have partners share answers. Then have each pair share answers with the team. Record all responses on flipcharts.

When all pairs have taken their turn, have the entire group discuss what the team or organization can do to make the hopes come true, and what can be done to prevent anything negative from happening.

"What I Want for Myself Out of This"

Once team members clearly understand the purpose of the project, it is useful to explore what each individual would like to see the team achieve over and above the team goals.

Allow members 3 to 5 minutes to list personal goals for their participation in the project. What do they want to learn or do, and why? Suggest they consider personal goals such as getting to know new people, exploring other aspects of the learning environment; feeling good about themselves as educators; learning quality principles, statistical methods, and other tools for problem solving; and other goals important to themselves.

Have each one read the list to the team. You may choose to just listen, discuss the ideas among the team, or record and save them.

Member Mapping

In preparation for this activity, find or draw a map showing the school, classroom, or office area the team is studying. Post it on the wall before the meeting. Then have members initial (or otherwise mark) the areas that they or their students use. After everyone has taken a turn, the team studies the map. Are there any patterns? How do members' and their students' roles and activities interact? Are significant areas or activities unrepresented or over-represented in this team? What else does this map show?

Group Conversation

Prior to the meeting, make a list of incomplete sentences, "conversation starters." You may use the list below, devise your own, or use a combination. Either post the list on a flipchart or write it on one sheet of paper that can be passed around the table.

Possible conversation starters include:
- Anybody will work hard if . . .
- People who run things should be . . .
- I would like to be . . .
- One thing I like about myself is . . .
- Nothing is so frustrating as . . .
- The teacher I liked best was a person who . . .
- Ten years from now, I . . .
- Every winning team needs . . .
- I take pride in . . .
- If you want to see me get mad . . .
- A rewarding role is one that . . .

Go around the table and have one team member at a time start a conversation on one topic, focusing on what this person has witnessed or experienced rather than on abstract principles. The whole team discusses the idea; when that conversation is done, the next person selects a new topic.

Alternatively, break the group into pairs or threes and distribute copies of the list to each group. Have these small groups do this exercise for 10 to 15 minutes. Each group then reports back to the entire team.

Drawing a Classroom or Office . . .

often helps team members come up with creative solutions to problems caused by the physical limitations of their work spaces.

If I Were Still at My Daily Workplace . . .

As a way to get to know each other's roles in the educational system, have members say what they would be doing if they weren't in the team meeting. Allow them to go into detail; other members can probe for more information. (Alternately, this can be a quick go-around of short, one-sentence explanations.)

After everyone's role has been discussed, turn the tide and suggest that members forget about their usual responsibilities until the meeting ends. Create an image of leaving their work outside the meeting room door as if hung on a coat rack; members can retrieve them when they leave the meeting.

Draw a Classroom/Office

Distribute paper and markers, and give each member 5 to 10 minutes to draw an ideal classroom, office, meeting room, or other appropriate environment. Tape the pictures on a wall and invite everyone to walk through the "gallery" to view the drawings. Discuss the pictures, clarifying and elaborating on the ideas they represent. Guide the discussion to issues of quality, process problems, problems in the learning environment, etc.

Team Name

Ask each person to write down as many names as possible for the team, at least five. Have members read their lists while you jot down the ideas on a flipchart. Add other ideas as they come up. Discuss the suggestions and choose a team name informally, or "sleep on it" and defer the decision to a later meeting.

Chapter 7

Common Denominators

Pair up members who don't know each other well. Have them search for traits they have in common that make them *unique* from other team members. For example, acceptable answers would be that both can wiggle their ears, have children born on the same day, or traveled to California/Europe for the first time this July. However, saying both are human beings or are participating in this training session would not make them *unique* since all participants share those traits. The answers may not be stated negatively; they cannot say, for example, that neither has ever broken a leg.

If there is time, form new pairs and repeat the exercise. At the end, have members share answers with the whole team.

II. Team-Building Exercises

In its early stages, a project team can benefit from exercises that help members develop productive working relationships. The exercises here let members practice working as a team so they will be more effective when they begin their improvement-related tasks: studying a process, gathering and analyzing data, preparing reports, and so forth. Often teams will find the information they get from these exercises is useful later in the project.

Though longer than warm-ups, most team-building exercises can be done in a single meeting (some will require the entire meeting). The instructions for the following exercises are generally written for the team leader, quality advisor, or other meeting facilitator (exceptions are noted in specific exercises).

Footnote: One other warm-up ("The Check-In") was given in Chapter 4, p. 4-30. "Superlatives" and "Background" are adapted from *A Handbook of Structured Experiences for Human Relations Training, Volume IV.* J. William Pfeiffer and John E. Jones, editors, La Jolla, CA: University Associates, Inc., 1975. "Group Conversation" is adapted from Volume II of the same series (1973). This annual publication is an excellent source of various group activities.

Exercise 1
Disruptive Group Behavior

Time 1.5 to 3 hours

Overview

In this exercise, the team agrees on methods for dealing with group problems that members choose to discuss. Through this exercise, the team develops a common understanding of acceptable team behavior. Team members decide how far a leader or facilitator can go in dealing with a problem, and how much disruptive behavior they will allow. Each member thus knows, and even helps determine in advance, the consequences of disruptive behavior.

This exercise is particularly effective when used after the second or third meeting, when members know at least a little about each other. It can also be used when disruptive patterns begin to develop in the team activities. This way, the team is involved in its own self-government from the beginning of the project, an important value to establish early on.

Instructions

1. Preparation.
Have a flipchart or chalkboard available, and pencil and paper for each member.

2. Introduce the exercise.
The goal is to focus the team on behavior that interrupts group activities or hinders the team's progress. While people may witness the same behavior and interpret it differently, some seeing it as a problem and others not, usually they can agree on whether it is disruptive, that is, whether it interrupts work the group is doing. Introduce this exercise as a tool used to establish guidelines for conducting business at meetings and to develop methods for dealing with disruptive behavior.

3. Brainstorm.
Direct the team to brainstorm about behaviors that could disrupt meetings or other team activities. Remind the team that in brainstorming there are no right or wrong answers. Do not critique responses. Crazy or silly answers are OK and can help the process. (You may even encourage these responses.)

Start with each member taking a turn giving one response at a time (about two to three rounds) until ideas start to snowball. Record the ideas on a flipchart or chalkboard as they are given. Do not change the wording. Include everything from minor disruption (noisily flipping through a stack of paper) to major disruptions (holding side conversations, walking out of the room, coming in late). Continue until all ideas have been exhausted. (See p. 2-41 for more instructions on brainstorming.)

4. Select one behavior.
Reduce the brainstormed list to the two or three most important types of disruptive behavior. This can be accomplished through multivoting (described on p. 2-43). Take a vote to decide which to discuss first.

5. Discuss types of responses to disruptive behavior.
Introduce the group to the concept of graded intervention—that the response to a problem can be anything from no action to confrontation in a meeting. Focus only on three levels: preventive measures, minimal intervention, high intervention. (These are adapted from material in Chapter 6, starting on p. 6-30.)

6. Discuss possible responses to this behavior.
Write the type of disruptive behavior at the top of a flipchart or chalkboard. Divide the rest of the page or board into three columns and label each in order:

#1 Preventive Measures
#2 Minimal Intervention
#3 Higher Intervention

Start with column 1, Preventive Measures. Have the team brainstorm possible ways to prevent the disruptive behavior. Record the ideas in the appropriate column. When the list for this column is complete, discuss the pros and cons of each idea. This discussion is extremely important. As the members discuss the brainstormed interventions, they are sorting out their values on such issues as "How much response to a problem is too much response." Often after discussions of this type, the team implicitly agrees on what behaviors are acceptable or unacceptable in the group. Reach consensus on which ideas best represent the team position on preventing this behavior.

Repeat this process for Minimal Intervention (column 2) and then Higher Intervention (column 3), each time reaching a consensus on the group's position about dealing with the behavior at that level of intervention.

7. Review the team decisions.
After all columns have been discussed, summarize the team's position on this disruptive behavior. Ask members if the summary is accurate. Discuss and revise the answers until the team is satisfied.

8. Repeat for another disruptive behavior.
Return to Step 5 and repeat the process on another type of disruptive behavior.

9. Critique.
When the team has discussed the two or three behaviors chosen in Step 4, critique the entire exercise.

Note: This exercise may also be applied directly to a classroom situation.

Footnote: This exercise was developed by John Criqui when he was the statistical coordinator for Microcircuit Engineering Corporation of Mount Holly, New Jersey. Criqui has had greatest success in using this exercise to help project teams develop a greater awareness of acceptable group behavior.

Suggested format for flipcharts:

Problem being discussed:		
Preventive Measures	Minimal Intervention	Higher Intervention

Exercise 1—Disruptive Group Behavior
Sample Filled-in Format

Results from a team that discussed problems between feuding members.

Preventive Measures	Minimal Intervention	Higher Intervention
Most feuds predate the team. One way to prevent disruptions is for the leader to know about the feud in advance and leave one of its members off the list of team appointment candidates. If this is impossible, then the feuding parties should be brought together prior to any meeting of the team so they can decide how they might work together on this team. Agreement to the Scientific Approach will force them to substantiate their conflicting opinions with data.	*Leader:* Talk to the feuding parties, either alone or together, but outside of the group. "When you two go at each other, I feel angry. It wastes the group's time and makes it difficult for anyone in the group to participate in the discussion without appearing to choose sides."	*Leader:* Set aside a meeting (with or without the combatants) in which the team discusses what to do about the problem. Ask the feuders to suggest ways to intervene. Agree on a process or mechanism to end the feuding (if not the feud). Alternatively, when the behavior appears, the facilitator may say: "Mr. Hatfield, state in one sentence the point you're trying to make on this issue without reference to anyone who might disagree with you . . . Mr. McCoy, do likewise." Then let the others on the team give their one-sentence statements. Record all the sentences on a flipchart and start from there.

Exercise 2
The Responsibility Matrix

Time: 1 to 1.5 hours

Overview

In Chapters 3 and 4, we identified tasks to be performed in preparing for a project and running meetings. The responsibility for most of these activities belongs to the team leader, quality advisor, or a team member. However, the team will run into many tasks that do not clearly belong to any one person or role. This exercise helps the group identify and assign the responsibility for these tasks. (Another tool for this purpose, "The Planning Grid," is described in Appendix 3.)

Instructions

1. Identify tasks.

Have the team list activities not clearly assigned to a person or group of people. Use the following examples to spur your own discussion (some of these may already be assigned in your team). Aim for a list of no more than 20 items.

Meeting responsibilities
- Sending out meeting material, agendas, and minutes
- Setting up the meeting room; cleaning up after meetings
- Taking minutes
- Facilitating meetings
- Arranging meetings with leadership team
- Helping the team when it's stuck
- Maintaining files
- Leading warm-ups
- Leading the meeting critique
- Containing digression and monopolizing; using other discussion skills

Project responsibilities
- Maintaining the picture book format
- Gathering data
- Plotting charts
- Maintaining files

Education/Training responsibilities
- Teaching problem-solving tools
- Teaching project-management skills
- Teaching meeting-management skills
- Teaching quality concepts
- Technology to assist team with problem-solving tools

2. Create a matrix.

Set up one or two flipchart pages to correspond to the matrix shown (next page). Then list the tasks you identified in the TASK column.

3. Work through the matrix.

Work through the matrix one task at a time, having each member mark (with an X or initials) the column representing the group or person he or she thinks is responsible for that task. (Note: Have each member use a different color marker when marking the columns to simplify later discussion.) Do this for every task listed.

4. Discuss the answers.

Discuss the answers, again working through the matrix one task at a time. Do not move to the next item until the team has reached consensus on which person or group is responsible for that task. You can decide to rotate a responsibility among people or groups, but you must clearly set down procedures for how and when to switch.

Exercise 2—The Responsibility Matrix
Sample Matrix

Instructions: Copy this form onto flipcharts. Enter tasks in the left column, then have team members mark who they think is responsible for each task. Discuss the answers as a group, and make final decisions regarding the responsibilities.

TASK	WHO			
	Team Leader	All Team Members	Quality Advisor	Leadership Team

Exercise 3
Observing and Interviewing in Pairs

Time: 1.5 to 2 hours for the excursion, 0.5 hour per pair for reporting and discussion

Overview

In this exercise team members pair up, tour a school, classroom, or office, and interview several staff members. They then return to the group and report on what they have discovered. Often the places assigned are in some way related to the project and involve internal customers or suppliers. This is an excellent way for team members to meet co-workers they may not have otherwise met, and to see how the process they are studying relates to other parts of the school and district.

Instructions

1. Preparation.

Review the team's mission and think about what other schools, departments, learning environments, or work areas could affect or be affected by this project. Decide which areas, both inside and outside the building in which you are meeting, the team should visit. Note: Administrators or supervisors of the areas selected for observation will probably be uneasy if this is done without their understanding and approval. Therefore, before selecting an area, explain this exercise and its purpose to the appropriate administrator and obtain his or her permission. Print up copies of the observation instructions (Step 4) and the interviewing instructions (Step 5).

2. Set assignments.

Divide the team into pairs, preferably putting together people who don't know each other well. Assign each pair an area to observe. Hand out copies of the observation and interview instructions to each pair.

3. Review assignments.

Have each pair of observers take approximately 15 minutes to review the observation instructions and the interview instructions and plan their observing. Give them 45 minutes, from the time they leave the meeting room, to complete the activity. Have each pair note what time they should return to the meeting room.

4. Observation instructions.

When the observers reach their assigned areas, they should first just watch what is going on. Before they leave the area, however, they should jot down their thoughts and reactions.

- View the area assigned with the eyes of a newcomer: How would this area look to someone unfamiliar with its appearance?

- Note the following: Is the area messy or neat? Congested or spacious? Chaotic or organized? Is it attractive, plain, or unsightly? Do the displayed materials reflect the lessons being taught? Colorful or bland? Is it noisy or peaceful? Fast-paced or leisurely? Welcoming or uninviting? What do you observe that leads you to those conclusions?

- Look for signs of the application of key quality principles and concepts and the application of the tools for problem solving. Is there any work that would be unnecessary if there were no problems in the process? Is there evidence that the instruction, curriculum, assessment, and administrative processes are in alignment?

- If people are present, note the following: Are they friendly, informal, aloof, or disagreeable with each other? Do they talk to each other? Look at each other? Do they work together or separately? Are they near to each other or far apart?

- Take notes on anything else of interest you observe.

5. Interview teachers or other staff.

Randomly select a few teachers or other staff members in the area. Introduce yourselves and explain that you belong to a team trying to better understand what happens in the school or office. Ask if they have a few minutes to answer questions. If they say no, thank them for their time and try someone else.

Possible questions to ask: What do you like best about working here? If you could improve one thing here, what would it be? When you and your peers notice problems or think of improvements, is there a way for you to communicate these ideas to your administrators? Are they ever acknowledged? How?

6. Reporting.

After the observers return to the meeting room, ask each pair to report what they saw or heard, and any conclusions they drew from the experience. Give each pair 10 to 15 minutes to report.

7. Assessment.

Lead a discussion on the following points (you may do this either after each pair reports or after all the reports):

- How did each pair divide up the task? How did they decide who did what?

- Did the pair have any trouble with operational definitions? (See p. 2-32.) Did both agree, for example, on what was meant by "messy" or "congestion" or "waste"?

- Did they get any "bad news" responses, such as negative comments from people about their roles, the educational environment, or this inquiry?

- How should team members respond when people distrust the motives for interviews and inquiries?

How might you prevent distrust of your inquiries the next time you do something like this?

- Would this exercise be different if members had done it alone rather than with a partner? More difficult? Easier?

- Was anyone surprised? Did participants learn anything they didn't expect to learn?

- Comment on each other's reports: How closely did the team stick to observation and factual data rather than inferences, judgments, or opinions?

Exercise 4
The Living Flowchart

Time: 1.5 to 3 hours

Overview

In this exercise, the people who work with a process meet and talk to each other as customers and suppliers. They discuss issues such as what they want or get from the steps of a process. This exercise helps participants identify the basic steps and substeps of a process, and explore the interdependence of all process steps. It works best, and is most educational, if the participants are asked to "represent" steps with which they are familiar, but that are not part of their main jobs.

Instructions

1. Preparation.
You may involve anywhere from 5 to 30 people in this exercise. Have several flipcharts or posterboards, post-its, and plenty of markers available.

2. Select a process to discuss.
If this activity is done by a project team—or a project team and its leadership team—the process used should be the process targeted for improvement. If you choose to involve a more diverse group of people, pick a process known by most of them. The quality advisor, team leader, or some other designated facilitator should actively lead the participants through this activity.

3. Flowchart the process, Part 1.
Identify the four to five major steps of the process, what would go at the top of a top-down flowchart (see p. 2-23). If there are fewer than eight people involved in this activity, have the entire group work together on this step. If there are more than eight people, divide them into two or more groups of about four to five members each. Have the small groups report on their versions of the process, then have everyone discuss the different versions until you come up with one version that is best.

4. Assign the major process steps.
Ask one or more people to represent each major step (and substep) you identified. The meeting facilitator may either assign steps to the participants, or let people select a step.

> Note: If participants are allowed to pick the step they want to represent, it cannot be one they work with every day. Rather, have them choose one they think they understand or know something about. This is important so the participants will begin to see the process, and their own roles in particular, from different viewpoints.

5. Assemble the flowchart.
Arrange the people or groups in the room so they represent the general sequence of steps in the actual process (see the cartoon on the facing page). That is, the person or people representing the first step will be at one end of the room; the people representing the second activity will be next to them; and so forth.

6. Flowchart the process, Part 2.
Each individual or small group takes its step, the one they represent, and divides it into four to six other substeps. These other steps would be the same as the columns in a top-down flowchart. If you have small groups, they can assign individual members to represent other substeps (the same way the small group represents a major step).

CURRICULUM

TEXTS AND OTHER RESOURCES

DESIGNING CURRICULUM

DISSEMINATION

PILOT STUDIES

PRODUCTION OF CURRICULUM

IMPLEMENTATION

TRAINING

7. Let the system talk.

The facilitator creates a lively interchange of ideas between participants by working through the process in no particular order. He or she chooses a step or substep and asks the person or group representing it one or two of the following questions:

- What contribution do you make to this overall process?

- Who is your internal customer? What do you believe they expect from you? How do you know?

- How do you keep in touch with what the external customer or learner wants?

- Who is your internal supplier? Pick one or two of your internal suppliers and tell them what you need from them. How could they make your life miserable?

The entire group should discuss the answers this person or group gives. After some discussion, shift the focus to another step or substep, asking its representatives the same kinds of questions. Whenever discussion slows down, ask questions of a different group. Keep shifting the focus unpredictably to keep group members involved and on their toes.

8. Wrap up the discussion.

After the participants have worked through most (if not all) of the substeps, everyone discusses the following:

- What did we learn from this activity? What did individuals learn about how their roles do or should function?

- What inadequacies in the real process came to light?

Exercise 5
Obstacles to Quality Improvement

Time: 2 to 2.5 hours

Overview

It is natural for team members to sometimes feel that they are banging their heads against a wall and getting nowhere. To overcome these feelings, have team members discuss the philosophy of Quality Leadership so they can identify obstacles that prevent them from reaching their goals.

The following instructions are written for an improvement project team of five or six members that divides into sub-groups of two or three people. However, this exercise is effective with many more participants, and you may want to invite others to join in this exercise or perhaps conduct this exercise jointly with other project teams. You can use this exercise comfortably with up to 17 small groups of no more than six people each, with each group assigned one or two items for discussion.

Instructions (For the quality advisor)

1. Preparation.
Determine how many groups will be involved. Make copies of the instructions on p. 7-21 and the "Obstacles to Quality Improvement" forms (p. 7-19) so each group will have one for each topic discussed (see Step 3 to determine this number). Review the instructions below and decide which of Deming's 14 Points and which corners of the Joiner Triangle each group will discuss.

2. Review the Joiner Triangle and Deming's 14 Points. (45 to 60 min.)

With the whole group assembled:
- Explain that the Joiner Triangle and Deming's 14 Points represent changes seen by some quality experts as necessary for an educational system to meet the needs of students, prosper, and prepare students for a bright future in today's global market.
- Go through each corner of the Joiner Triangle (p. 1-4) and answer questions to clarify the message of the Triangle (do not yet discuss the pros and cons of that message).
- Instruct team members to read the 14 Points (see p. 2-4 to 2-7) and answer questions to clarify their meaning (again without discussing the pros and cons).

3. Assign Points and Corners. (10 min.)
Hand out copies of the instructions (on p. 7-21 and repeated below) and answer any questions. Each group will discuss at least one Triangle corner: The number of Points discussed depends on the number of groups. (For example, if there are three groups, one group will discuss four of the 14 Points, and the other two groups will each discuss five of the Points; if there are five groups, one group will only get two Points, while the other four will each get three Points.) Note: If there are many small groups, allow for duplication so each group discusses at least four or five items (one of which is a corner).

Assign Points and corners in a round robin, continuing until all items have been assigned: "Group One, take Points 1 and 7, and the 'all one team' corner; Group Two, take Points 2 and 8. . . ."

4. Identify Obstacles to Quality Improvement (10 to 15 min. per assigned point and triangle corner)
Have groups complete the top half of a form (shown right) for each Point and corner assigned to them. Part I of the instructions they will receive is as follows:

A. Review the corner of the Joiner Triangle assigned to your small group. Ask what will make it difficult to implement this corner of the triangle in your educational system. Record these obstacles on a flipchart. Repeat for each Deming Point assigned to you.

Exercise 5
Obstacles to Quality Improvement: Sample Form

Instructions: Create a form like this the size of a half-page. Make enough copies so each group will receive at least one for each Point and corner it will discuss (they may need more, so be sure there are plenty of extras). One group fills out Part 1 of this form for each asigned item, then hands the forms to another group, which completes the second half.

Part 1: The Obstacle
The first group fills out the top part of this form, leaving the "To:" space blank until instructed to fill it in.

From: _____   To: _____

Which Deming Point or Joiner Triangle corner is being discussed?

Describe an obstacle related to this Point or Corner. (Enter only one per page. Use a separate form for other obstacles.)

Part 2: Overcoming the Obstacle
Filled out by the second group.

Describe ways to overcome this obstacle.

B. Review your lists and select three or four items that your group agrees are the most substantial obstacles to implementing quality in your educational system.

C. Fill out Part 1 of an "Obstacles to Quality Improvement" form for these main obstacles as follows:

FROM: Enter the names of the people in your group.

TO: Leave this space blank for now.

WHICH POINT . . . Indicate which Triangle corner (by name) or Deming Point (by number) you are describing on this sheet.

DESCRIBE ONE . . . Write here one obstacle you identified for the specific Point or corner. Leave the bottom half of the form blank.

Take a new form and fill out Part 1 for the next obstacle you identified for that point or corner. Repeat until you have a form for each of the three or four substantial obstacles your group identified for each assigned Point or corner.

D. Divide your partially completed "Obstacles to Quality Improvement" forms into stacks, one for each of the other groups. Try to mix Points and corners in each stack. When you have assembled a stack for each of the other groups, write the names of the group members after the word TO: on each form in their stack. DO NOT deliver these stacks to the other groups until you are instructed to do so by the facilitator.

Chapter 7

5. Deliver the stacks. (10 min.)

When all groups have completed the top halves of their forms and separated them into piles, instruct them to deliver the stacks to the appropriate group members.

6. Identify ways to overcome the obstacles. (5 min. for each form in a team's stack)

Each group should have the forms they received from other groups. Tell them to review Part II of the instructions for the "Obstacles to Quality Improvement" forms. They will review the forms one at a time, discuss the obstacle described, think of ways to overcome that obstacle, and decide which method they think is best. Then have them enter that response legibly on the lower half of the form, continuing on until they have completed each form in their stack.

7. Reports and Discussion. (Approximately 60 min.)

After all groups have completed Step 6, select one corner of the Joiner Triangle and one of Deming's 14 Points and invite any group that discussed an obstacle to this item to report. The group describes the obstacle and summarizes the suggestions for overcoming it. When that group is done, ask if other groups discussed obstacles to that item. Allow the entire team to discuss the answers as you go along. Move to the next Point or corner. Continue until reports are made on each obstacle to each corner of the triangle and each of the 14 Points assigned. Allow the entire group to discuss some of the more controversial or deeply felt issues that emerge from the reports. Sometimes this exercise produces too much information to report in the time available. If this is the case, tell the groups to report on only the obstacles or ways of overcoming obstacles that stand out as most important in their judgment.

A Final Note: Save the completed forms! The insights and opinions generated in this exercise may be invaluable to others in the educational system. The implementation coordinator and administrators of your school district might benefit from these discussions. If team members are uncomfortable having their names on the forms, remove the names. Send the forms, with or without names, to people in your school system responsible for quality implementation.

Exercise 5—Obstacles to Quality Improvement
Instructions for the Obstacle to Quality Improvement Forms

Instructions: Each participant should receive a copy of these instructions.

Instructions for filling out the Obstacle to Quality Improvement forms

Part I

A. Review the corner of the Joiner Triangle assigned to your small group. Ask what will make it difficult to implement this corner of the triangle in your educational system. Record these obstacles on a flipchart. Repeat for each Deming Point assigned to you.

B. Review your lists and select three or four items that your group agrees are the most substantial obstacles to implementing quality in your educational system.

C. Fill out Part 1 of an "Obstacle to Quality Improvement" form for these main obstacles as follows:

FROM: Enter the names of the people in your group.

TO: Leave this space blank for now.

WHICH POINT... Indicate which Triangle corner (by name) or Deming Point (by number) you are describing on this sheet.

DESCRIBE ONE... Write here one obstacle you identified for the specific point or corner. Leave the bottom half of the form blank.

Take a new form and fill out Part 1 for the next obstacle you identified for that Point or corner. Repeat until you have a form for each of the three or four substantial obstacles your group identified for each assigned Point and corner.

D. Divide your partially completed "Obstacle to Quality Improvement" forms into stacks, one for each of the other groups. Try to mix Points and corners in each stack. When you have assembled a stack for each of the other groups, write the names of the group members after the word TO: on each form in their stack. DO NOT deliver the stacks to the other groups until you are instructed to do so by the facilitator.

Part II

Review each form you received. Discuss the obstacles one at a time and, for each, discuss ways to overcome the obstacle. Reach agreement on what you think is the best way to overcome this obstacle and enter that response legibly on the lower half of the form. Do the same for the next obstacle until you have completed each form.

Exercise 6

Identifying the Consequences of Management by Results

Time: 1.5 to 2 hours (one full team meeting)

Overview

Most educational systems are so used to operating under Management by Results that it is very, very difficult for staff to fully appreciate the difference that Quality Leadership can make. After all, if you have to spend your time fighting fires, there isn't time to prevent them. Even in school systems where Management by Results appears to work well, there is always room for improvement.

We could spend pages and pages recounting stories of how other people distort systems and processes to meet deadlines or arbitrary numerical goals. But hearing what's happened in other schools will not convince you or others in your school system that you have similar problems. This exercise is designed to help you start reexamining how work gets done in your school system; to open your eyes to the opportunities for improvement that exist in your own learning environment.

One caution before you proceed: Use this exercise as a constructive discussion of what team members can do to improve the learning environment. Do not use it as an excuse to point fingers at any individual or group.

Instructions

1. Preparation.

The team leader provides each team member with a copy of Dr. Deming's 14 Points (pp. 2-4 to 2-7). Set up a flipchart to correspond with the chart shown on the next page. (You may also hand out smaller versions to team members.) Using this chart as a guide, write down the column headings on the top of a flipchart page. You will use this chart to record answers given in Steps 3 to 6. Either prior to or at the beginning of the meeting, have team members review the description of Management by Results and its problems.

2. Discuss examples.

As a team, discuss how the examples of Management by Results described in the text relate to your school system. What kinds of behavior have team members seen that are similar to the ones we describe? Have each person take a few minutes to write down examples of fire fighting or process distortion they have seen, without naming those involved. When everyone is finished, share answers among the group and record them on the flipchart.

3. Identify potential improvements.

After the list of examples is complete, identify the behaviors or situations that team members believe they can improve. Hold a multivote (p. 2-43) to identify the ones that generate the most concern in the group.

4. List the highest priority items.

List the items that scored highest in the left-hand corner of the flipchart. Team members may also fill in blank copies of the chart if they wish.

5. Compare with Dr. Deming's 14 Points.

Compare the behavior described in this example with Dr. Deming's 14 Points. Which point(s) does the behavior violate? Record ideas in the appropriate column of the flipchart.

6. Discuss problems caused by the situations.

Discuss what problems arise because of this situation or behavior. Can you see any pattern in when the behavior or problem appears?

Exercise 6—The Consequences of Management by Results
Sample format for recording answers

Instructions: Use this format to record team answers on flipcharts.

Example of behavior seen under Management By Results.	Which of Dr. Deming's 14 Points does this violate?	What problems does this behavior create?	Alternatives that are more consistent with Quality Leadership.

7. Discuss alternate ways to deal with problems.
Discuss alternate ways of dealing with these problems, particularly ways that are consistent with Quality Leadership principles. What are the long-term goals? What are some short-term steps that will take you along that path? What can you as a team do to improve the situation? (Part of your answer may be meeting with administrators or supervisors to discuss the group's conclusions.)

8. Repeat discussion for each example.
Repeat Steps 3 through 6 for as many examples as you can fit in the meeting. Reserve 15 minutes at the end to discuss patterns you have found and to form plans for following up on the ideas generated in the discussion.

Exercise 7

Information Hunt—A Preliminary Look at a Process

Time: Each team member will put in 15 to 60 min. for each question; allow 15 min. per question for team discussion. This time may be spread over several weeks.

Overview

A series of questions is presented on the following page. Exploring the process to find the answers will introduce team members to the process you're studying and let you identify key process characteristics and conditions. The goal is to get the best answers you can in the time allotted. The team may decide to dig further, and spread this exercise over several meetings. (Note: The information gathered will be useful background should the team ever use the strategy, "Describe a Process," p. 5-52.)

Instructions

1. Preparation and start-up.

Copy the list of questions on p. 7-25 and hand it out to each team member. Select several questions that seem most relevant to the process you are studying. Don't attempt to answer the entire list of questions the first time around. You can work through them over several weeks. Divide the chosen questions among team members, who will work either individually or in pairs.

2. Investigation.

Have individuals or pairs answer their assigned questions independently. Tell them to seek a balance between carefully gathering objective information and using educated opinions. They should use available data to answer the questions if they are fairly certain the data are reliable; avoid additional data collection unless it can be done easily. They should seek opinions from people involved in the process who are in the best position to know the answers.

3. Discussion.

As members of pairs complete their answers, have them discuss their findings with the entire team. If you are spreading the assignment over several weeks, reserve time at team meetings to review the assignments completed by that meeting.

4. Complete the list.

As members or pairs complete the assignment, give them another question to answer. Continue until all relevant questions have been answered and discussed.

Exercise 7—Information Hunt
Questions to Ask about a Process

Instructions: Give a copy of these questions to each team member.

The process being studied is_____

_____.

(All the following questions refer to this process)

1. Who are its external customers? What individuals, groups, or systems outside our educational system rely on or could benefit from this process? Who has (or could have) expectations about this process?

2. How do we know what the external customers, including future employers, like or don't like about this process? What satisfies or dissatisfies them?

3. Who are its internal customers? It's learners? Describe those within our educational system who do (or could) rely on the successful operation of this process or the desired learning outcome.

4. How do we determine what the learners and other internal customers like or don't like about this process? What satisfies or dissatisfies them?

5. What are the operational definitions of quality in this process or of desired learning outcomes? What specifically determines whether the process is working well or poorly?

6. What data are kept regarding quality? Who uses this information? How do they use it? Are the formats suited to how they are used?

7. What are the most common mistakes that occur? What is the operational definition for each mistake? What proportion of these is commonly assumed to be a teacher's or staff member's fault? What proportion do we usually attribute to the system? How do people arrive at these conclusions?

8. By what process do we inspect, evaluate, and report problems regarding:
    A. Planning required for this process
    B. Incoming materials, supplies, and information critical to this process
    C. The process itself
    D. The outcomes

9. List the critical elements of this process: technology, people, time, information, etc.

10. List the suppliers of curriculum, instruction, or materials of each critical element.

11. Describe the educational system's procedures for purchasing materials or ingredients brought in from outside the school. To what extent is "low bid" a governing factor in our purchasing decisions?

12. Describe the impact of the most common mistakes in the process. What do they cost in time, money, or staff pride?

13. Who is responsible for quality in this process? Who is responsible for detecting mistakes? Who is responsible for identifying and correcting the causes of mistakes?

Exercise 8
Meeting Skills Checklist

Time: 30 to 45 minutes

Overview

Having team members evaluate their meeting *skills* is an excellent alternative to evaluating the meeting itself. This exercise may precede or follow activities involving role behavior, such as the Responsibility Matrix (p. 7-12).

Use this exercise after the team has had four or five meetings and has begun to establish patterns and routines of behavior.

Instructions

1. Preparation.
Make enough copies of the "Meeting Skills Checklist" (facing page) to distribute to the team. On a flipchart, draw 21 rows and 4 columns. Label the first column "Behavior" and the last three "Never," "Occasionally," and "Often," in sequence. Number each row and copy keywords from the corresponding sentences provided (unless you want to copy down the entire sentence!).

2. Fill out forms.
Hand out copies of the checklist and have each member individually complete one.

3. Compile answers.
Transfer individual ratings to the previously prepared flipchart that duplicates the checklist. Have each member enter a checkmark or initials on the line under the appropriate column.

4. Discuss the answers.
Any surprises? Which areas seem to be weakest? What can you do to help yourselves and each other? Should you do this in the future to see whether there is a shift? When?

> **Note**
> Team members can also use this checklist on their own so they can work to improve the skills each is weakest in.

Exercise 8—Meeting Skills Checklist

Instructions: Either photocopy this page and the next page or create your own version. Have team members work through it, first individually and then as a team.

Behavior	Never	Occasion-ally	Often
1. I suggest a procedure for the group to follow, or a method for organizing the task.			
2. I suggest a new idea, new activity, new problem, or a new course of action.			
3. I attempt to bring the group back to the agenda when joking, personal stories, or irrelevant talk goes on too long.			
4. I suggest, when there is some confusion, that the group make an outline or otherwise organize a plan for completing the activity.			
5. I initiate attempts to redefine goals, problems, or outcomes when things become hazy or confusing.			
6. I elaborate on issues with concise examples, illustrations.			
7. I suggest resource people to contact and bring in materials.			
8. I present the reasons behind my opinions.			
9. I ask others for information and/or opinions.			
10. I ask for the significance and/or implications of facts and opinions.			
11. I see and point out relationships between facts and opinions.			
12. I ask a speaker to explain the reasoning or what tools were used to lead him or her to a particular conclusion.			

Exercise 8—Meeting Skills Checklist, continued

Behavior	Never	Occasion-ally	Often
13. I relate my comments to previous contributions.			
14. I pull together and summarize various ideas presented.			
15. I test to see if everyone agrees with, or understands, the issue being discussed, or the decision being made.			
16. I summarize the progress the group has made.			
17. I encourage other members to participate and try to unobtrusively involve quiet members.			
18. I actively support others when I think their point of view is important.			
19. I try to find areas of agreement in conflicting points of view and try to address the cause of the problem (e.g., "How could we change our solution so that you could support it?" or "It sounds to me that we all agree to X, Y and Z").			
20. I use appropriate humor to reduce tension in the group.			
21. I listen attentively to others' ideas and contributions.			
22. I use appropriate technology.			

Exercise 9
Discussing Your Mission

Time: 1 to 1.5 hours, plus some preparation time

Overview

A team that understands its mission can determine its goals more easily. The primary purpose of this exercise, therefore, is to have a team explore its mission in depth. However, this is also a chance for members other than the team leader and quality advisor to get experience planning and facilitating meetings.

Two team members—and we suggest using people other than the team leader and quality advisor—plan and run a meeting to discuss the mission statement. The objectives are two-fold: to understand the mission, and to learn what planning and facilitating involve.

The format for this exercise is a combination of the regular meeting agenda items (p. 4-34) and the Plan-Do-Check-Act strategy (p. 5-44). You can easily adapt this combination to discuss other important issues.

Instructions

(for the team members planning the meeting)

TASK: Your task is to convene a meeting with your group to discuss your team's mission.

1. Plan the meeting.

A. Review the meeting skills discussed in Chapter 4, and the discussion of roles in Chapter 3.

B. Decide when and where the meeting will be held (if outside regular meeting time).

C. Clarify roles: The two roles you must fill are facilitator and scribe. You may switch the roles during the meeting, but each turn should last at least 30 minutes. The facilitator runs the meeting, keeps the meeting focused, and moderates discussion. The scribe keeps track of time and records notes on flipcharts.

Optional: You may ask the team leader or quality advisor to be an observer during the meeting. Observers evaluate the meeting process; they don't judge meeting content. You could also ask an observer to give you feedback on your skills as facilitator.

D. Select a warm-up, either one described earlier in this chapter or one of your own.

E. Decide how to structure the meeting discussion. The procedure on the following page is offered as a guide.

2. "Do" and "Check" the meeting and discussion.
Carry out the plan, which is the "Do" activity in the Plan-Do-Check-Act cycle. Try to stay close to your agenda. Make sure you evaluate the meeting and review the discussions. This is the "Check" step. (Refer to the meeting evaluation section, p. 4-31).

3. Act on the team's conclusions.
Record what you learned about your mission, the conduct of meetings, and the various roles. File these records with other team documents. Send copies of the conclusions about your mission to the leadership team. Either have the team leader discuss the issues with the leadership team, or include this topic on the agenda of a joint meeting with the leadership team.

Exercise 9—Discussing Your Mission
Suggested meeting format.

Instructions: Use these suggestions to create an agenda appropriate for your team.

1. Have the team generate a list of criteria for a good mission statement. What do members think they should understand about a task so they can set proper goals for the project?

2. Have someone read and explain your team's mission statement (you may ask the team leader or quality advisor to do this).

3. Have the team discuss any of the following questions. Either write them on flipchart pages before the meeting and post these pages on the wall, or hand out prepared sheets (and have a transparency as well). Ask only one question at a time. After the first three questions, you might divide the team into two smaller groups, give each small group a different question, and have them discuss the question and then report back to the other small group.

   • Is it clear what administration expects of us? What desired outcomes are expected?

   • Does our project cover only part of a larger process? Where do we fit in? Where does our part of the process start and end?

   • Are the boundaries of the project clear? What will be outside our consideration?

   • Are the goals realistic?

   • What resources, inside or outside the department or school, will we need to successfully complete the project?

   • Will this project work? Does the mission fit in with our knowledge about the process or system?

   • Do we have the right people on this team to accomplish the mission?

   • What people not on the team will be crucial to our efforts?

   • Who will support our efforts? Who will be opposed? Who will be neutral? How can we reach all of these people associated with the process?

   • Is it clear where this project fits into the system's overall improvement plan?

4. Summarize the team's reactions.

5. Compare your findings to the list of criteria you generated. Have you answered all your questions? Are there missing pieces? Can the quality advisor or team leader answer some of these questions?

6. Create an agenda. Use the model agenda on p. 4-34 or create your own. List time estimates for each exercise you include. Remember that the evaluation should address both what the team learned about the mission and what you learned about planning and running a meeting.

7. Determine supplies you will need. Will you need extra flipchart pads? paper? pens? markers? tapes? transparencies? Who is responsible for getting these supplies?

Exercise 10
Observing Group Process

Time: Duration of the meeting; occurs regularly at team meetings

Overview

This "exercise" is really a series of exercises. Use them periodically throughout a project to improve interactions and, therefore, how well the project is run.

One team member is designated as an observer. The observer does not participate in the meeting. He or she simply watches for specific behaviors during discussions, and takes notes on forms like those provided. At the end of the meeting, or during a predetermined evaluation period, the observer reports his or her observations. Then the whole team talks about what behavior to encourage, what to discourage, and what deserves further discussion. This information helps the group study and improve how members interact.

General Instructions

1. Preparation for the exercise.

A. *Choose the appropriate observation form.*
The following pages contain ten forms and checksheets for observing a group. Each is ranked as Beginner, Intermediate, or Advanced, depending on the difficulty or level of sophistication required. Plan on working through the observation forms in sequence from Beginner to Advanced, over a period of months. Thus, the first time you use this exercise the designated observer will use one of the Beginner forms. Each subsequent turn will involve a different Beginner form until you have used them all. Then move to the Intermediate forms; after using all of those, move to the Advanced Forms. Allow enough time between "observed" meetings for the team to work on the behavior studied. Therefore, use this exercise only occasionally, perhaps every three or four weeks.

B. *Select an observer.*
Typically, one observer works for the entire meeting. You may, however, use two observers per meeting (never more than two), each working half of the meeting (approx. 45 minutes). The team leader and quality advisor can select the observer, ask for volunteers, or help the team devise a procedure for rotating the responsibility.

C. *Decide when and how the observer will report.*
Observers are allowed to report only during a predetermined meeting evaluation time. You may include this report in the regular evaluation during the meeting (which will typically be at the end, or occasionally, the middle), or designate a special time to discuss the observer feedback. Decide in advance whether you want the observer to report first, before other team members comment, or after everyone else has commented.

2. Instructions for the observer.

A. *Do not participate in the meeting content.*
While acting as an observer, a team member sits apart from the meeting circle in a chair obviously separate from the group. The observer *does not* participate in discussions. The observer ignores the topics discussed (content), and pays attention solely to the discussion methods and interactions among members (process). Observers may join the group when their turns are over and contribute to discussions. But they must reserve their observation comments for the meeting evaluation (either at the end or midpoint of the meeting).

B. *Guidelines for reporting observations.*
- Report what you see and hear. Avoid reporting what you *think* was going on in other people's minds.

- Be descriptive and follow an order. For example, you could report on categories of observations, recurring patterns of behavior, or a chronological sequence of what happened during the meeting (Member A did this; B replied . . .).

- If what you record compliments or criticizes an individual, use the guidelines for constructive feedback in Chapter 6 (starting on p. 6-21).

3. Conduct the meeting.
Hold the meeting as usual, except for having the observer sit apart from the rest of the team.

4. Have the observer report.
If the group is unfamiliar with the form used to record observations, the observer explains it before describing the observation data. That will let the team members better understand the observations they are about to hear.

5. Have everyone discuss the data or observations.
Ask everyone for their own observations: Do they differ from those of the official observer?

CAUTION: Sometimes an observer's feedback will criticize individuals. The challenge for the team is to see how the group can deal with the problem (see Chapter 6), not whether it should change an individual. Still, the team leader should be prepared to deal with hurt feelings, especially the first few times this exercise is used— when team members are not yet skilled in constructive feedback techniques. For the same reason, observers should be careful when giving feedback to individuals.

General comments on Intermediate and Advanced Observation:

One way to make this exercise more challenging is to add more behaviors the observer watches at a given session. Therefore, you can combine two or more of the basic forms to increase the difficulty, which is what several of our intermediate and advanced formats do.

Giving the observer a blank page is another way to increase the difficulty. The observer simply notes whatever comes to mind. It requires sophistication and skill to get beyond noting the obvious behaviors and to see the subtle dynamics of group interactions.

Exercise 10—Observing Group Process
Observation Format 1 (Beginner)   Basic Observation

Instructions

1. Select a meeting characteristic to observe.
Select one or two of the following characteristics of the meeting process:
- Who talks?
- How often does each member talk?
- How many interruptions are there?
- How many statements* of agreement and disagreement are there?
- How often do discussions get sidetracked?

(*Decide how you will operationally define "statement." Does it include a simple murmur and nod of the head? Does it have to be something more complete? This choice is up to the observer.)

2. Create an appropriate, simple form.
At the top of a sheet of paper, write down what you have decided to watch. You can either leave the rest of the space blank for free-form notes, or list names or items that you can check or mark as needed.

3. Review the general instructions for observers (p. 7-31 to 7-32).

4. Practice observing the group.
At the meeting, watch the group for 10 to 15 minutes without taking notes. Practice ignoring what they say; pay attention only to *how* the group manages the process of discussion.

5. Observe and take notes.
Once you've gotten used to watching the group process, mark the time on the form and begin filling it in. If your form doesn't work, feel free to change it. The same holds true for operational definitions. Remember: Do not speak during the meeting.

6. Have the observer report.
If the group is unfamiliar with the form used to record observations, the observer explains it before describing the observation data. That will let the team members better understand the observations they are about to hear.

7. Discuss the conclusions.
Have everyone discuss the data or observations. Ask everyone for their own observations: Do they differ from those of the official observer?

Exercise 10—Observing Group Process
General Instructions for Observation Formats 2 through 5

1. Background.
The next four forms are very similar. Each asks the observer to look at four different behaviors at once. Each combination of four was chosen because it includes some behaviors that happen all the time and some that are rare. You can easily modify the formats yourself, adding more categories to make it harder or eliminating some to make it simpler. However, we recommend adding items only if you are experienced enough to know which behaviors can be monitored simultaneously and provide a balance for the observer—otherwise the observer may end up with too much or too little to do.

2. Review the form before the meeting begins.
Brief descriptions of the behaviors are provided on the form. If questions remain, the team leader or quality advisor may help clarify the instructions. Or refer to Chapters 4 and 6 for more details.

3. Review the instructions for observers (page 7-31).

4. Practice observing the group.
At the meeting, watch the group for 10 to 15 minutes without taking notes. Practice ignoring what they say; pay attention only to *how* the group manages the discussion process.

5. Observe and take notes.
Once you've gotten used to watching the group process, mark the time on the form and begin filling it in. Remember: Do not speak during the meeting.

6. Have the observer report.
If the group is unfamiliar with the form used to record observations, the observer explains it before describing the observation data. That will let the team members better understand the observations they are about to hear.

7. Discuss the conclusions.
Have everyone discuss the data or observations. Ask everyone for his or her own observations: Do they differ from those of the official observer?

Exercise 10—Observing Group Process
Observation Format 2 (Beginner)

Instructions: Make notes below whenever you observe examples of these behaviors. Be as specific as possible when describing what happened.

Initiating	Gatekeeping
Gets a conversation going; keeps it going by defining problems, suggesting procedures, proposing tasks, stimulating ideas.	Helps to keep communication channels open, helps others to participate, controls dominating speakers, encourages noncontributors.

Information or Opinion Seeking	Sharing Feelings
Draws out relevant information, opinions, ideas, suggestions, or concerns from the group.	Shares personal feelings with the team, getting others to express their feelings.

Exercise 10—Observing Group Process
Observation Format 3 (Beginner)

Instructions: Make notes below whenever you observe examples of these behaviors. Be as specific as possible when describing what happened.

Initiating	Encouraging
Gets a conversation going, keeps it going by defining problems, suggesting procedures, proposing tasks, stimulating ideas.	Is friendly, warm, and responsive; uses eye contact and "uh-huhs."

Information or Opinion Giving	Group Sensitivity
Shares relevant information, opinions, beliefs, suggestions, and concerns.	Senses and expresses group feelings and moods. Aware of significant shifts in tone.

Exercise 10—Observing Group Process
Observation Format 4 (Beginner)

Instructions: Make notes below whenever you observe examples of these behaviors. Be as specific as possible when describing what happened.

Clarifying and Elaborating	Harmonizing/Compromising
Clears up confusion, gives examples, points out issues and alternatives, shares interpretations of what's been said.	Reduces tension, works out disagreements, admits error, changes proposals to help the group, looks for middle ground.
Summarizing	**Approval/Acceptance**
Pulls together what's been said, organizes related ideas, restates suggestions, offers conclusions for the group to accept or reject.	Nonverbal or verbal approval of another member's participation.

Chapter 7

Exercise 10—Observing Group Process
Observation Format 5 (Beginner)

Instructions: Make notes below whenever you observe examples of these behaviors. Be as specific as possible when describing what happened.

Terminating	Checking Decisions
Moves the group towards decision or action (checking for consensus, agreement, or disagreement).	Monitors how the group makes decisions, whether by verbal agreement, nonverbal agreement, minority opinion, consensus, and so forth.
Use of Data	**Gatekeeping**
Presents data to back up statements, suggests what data to collect to verify opinions.	Helps to keep communication channels open, helps others to participate, controls dominating speakers, encourages noncontributors.

Exercise 10—Observing Group Process
Observation Format 6 (Intermediate)

Instructions: The figure below represents a table. Enter the names of team members along the sides of the square, corresponding to where they sit during the meeting. When someone speaks, draw an arrow from the speaker to the person addressed by the remark. Use a slash mark across that arrow each time the pattern is repeated. If the recipient answers the remark, draw a separate arrow from this person (who is now the speaker) to the first person (who is now being addressed). If a remark is to no one in particular, draw the arrow from the speaker to the center of the square.

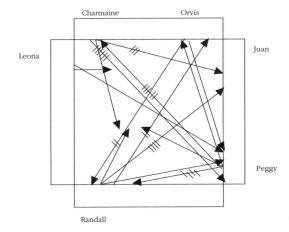

A sample sociogram

In this discussion, Charmaine addressed many remarks to Peggy (who answered her most of the time) and to Juan, who did not answer. Orvis spoke to Randall twice (who answered twice) and to Peggy, who responded. Juan was spoken to but never answered: Leona spoke but was never answered. Randall addressed remarks to Orvis, Juan, and Peggy (who spoke to Randall more often than she was answered). Charmaine, Leona, Peggy, and Randall all made remarks that were addressed to no one in particular. Note: This would normally be hand-drawn.

Exercise 10—Observing Group Process
Observation Format 7 (Intermediate)   Group Task Needs

Instructions: Copy the chart below or create a version on your own. Enter the names of team members along the top. Enter checkmarks or comments in the appropriate boxes when you see one of the behaviors.

Initiating Gets a conversation going; keeps it going by defining problems, suggesting procedures, proposing tasks, stimulating ideas.						
Information or Opinion Seeking Drawing out relevant information, opinions, ideas, suggestions, or concerns from the group.						
Information or Opinion Giving Shares relevant information, opinions, beliefs, suggestions, and concerns from the group.						
Clarifying and Elaborating Clears up confusion, gives examples, points out issues and alternatives, shares interpretations of what's been said.						
Summarizing Pulls together what's been said, organizes related ideas, restates suggestions, offers conclusions for the group to accept or reject.						
Terminating Moves the group towards decision or action (checking for consensus, agreement, or disagreement).						
Use of Data Presents data to back up statements, suggests what data to collect to verify opinions.						

Exercise 10—Observing Group Process
Observation Format 8 (Intermediate)　　Group Relations Needs

Instructions: Copy the chart below or create a version on your own. Enter the names of team members along the top. Enter checkmarks or comments in the appropriate boxes when you see one of the behaviors.

Encouraging Is friendly, warm, and responsive; uses eye contact and "uh-huhs."					
Approval/Acceptance Nonverbal or verbal approval of another member's participation.					
Group Sensitivity Senses and expresses group feelings and moods. Aware of significant shifts in tone.					
Harmonizing/Compromising Reduces tension, works out disagreements, admits error, changes proposals to help the group, looks for middle ground.					
Gatekeeping Helps to keep communication channels open, helps others to participate, controls dominating speakers, encourages noncontributors.					
Sharing Feelings Shares personal feelings with the team, getting others to express their feelings.					

Chapter 7

Exercise 10—Observing Group Process
Observation Format 9 (Advanced)   **Problem Solving**

Instructions: Read the background and questions given below. During the meeting, record your observations in the space provided or on a separate sheet. Refer to the general instructions given on pp. 7-31 to 7-32.

Before you can improve the team's problem-solving process, you must understand how it works now. During the meeting, track discussions concerning problems facing the group or any single member. Listen specifically for the information below, but add to this any other impressions you have. Use the space at the bottom of the page to record your observations. Reminder: Listen carefully to the participants. Do not interfere with the process.

Notes

Specific Patterns to Watch For

- How did the facilitator define the problem?
- Did anyone ask for clarification?
- How long did it take for the group to understand the problem?
- How committed did the group seem to solving the problem?
- Who seemed most influential in shaping the discussion?
- Was a decision reached? If not, why not? If yes, who was most influential in the choice?
- Did people listen to one another?

Exercise 10—Observing Group Process
Observation Format 10 (Very Advanced)
Studying Patterns of Participation

Instructions: Copy the form below (consider using legal size to allow adequate room). If you redraw the figure, be sure to include the timing matrix, a small sociogram, and spaces for notes on decision patterns, topic patterns, and roles. Enter team members' names in spaces on the left of the matrix. For the first hour, make a checkmark each time a person participates during the time period indicated by the columns. Use the sociogram, too, to indicate interaction patterns. Look for patterns that appear (e.g., Does Irma always contradict Joseph? Does everyone try to change the subject when it comes time to assign tasks?). At the end, summarize your observations at the bottom of the page and report to the team.

Sociogram: Indicate where each team member is sitting around the table. Draw lines indicating interactions between members.

Names	1st 10 min	2nd 10 min	3rd 10 min	4th 10 min	5th 10 min	6th 10 min

Decision Patterns   **Topic Patterns**   **Roles**

SUMMARY

This chapter is a compendium of activities you can use to create understanding in a team and get everyone working in unison. The experienced team leader will most likely use this chapter only occasionally, preferring instead to build a private collection of tried-and-true approaches to team activities. (In fact, several exercises here were contributed by experienced team leaders we know.) Therefore, use this collection as a start; keep looking around for other exercises that will benefit your team.

Appendix 1
Further Reading

Management Principles

Aquayo, Rafael. *Dr. Deming: The American Who Taught the Japanese About Quality.* New York: Lyle Stuart, 1990.

Argyris, Chris. *Integrating the Individual and the Organization.* New York: John Wiley & Sons, Inc. 1964.

Bayless, David L., Gabriel A. Massaro, et al. "The Quality Management Approach as Implemented in a Middle School." *Journal of Personnel Evaluation in Education,* Vol. 6, No. 2, December, 1992.

Bennett, David A., and **D. Thomas King.** "The Saturn School of Tomorrow." *Educational Leadership,* May, 1991.

Bennis, Warren, and **Burt Nanus.** *Leaders.* New York: Harper & Row. 1985.

Blake, Robert, and **Jane Mouton.** *Managerial Grid.* Houston, Tex.: Gulf Publishing. 1964.

Bonstingl, John Jay. "The Total Quality Classroom." *Educational Leadership,* March, 1992.

David, Jane L. "What It Takes to Restructure Education." *Phi Delta Kappan,* May, 1991.

Deming, W. Edwards. *Out of the Crisis.* Cambridge, Mass.: MIT, Center for Advanced Engineering Study. 1986. The classic.

_____ *The New Economics for Industry, Government, Education.* Cambridge, Mass.: MIT, Center for Advanced Engineering Study. 1993.

Fuller, F. Timothy. "Eliminating Complexity From Work: Improving Productivity By Enhancing Quality." *National Productivity Review,* Autumn, 1985: 327-344.

Gitlow, Howard, and **Shelly Gitlow.** *The Deming Guide to Quality and Competitive Position.* Englewood Cliffs, N.J.: Prentice-Hall. 1987.

Glasser, William. "The Quality School." *Phi Delta Kappan,* February, 1990.

Glickman, Carl. "Pretending Not to Know What We Know." *Educational Leadership,* May, 1991.

Gordon, Thomas. *Leader Effectiveness Training: L.E.T.* New York: Bantam Books. 1977.

Hunter, William G. "Managing Our Way to Economic Success: Two Untapped Resources." *Report No. 4.* (1986). Center for Quality and Productivity Improvement (610 Walnut St., Madison, WI 53705).

Imai, Masaaki. *Kaizen, The Key to Japan's Competitive Success.* New York: Random House Business Division. 1986. (Random House, Inc., 201 E. 50th St., New York, NY 10022)

Ishikawa, Kaoru. *What Is Total Quality Control?: The Japanese Way.* Englewood Cliffs, N.J.: Prentice-Hall. 1985.

Joiner, Brian L. *Fourth Generation Management: The New Business Consciousness.* New York: McGraw-Hill, 1994.

Joiner, Brian L., and **Peter Scholtes.** "The Quality Manager's New Job." *Quality Progress,* October, 1986: 52-56.

Juran, Joseph M. *Juran on Planning for Quality.* New York: The Free Press (Macmillan, Inc.) 1988.

_____ "The Quality Trilogy," *Quality Progress,* January, 1988.

_____ *Quality Control Handbook.* New York: McGraw-Hill, Inc. 1974.

_____*Managerial Breakthrough.* New York: McGraw-Hill, Inc. 1964.

Kepner, Charles H., and **Benjamin B. Tregoe.** *The New Rational Manager.* Princeton, N.J.: Princeton Research Press. 1981.

Knowles, Malcolm S. *Using Learning Contracts: Approaches to Individualizing and Structuring Learning.* San Francisco: Jossey-Bass Publishers. 1986.

_____ *The Adult Learner: a Neglected Species (3rd ed.).* Houston, Tex.: Gulf Publishing Company. 1984.

_____ **and Associates.** *Andragogy in Action: Applying Modern Principles of Adult Education.* Washington, D.C.: Jossey-Bass Publishers. 1985.

Latzko, William. *Quality and Productivity for Bankers and Financial Managers.* Milwaukee, Wis.: American Society for Quality Control. 1986.

Likert, Rensis. *New Patterns of Management.* New York: McGraw-Hill, Inc. 1961.

Melvin III, Charles A. "Restructuring Schools by Applying Deming's Management Theories." *Journal of Staff Development,* Summer, 1991.

Pines, Ellis. "From Top Secret to Top Priority: The Story of TQM." *Aviation Week and Space Technology,* May 21, 1990.

Rhodes, Lewis A. "Why Quality is Within Our Grasp, If We Reach." *The School Administrator,* November, 1990.

_____"Beyond Your Beliefs: Quantum Leaps Toward Quality Schools." *The School Administrator,* December, 1990.

Roach, Carol S. "Outcome-Based, Long Range Planning: Development." *The Curriculum Leader, No. 18.*

Satir, Virginia. *Making Contact.* Millbrae, Calif.: Celestial Arts. 1976.

_____ *Peoplemaking.* Palo Alto, Calif.: Science and Behavior Books, Inc. 1972.

Schein, Edgar. *Organizational Culture and Leadership.* San Francisco: Jossey-Bass Publishers. 1985.

Scherkenbach, William W. *The Deming Route to Quality and Productivity.* Rockville, MD: Mercury Press/Fairchild Publications. 1987. (Available from: Continuing Engineering Education, The George Washington University, Washington, D.C. 20052, [800] 424-9773.)

Scholtes, Peter R. "An Elaboration on Deming's Teachings on Performance Appraisal." Madison, Wis.: Joiner Associates Inc. 1987. (Available from Joiner Associates Inc.)

_____ "Total Quality or Performance Appraisal: Choose One." Madison, Wis.: Joiner Associates Inc. 1993. (Available from Joiner Associates Inc.)

_____and **Heero Hacquebord.** "Beginning the Quality Transformation, Part I." *Quality Progress,* July, 1988: 28-33.

_____and **Heero Hacquebord.** "Six Strategies for Beginning the Quality Transformation, Part II." *Quality Progress,* August, 1988: 44-48.

Stampen, Jacob O. "Improving the Quality of Education: W. Edwards Deming and Effective Schools." *Contemporary Education Review,* Winter, 1987.

Townsend, Patrick. *Commit to Quality.* New York: Wiley & Sons. 1986.

Tribus, Myron. "Selected Papers On Quality and Productivity Improvement." (Available from Mr. G.N. Wright, National Society of Professional Engineers, Washington Engineering Center, 1420 King Street, Alexandria, VA 22314, [703] 684-2800.

_____"The Application of Quality Management Principles in Education, at Mt. Edgecumbe High School, Sitka, Alaska. *An Introduction to Quality for Schools, American Association for High School Administrators,* 1991.

_____ *Quality First: Selected Papers on Quality and Productivity Improvement.* Knoxville, TN: SPC Press. 1993.

Tveite, Michael. "The Theory Behind the Fourteen Points: Management Focused on Improvement Instead of Judgment." *An Introduction to Total Quality for Schools, American Association of School Administrators,* 1991.

Walton, Mary. *The Deming Management Method.* New York: Perigee Books. 1986. A good, easy-to-read starting point.

Tools

"Continuing Process Control and Process Capability Improvement." (To order, contact: P.T. Jessup, Statistical Methods Associate, Statistical Methods Office, Operations Support Staff, Ford Motor Company, Room 524, World Headquarters, P.O. Box 1899, Dearborn, MI 48121-1899.) A basic guide to S. P. C.

The Memory Jogger for Educators. Goal/QPC, 13 Branch St. Metheun, MA 01844, (508) 685-3900.

Finn, Lynda, Tim Kramer, and **Sue Reynard.** "Design of Experiments: Shifting Quality Improvement Into High Gear." Madison, Wis.: Joiner Associates Inc. 1987. (Available from Joiner Associates Inc.)

Hoffeir, Glen. *The Toolbook.* Markon, Inc. Box 423, Windham, NH 03087, (603) 898-3919.

Hunter, William G. "Some ideas about teaching design of experiments with 25 examples of experiments conducted by students." *The American Statistician,* Vol. 31, No. 1. 1977. A paper showing how to get students in a statistics course to carry out simple statistically designed experiments. These same approaches could be used at the elementary and secondary school levels.

Ishikawa, Kaoru. *Guide to Quality Control.* Tokyo: Asian Productivity Organization. 1976. (Available exclusively from UNIPUB, One Water St., White Plains, NY 10601, [800] 247-8519.) A best-seller in the area of basic statistical approaches for quality improvement. Originally written for factory foremen in Japan, but has a much wider appeal. It has good examples, including a number of case histories that you might start with.

Joiner, Brian L. "The Key Role of Statisticians in the Transformation of North American Industry," *The American Statistician,* Vol. 39, No. 3: 224-227 (1985). A description of the role that statisticians need to play to help change the American style of management. (Available from Joiner Associates Inc.)

Kume, Hitoshi. *Statistical Methods for Quality Improvement.* Tokyo: The Association for Overseas Technical Scholarship, 1985. (Available from UNIPUB, One Water St., White Plains, NY 10601, [800] 247-8519.) A book on statistics for manufacturing processes. Skip the parts on testing hypotheses (esp. Ch. 9).

Landwehr, James M., and **Ann E. Watkins.** *Exploring Data.* Prepared for the American Statistical Association—National Council of Teachers of Mathematics Joint Committee on the Curriculum in Statistics and Probability. 1984. A wonderful presentation of some basic graphical statistical procedures. It shows how they can be used at the grade school level to teach students how to learn from data.

Wheeler, Donald J., and **David S. Chambers.** *Understanding Statistical Process Control.* Knoxville, TN: Statistical Process Controls, Inc. 1986. (Order from Statistical Process Controls, Inc., 7026 Shadyland Dr., Knoxville, TN 37919, [615] 584-5005.) The best current book on statistics for manufacturing processes. Skip the part on acceptance sampling.

Other Items of Interest

The Deming Library video series. Available from Films Incorporated (800) 323-4222.

Joiner Associates Inc. *Fundamentals of Fourth Generation Management.* This is a new video program that teaches the basic principles of the quality-oriented approach to management. Available from Joiner Associates (800) 669-8326.

Appendix 2
Picture Book Format

This Picture Book Format was adapted from a classic quality improvement anecdote published in the booklet "The Quest for Higher Quality: The Deming Prize and Quality Control" published by RICOH of America.

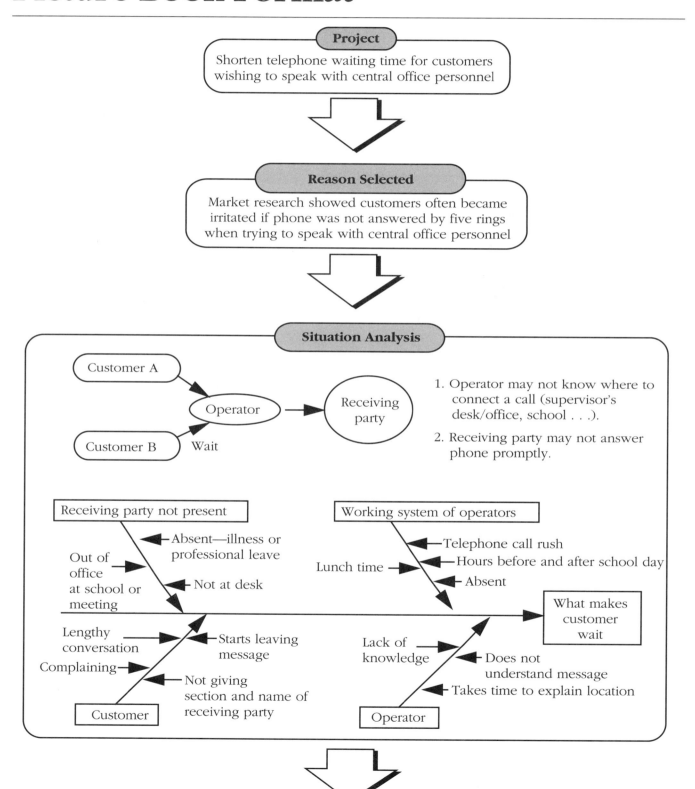

Project

Shorten telephone waiting time for customers wishing to speak with central office personnel

Reason Selected

Market research showed customers often became irritated if phone was not answered by five rings when trying to speak with central office personnel

Situation Analysis

Customer A

Operator

Receiving party

Customer B   Wait

1. Operator may not know where to connect a call (supervisor's desk/office, school . . .).
2. Receiving party may not answer phone promptly.

Receiving party not present

Absent—illness or professional leave

Out of office at school or meeting

Not at desk

Lengthy conversation

Starts leaving message

Complaining

Not giving section and name of receiving party

Customer

Working system of operators

Telephone call rush

Lunch time

Hours before and after school day

Absent

What makes customer wait

Lack of knowledge

Does not understand message

Takes time to explain location

Operator

Data Collection

Check Sheet

Reason / Date	No one present at the desk or office receiving the call	Receiving party not present	Only one operator		Total
June 4	\\\\	⫶⫶ \	⫶⫶ ⫶⫶ \	⫶	24
June 5	⫶⫶	⫶⫶ \\\	⫶⫶ ⫶⫶ \\\\	⫶	32
June 6	⫶⫶	\\\\	⫶⫶ ⫶⫶ \\	⫶	28
⋮	⋮	⋮	⋮	⋮	
June 15	⫶⫶	⫶⫶	⫶⫶ \\\	⫶	25

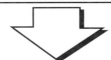

Data Analysis

Reasons why callers had to wait

		Daily average	Total number
A	One operator (partner out of the office)	14.3	172
B	Receiving party not present	6.1	73
C	No one present at the desk or office receiving the call	5.1	61
D	Section and name of receiving party not given or not known	1.6	19
E	Inquiry about school locations	1.3	16
F	Other reasons	0.8	10
	Total	29.2*	351

*6% of calls had long waits

Pareto Diagram

A	One operator (partner out of the office)
B	Receiving party not present
C	No one present in the area receiving the call
D	Section and name of receiving party not given or not known
E	Inquiry about school locations
F	Other reasons

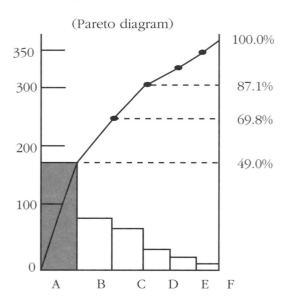

(Pareto diagram)

Goal

Reduce calls with long waits to zero

Actions

1. Helper operator brought in to substitute while each of two regular operators went to lunch.

2. Asked all central office personnel to leave messages when leaving their desks.

3. Compiled directory listing central office personnel and their respective roles.

Evaluation

Comparisons of before and after

	Reasons why callers had to wait	Total number Before	Total number After	Daily Average Before	Daily Average After
A	One operator (partner out of the office)	172	15	14.3	1.2
B	Receiving party not present	73	17	6.1	1.4
C	No one present in the area receiving the call	61	20	5.1	1,7
D	Section and name of receiving party not given or not known	19	4	1.6	0.3
E	Inquiry about school locations	16	3	1.3	0.2
F	Other reasons	10	0	0.8	0
	Total	351	59	29.2 *	4.8

Period: 12 days from Aug. 17 to 30

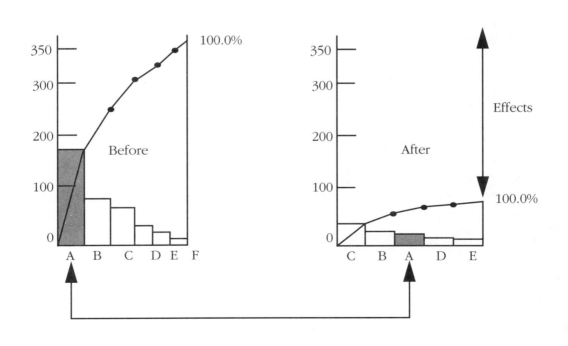

Appendix 3
The Planning Grid

The planning grid is a tool for short-term planning, used for single events or simple projects. (Longer-term projects or more complex tasks may involve the use of many planning grids—or other kinds of tools—at various points along the way.) The Grid helps you or your group organize all the key elements needed to reach a predetermined goal. It does not help you choose the goal, it only helps you reach it. The set-up is shown on the next page.

To create a Planning Grid

1. Specify the final outcome.
How will you know when this project or task is successfully completed? What will you have accomplished? Arrive at consensus and put it in writing.

2. Identify the final step and its product.
What will be the action that officially indicates the completion of the project or task? For example: developing the format for a learning contract, implementing a flawless fire drill or building evacuation procedure, the submission of an evaluation report, filing the project documentation.

3. Identify the starting point and its product.
What will be (or was) the first action that indicates the beginning of this task or project? For example: writing the first draft of an announcement, developing a list of people to involve in a training session, convening the first meeting.

4. Brainstorm a list of separate, distinct activities that will take place between the starting and ending points.
Follow the rules of brainstorming here. You want to elicit as many ideas as possible, not judge their appropriateness at this point.

5. Refine the brainstormed list.
Clarify what is unclear; eliminate redundancy; subdivide tasks that are too large; combine those that are too small.

- Enter as a single item any activities that cluster together by virtue of occurring in uninterrupted chronological sequence, being dependent on each other, and probably being done by the same person.

- Enter as separate items any sequences of activities in which there are lengthy interruptions, or different deadlines that may be concurrent but not dependent on each other for completion, or that could be divided up among different individuals without harming the effectiveness of the sequence.

For example, "1. Design Training/2. Announce Training/ 3. Conduct Training" are normally entered as separate items because they are not a continuous set of events. There will be interruptions between and probably within each step, different deadlines, and Step 2, in particular, can be done by a different person without detriment. On the other hand, "Design Questionnaire/Test Questionnaire/Finalize Questionnaire" could be entered as the single item "Design/Test/Finalize Questionnaire." This latter activity has a single, common deadline, and benefits from the continuity of having the same person or people involved in all three steps.

6. Prepare the Grid.
- Look over the categories of information described on the next page. Decide whether to add any of the optional categories to your grid.

- Divide a flipchart page into columns, one for each category you decide to include. Enter the titles (shown above) into the column headings. Replace the generic titles given with ones specific to your project whenever appropriate.

Format for the Planning Grid

Step Number	Sequential Steps or Individual Activities	Product	Responsibility	Due Date	Whom to Involve/ Contact	Budget and Cost	Other Categories

7. Arrange the list of tasks/steps in sequence down the left column of the planning grid.

You may want to use self-stick notes so you can easily rearrange items until you get a sequence that seems right.

8. Fill in the Product column for each item.

9. Enter a tentative date for each item.

You need to complete this step before others because the time available for performing a task sometimes affects the nature of the project. ("Do what you can in the next 30 days!") Due dates also indicate when the person responsible for that item must be available. If a person cannot be available during the specified time, someone else should probably be the champion of that step. If you have an inflexible deadline, start at the end of the list and work backwards. Use your prior experience and any knowledge about similar activities to set realistic deadlines.

10. If necessary, revise items.

After setting deadlines, you may find that some items need to be reworked.

11. Complete the remaining columns.

Missing Deadlines

If a deadline cannot be met, your options are:
- Delete some steps
- Get the deadline moved
- Redefine the steps so they can be finished in less time
- Redeploy personnel to accelerate activities
- Ignore the deadline

If it appears unlikely that a deadline will be met, the planner should review the plan to see whether it can be improved and speeded up without compromising quality. In a quality-focused organization, seldom should a deadline be allowed to override the quality of the work. It is essential, however, to improve processes so that high quality takes less time. It is also essential to eliminate unnecessary work, which can only decrease the time required. In the same vein, keep track of how good you are at predicting deadlines; explore reasons for missed deadlines and look for ways to improve in the future.

Definition of Terms

Step Number

Simple numbering is used most frequently to indicate the sequence of events, but you may use some other code if you like.

Sequential Steps or Activities

Enter, in chronological order, each activity that is part of this task. For example, if the step involves "data collection," then the activities might be: 1. Develop operational definitions, 2. Prepare checksheets, 3. Test and refine checksheets, 4. Train staff who will collect data.

Product

Each discrete step results in some product, for example, a report, a tangible change, a decision, a phone call, a meeting. There is always something that indicates the completion of a step. Enter here a word or phrase describing what that completion sign is for this step.

Responsibility

Enter here the names of one or two people who are responsible for seeing that this task gets done. Note: They do not necessarily carry out the action themselves. They may just coordinate the actions of others.

Due Date

The calendar date when this step should be finished.

Whom to Involve/Contact

If appropriate, enter here the names of people who should be part of the team working on this task, or who should at least be contacted and informed of progress or events.

Optional Columns

Budget/Cost

If funds have been allocated for this activity, or if there is a limit to expenditures, enter that figure.

Customers

This column lets you keep track of people who are particularly interested in or concerned about the successful outcome of this step, or the project as a whole. Typically, this includes people whose work depends on what your team accomplishes (that is, internal customers).

Limitations/Specifications

Enter here any constraints under which the people involved with this step must operate, such as amount of time per week they can spend on the task, how many other people they can call on for help, the maximum time they can stop a process (if at all), and so forth. Note: You may also enter time and money limits here, though the categories of "budget" and "due date" usually indicate the same thing.

Hazards/Pitfalls

Past experience with this activity may lead you to expect trouble in some form. Enter here any information that will help the team avoid pitfalls.

By-products

Many times a team will be given secondary objectives: "While you're at it, see if you can find this out." Though such commissions should not be allowed to interfere with the primary goals of the project, they should be allowed if they may lead to useful information without causing too much disruption.

Index